Second Edition

Creating
Great
Web
Graphics

Laurie McCanna

First Edition—1996

McCanna, Laurie.
    Creating great Web graphics / by Laurie McCanna. -- 2nd ed.
      p.   cm.
    ISBN 1-55828-550-4
    1. World Wide Web (Information retrieval system) 2. Computer
graphics. 3. Web sites--Design. I. Title.
   TK5105.888.M374 1997
   006.6--dc21   97-20212
                                    CIP

Printed in the United States of America.

10 9 8 7 6 5 4 3 2 1

Trademarks

Chapter opening illustrations by *Natalie Fortin*

Associate Publisher: Paul Farrell

Managing Editor: Shari Chappell

Editor: Debra Williams Cauley

Copy Edit Manager: Karen Tongish

Design and Production: Maya Riddick

Technical Editor: Georgia Rucker

Copy Editor: Suzanne Ingrao

Dedication

For Tim, Adrian, and Teague

Acknowledgements

Thanks to Gayle Hefley for contributing the Mac information. Thanks also to all of the Web Diner crew members who've offered their talents to help other folks learn how to use the Web. Last but not least, thanks to the folks at MIS:Press who made this book a reality.

CONTENTS

Part 1 • Creating Simple Web Graphics

Part 2 • Intermediate Web Graphics

Part 3 • Advanced Web Topics

INTRODUCTION

Creating Great Web Graphics is the book that will help you to create professional-looking graphics, even if you don't have an artistic bone in your body. With instruction, you will be able to design eye-catching Web pages. You'll find recipes for icons, page backgrounds, unusual edges, and type, accompanied by valuable advice and tricks to help you create cool graphics that load quickly. And if you are fortunate enough to be graphically gifted, this book will inspire you to produce even more imaginative and wonderful artwork for your Web site.

Each chapter tackles a specific topic followed by a step-by-step demonstration in both Photoshop version 4.0 for Windows or the Macintosh and Corel PhotoPaint version 7 for Windows. Photoshop is the standard tool for creating bitmapped graphics; Corel PhotoPaint, in its most recent revision, is a very close cousin of Photoshop. In addition, I'll discuss techniques for making graphics look great at low resolution.

The Web has more in common with fast-paced television than it does with traditional paper printing. You may create beautiful graphics, but if the files are too large, no one will stay at your Web site long enough to see your artwork since it will take so long to download. Creating fast-loading, great-looking graphics is the only way to immediately engage the visitor and keep him or her coming back for more.

But a Web site is more than just graphics. On a Web site, you can express your most passionate beliefs, self-publish your own creative writing or poetry, garner publicity for your favorite nonprofit group, or present your business to a new audience. A Web site can be a new world of information, connections, and possibilities.

ANATOMY OF A WEB PAGE

Graphics are used in a number of ways on a Web page. Take a look at Figure I.1. The word *collage* at the top of the page is actually a graphic. And the graphic that repeats, or "tiles," creates the subtle background behind the text.

You no doubt know that the software application used to view Web pages is called a *browser*. Throughout the book I have used the two most popular: Netscape and Internet Explorer. But browsers are not just for desktop computers anymore. You can browse the Web via your television set, or with a palmtop application (sometimes called PDAs). These types of applications have their own proprietary browsers and

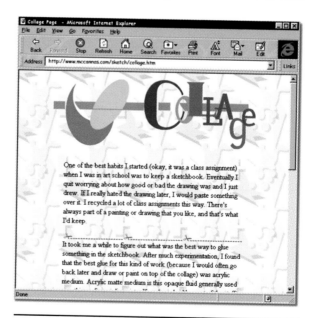

Figure I.1 A basic Web page.

may display pages differently from Netscape Navigator or Internet Explorer. Therein lies one of the most challenging aspects to creating Web graphics: Each browser views a given Web page differently, which you'll need to keep in mind as you go about your design work.

Web pages are created with the *HyperText Markup Language* (HTML), a cross-platform language that enables you to create an HTML page with the same codes for viewing by UNIX, Mac, or Windows users. An HTML page can be created in a WYSIWYG HTML Editor software application; or, if you learn the HTML codes, you can simply create your entire Web page in a word processor. Using HTML, you can add background images or colors, place images, and specify links to other pages or Web sites. With HTML, each element is placed on the page with an HTML code. For example, the Collage graphic in Figure I.1 is named **collage.gif.** It was inserted into the Web page with the HTML code `<IMG SRC="collage.gif">`. Spacing and alignment of Web page elements are also controlled with HTML.

Be aware that the codes for HTML are some of the fastest-changing elements of Web specifications. Refer to the Quick HTML Reference at the end of the book for a current list of the tags you can use with graphics. You can find out more about HTML by reading books such as *Teach Yourself Web Publishing in a Week* by Laura LeMay or the *World Wide Web Bible* by Bryan Pfaffenberger.

One final note about the Internet-technical side of Web graphics: Graphics files are always binary files, never text files. This can be important when you transfer files from your computer to your Web server. If your graphics don't show up on your Web page, they may have transferred as text or ASCII files, which can corrupt your graphics. Other common errors resulting in transfer glitches include typos in the name of the graphics file or not specifying the correct file or the correct path to the file in the IMG SRC tag.

GETTING STARTED

Before you begin the projects in this book, you should be familiar enough with your paint program to perform a few basic tasks, including how to set the foreground and background colors for an image, how to use the Marquee tool in Photoshop or Masking tool in PhotoPaint, and how to save a file.

Photoshop comes with very well-written documentation and an online Help function, which you can access from the menu bar within Photoshop, as shown in Figure I.2.

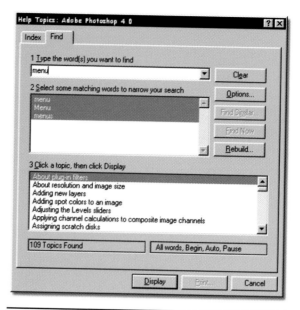

Figure I.2 Using Photoshop's Help function.

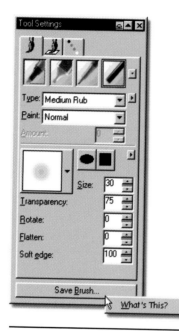

Figure I.3 Using the right mouse button in PhotoPaint.

Corel has integrated the use of the right mouse button into PhotoPaint. Thus, in PhotoPaint, a good way to get an overview of any tool is to double-click on the tool. This will access the Tool Settings roll-up. From there, using the right mouse button, right double-click on anything to receive more information about that function. "What's This?" (Figure I.3) will lead to a definition of the tool or option you have clicked on. In addition, there is an extensive online Help function within PhotoPaint, accessible from the menu bar within PhotoPaint (see Figure I.4).

PhotoPaint also includes a set of tutorials. You can launch these by selecting **Help/CorelTutor**. Select the tutorial you're interested in, as in Figure I.5, and CorelTutor will walk you through that task.

TURBOCHARGING YOUR PAINT PROGRAM FOR THE WEB

Creating Web graphics is very different from creating graphics for print materials, so there are a few defaults you'll want to change within Photoshop or PhotoPaint before you begin practicing the examples in this book. First, change the default measurement units from inches to pixels. In Web graphics, inches are irrelevant. In graphics for print, a 300 x 300 pixel image set to 300 pixels per inch will always ouput as a one-inch square graphic, whereas on your Web page, a 300 x 300 pixel image might take up half of your Web site visitors' screen, or conversely, only a tiny portion of the screen if they have a higher display setting on their

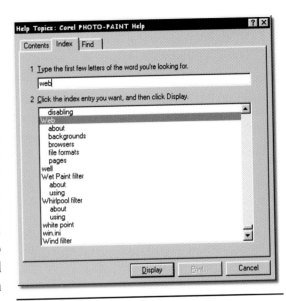

Figure I.4 Using PhotoPaint's Help function.

computer monitor. In short, the size of the image is dependent on the monitor resolution.

To change the units of measurement, in Photoshop, select **File/ Preferences/Units & Rulers**. Set the ruler units to **Pixels**. In Corel PhotoPaint, select **Tools/ Options**. Select the **General** tab, and then select **Units, Pixels**.

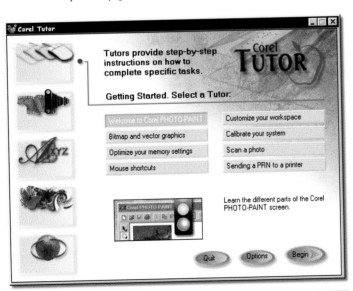

Figure I.5 PhotoPaint's tutorials.

Another setting you'll want to change in Photoshop is the default that embeds a thumbnail preview image in each graphic you save so that you can preview the image without opening the entire file. Unfortunately, saving a Web graphic with an embedded thumbnail image can more than double the file size of your Web graphic. If you have been wondering why your GIFs or JPEGs are twice as big as any other JPEGs (in file size), that pesky thumbnail is probably the culprit. To disable the embedded preview in Photoshop, select **Files/Preferences/Saving Files**, then select **Image Previews, Never Save.**

Color and the Web is covered in Chapter 5, but in the meantime you may want to set your on-screen color palette to use the 216 colors that won't dither to accommodate people viewing the Web with a monitor set to 256 colors using Internet Explorer or Netscape Navigator. You can download the Web palette from the Adobe Web site at http://www.adobe.com. Once you have downloaded the file, from within Photoshop, select the flyout palette on the color swatches palette, and select the Web palette you have down-loaded from Adobe's Web site.

You can also set the PhotoPaint color palette to a set of nondithering colors, which will not dither for Netscape or Internet Explorer users whose monitors are set to 256 colors. To change the color palette, select **Image/Color Palettes**, then select **Microsoft Internet Explorer** or **Netscape Navigator**, as shown in Figure I.6. The Microsoft Internet Explorer and Netscape Navigator palettes contain the same colors, arranged in a different order in each palette. This will change your on-screen color palette—seen in Figure I.6 at the right edge of the screen—to this non-dithering set of colors.

ABOUT THIS BOOK

If you are a beginning user of Photoshop or PhotoPaint, I recommend that you work your way through the tutorials in this book first and then go back to try some of the recipe variations. By the time you finish, you should be comfortable with all the basic tools in the paint package that you use. I hope that the recipes inspire you to experiment further with the tools in your paint program. A wonderful thing about working on the computer is that there is rarely only one way to achieve an effect.

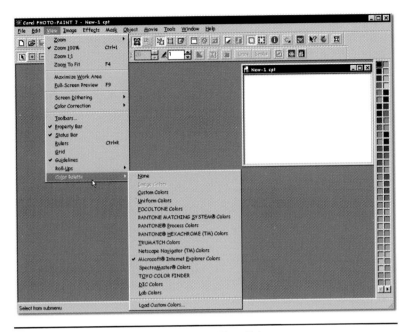

Figure I.6 Changing the color palette in PhotoPaint.

For experienced Photoshop or PhotoPaint users, I suggest that you read Chapter 1 for information on anti-aliasing and saving files. Then you may want to work through the recipes in the following chapters and read Chapters 5, 8, and 10 through 14 for more technical information on creating Web graphics.

This book is organized into three main sections: Creating Simple Web Graphics, Intermediate Web Graphics, and Advanced Web Topics.

In the first section, Chapters 1 through 4, you'll learn about anti-aliasing, creating a drop shadow, making colored ball and beveled-edged icons, and how to create seamless pattern tiles. Chapter 1 explains anti-aliasing, which helps to remove jagged edges and produce smoothness in Web graphics. Chapter 2 is a step-by-step demonstration of how to create those ever-popular colored ball icons, followed by 15 different variations for both Photoshop and PhotoPaint in the Recipes section. Chapter 3 explains two different methods of creating beveled-edged icons, again followed by 15 variations in the Recipes section. In Chapter 4, you will learn to create seamless pattern tiles to use as Web page backgrounds, as shown in Figure I.7. Chapter 4 also covers several methods of seamless pattern tile creation, including using the Clouds filter in Photoshop and making custom Image Lists in PhotoPaint.

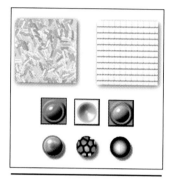

Figure I.7 Simple icons and seamless background tiles.

In the second section, Intermediate Web Graphics (Chapters 5 through 8), you'll discover tips on designing Web pages with color, how to fix a bad scan, how to create a hand-tinted photo, how to create interesting edges on images, and how to index colors. I delve into using color and overall design techniques in Chapter 5, including how to troubleshoot a Web page design. The whole spectrum of Web color issues and non-dithering Web palettes is covered, and a helpful hexcode color chart is included. I also explain several methods of finding the color hexcode in Chapter 5. Scanning is a big issue, and Chapter 6 discusses how to compensate, tweak, and correct bad scans. Two example sections in the chapter demonstrate the different effects you can achieve using the filters that come with Photoshop or PhotoPaint. In addition, Chapter 6 describes how to colorize a grayscale photograph, as shown in Figure I.8.

Adding creative edges on Web graphics is a great way to add interest, and Chapter 7 gives 15 methods for doing so. Chapter 7 also shows two methods for matching graphics from a collection of graphics whose colors and styles do not coordinate, a common situation if you're converting existing documents and artwork for the Web. Chapter 8 explores some of the more important technical issues in designing for the Web, including indexing, transparency, and a step-by-step guide for creating smaller graphics files.

In the final section of the book, Advanced Web Topics, you'll discover how to create text with a drop shadow (see Figure I.9), importing and exporting tips, how to speed up your work, and information on copyright and the Web.

Figure I.8 Colorizing a scanned photograph.

Figure I.9 Creating text effects.

Enlivening text with a glow or drop shadow is another great way to add some zip to a Web page, so Chapter 9 gives 15 examples of type treatments. Then, because it's rare to work with files in one format, Chapter 10 discusses importing and exporting files. Chapter 11 alleviates the drudgery of repetitive work with speed tips. Chapter 12 discusses copyright and the Web, a very important topic whether you are creating original work or planning to use artwork created by someone else.

In Chapter 14, you'll learn how to add motion to your Web pages using simple GIF animation techniques, as seen in Figure I.10. Chapter 13 covers some basic HTML tags for adding images and links to a Web page.

The end of the book contains a quick HTML reference chart and a Glossary, followed by a helpful Resources section, which contains a wide selection of Web sites you can visit to download movies and artwork, browse tutorials, publicize your Web site for free, and much more.

Figure I.10 Creating a GIF animation.

PART 1
CREATING SIMPLE WEB GRAPHICS

1 THE IMPORTANCE OF BEING ANTI-ALIASED, OR WHY BEING FUZZY IS SHARP

Anti-aliasing is the most important tool for working with low-resolution graphics. It minimizes the stair-stepping, or "jaggies" of diagonal edges so apparent in less professionally designed graphics. By creating a transition between two adjacent colors, which appears as a slight blur, the edges become crisper.

When you're working at screen resolution, you're using far fewer pixels, roughly a third that you would if you were working at normal print resolution; thus every pixel counts. Anti-aliasing is especially helpful in increasing the legibility of type in graphics. In this chapter we'll work through two examples using anti-aliasing: The first uses type, and the second a simple graphic.

In these examples, we'll be using a setting of 96 dpi, dots per inch. Whereas the dpi settings used in paint programs are meaningful when applied to print graphics, where they determine the resolution and size of the ultimate output of the image, in Web graphics, you can't control the size of the image or its resolution with the dpi setting.

Web browsers display images and pages at the resolution of the monitor being used to view the images. Examine Figures 1.1 and 1.2, which show the same Web page viewed at two different monitor resolutions. If you are using Photoshop or Corel PhotoPaint, chances are that you are using a higher-end computer with a higher-display resolution, which is why we'll be using 96 dpi in creating the images. The dpi setting does control how the images display in Photoshop or PhotoPaint. The most common resolution for computers is probably 640 x 480. There is no way to measure this, and there is a wide range of possible monitor resolutions. We'll discuss this topic more in Chapter 5.

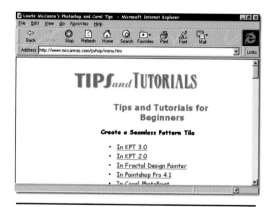

Figure 1.1 The Web page viewed at a display of 640 x 480.

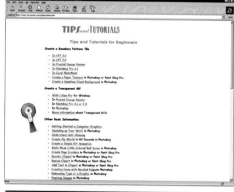

Figure 1.2 The same page, viewed on the same computer, but with the display set to 1200 x 800 resolution.

Photoshop

Getting Anti-Aliased

All of the Photoshop examples in the book assume that you are using RGB mode, 96 pixels per inch, and the paper color set to white, unless otherwise noted. If you're used to creating graphics for print, it might be useful to note that for Web graphics, pixels per inch is equal to dots per inch, and you won't want to use CMYK color, because RGB has a greater range of color.

1. Open a new file by selecting **File** from the menu bar, then **New**. Select a width of 300 pixels and a height of 100 pixels. The paper color should be set to white, and the color mode should be set to RGB, which is the color model that monitors use. The most common resolution for monitors is between 72 and 96 pixels per inch. Web graphics will automatically display at the resolution of the viewer's monitor.

2. Choose black as your foreground color. (The type will be filled with the foreground color.)

3. Select the **Type** tool, then click on your image. This will bring up the Type Tool dialog box. Make sure that the **Anti-Aliased** checkbox is checked. Set the type size to about 14 points, and type **This is anti-aliased type**.

4. To reposition your type, move the cursor over the type until it changes into an arrow, and then drag the type into position. If you prefer, you can nudge the type into position one pixel at a time by using the **Control (Command)** key in conjunction with the arrow keys on your keyboard.

5. Select the **Type** tool, then click on your file. Type **This is NOT anti-aliased type**. Be sure to deselect the **Anti-Aliased** option, as shown in Figure 1.3.

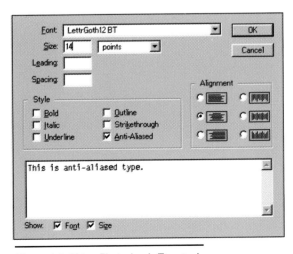

Figure 1.3 Using Photoshop's Type tool.

If you have your Layers palette open in Photoshop (you can open it by selecting **Window/Show Layers**), you'll notice that Photoshop automatically places the type you have created on a new layer.

Compare the two lines of type, as in Figure 1.4. See the difference a little anti-aliasing can make!

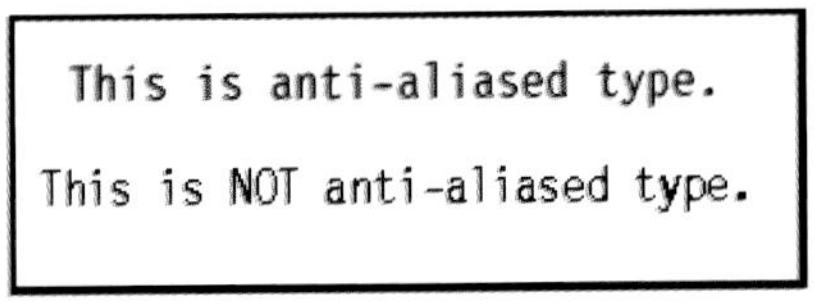

> This is anti-aliased type.
>
> This is NOT anti-aliased type.

Figure 1.4 Comparing anti-aliased and non–anti-aliased type.

Anti-Aliasing Other Types of Graphics

Often, you'll be presented with a bitmapped image that looks great—except for its jagged edges. If you need to anti-alias an entire image, your best bet is to resize the image using the **Image/Image Size** option. When Photoshop resizes an image, it automatically anti-aliases the edges for you. I'll discuss anti-aliasing imported files more in Chapter 11.

Many of the tools within Photoshop are automatically anti-aliased as well, including the Paintbrush, Airbrush, and Blur tools, all available from the Tool palette. Additionally, any of the selection tools, including Elliptical Marquee and Lasso can have an anti-aliased edge by selecting the **Anti-Alias** checkbox in the Options palette. And for those little touch-ups, I've found the Smudge tool in Photoshop to be perfect:

1. Start with a new file 100 x 100 pixels. Double-click on the **Pencil** tool to open the Options/Brushes palette.

2. Set the brush size to the smallest size (1 pixel) and draw a triangle by holding down the **Shift** key and clicking in three places. You can fill the triangle with red if you like, as shown in Figure 1.5.

3. Select the **Smudge** tool. Double-click on it to open the Options palette, if it isn't already open.

4. Set 50% pressure in the Options palette, and select a small brush size. Holding down the **Shift** key, **Shift+click** at two points on the triangle, across a jagged edge. In Figure 1.5, the right edge of the triangle has been anti-aliased.

Figure 1.5 Right side of triangle has been anti-aliased.

PHOTOPAINT

Getting Anti-Aliased

All of the PhotoPaint examples in the book assume that you are using 24-bit RGB color, 96 pixels per inch, and that the paper color is white unless otherwise noted. If you're accustomed to creating graphics for print, you won't want to use CMYK color, because RGB color has a greater range. Select black as your paint color, that is, the color the type will be filled with. You can select the fill color by clicking on the **Paint** color swatch at the bottom of the screen.

1. Open a new file by selecting **File** from the menu bar, then **New**. Set the paper color to white. Set the image size to **Custom**, with a width of 300 pixels and a height of 100 pixels. The default color mode in PhotoPaint is 24-bit RGB, the color model that monitors use. Most PC monitors display at somewhere between 72 and 96 pixels per inch, so set the resolution to 96 pixels per inch.

2. Double-click on the **Text** tool. This will bring up the Tool Settings dialog box, as shown in Figure 1.6. Make sure that the **Anti-aliasing** checkbox is checked. Set the type size to about 14 points, click on your file, and type **This is anti-aliased text**. If you need to reposition your type, drag the type into position. If you have the Objects palette open (you can open it by selecting **View/Rollups/Object Palette**), you'll notice that PhotoPaint automatically creates the type as an object separate from the background layer.

3. Click on your file with the Text tool. Type **This is NOT anti-aliased text**. Deselect the **Anti-aliasing** option.

Compare the two lines of type as shown in Figure 1.7. You can see how anti-aliasing creates more legible type. If you want to save this file, you'll need to apply **Objects/Combine/All Objects with Background** first.

> This is anti-aliased text.
>
> This is NOT anti-aliased text.

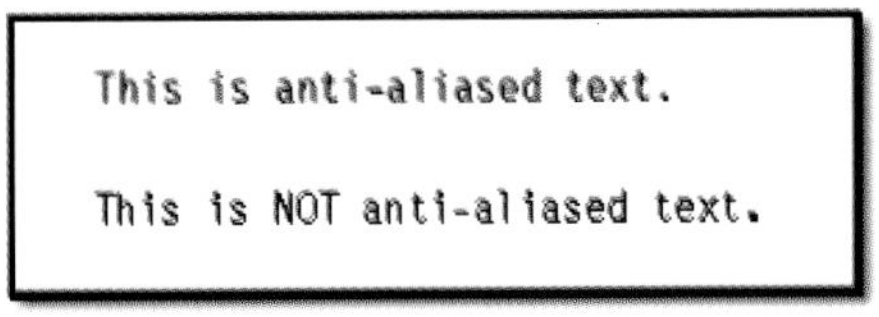

Figure 1.7 Comparing anti-aliased and non-anti-aliased type.

Figure 1.6 PhotoPaint's Text Tool Settings roll-up.

Anti-Aliasing Other Types of Graphics

If you need to anti-alias an entire bitmap image, the preferred option is to resize the image using **Image/Resample** with the process set to **Anti-aliased**. PhotoPaint has introduced the option of resampling a bitmapped file when you open it, but this does not anti-alias the image when it resamples, so it's best to open the file, then use **Image/Resample**. (I'll discuss anti-aliasing imported files, including CorelDRAW files, in Chapter 10.)

Many of the tools within PhotoPaint are automatically anti-aliased. In the Tool Settings palette (shown in Figure 1.8), if you indicate an amount in the Soft Edge box, the tool will be anti-aliased.

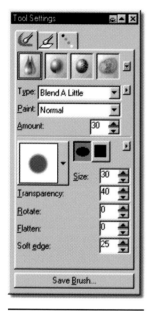

Figure 1.8 Tool Settings roll-up for the Effects tool.

If you've created a mask and want the edges of the mask to be anti-aliased, use the checkbox on the Mask roll-up, with the amount set to 1 or 2 pixels. And for those little touch-ups, I've found the Effects tool in PhotoPaint to be the best answer:

1. Start with a file 100 x 100 pixels. Click and hold on the **Rectangle** tool to reveal the Line tool. Double-click on the **Line** tool to open the Tool Settings roll-up. Set the size to 1 pixel.

2. Deselect the **Anti-aliasing** checkbox. Normally, you would leave this checked, but for this example we want to demonstrate the contrast between an anti-aliased and aliased edge.

3. Use the Line tool to draw a triangle by clicking in three places. Double-click to finish the triangle. You can fill the triangle with red, using the Fill tool, if you like.

4. Double-click on the **Effects** tool, which will bring up the Tool Settings roll-up. Select **Size, 4**; **Transparency, 50**; **Rotate, 0**; **Flatten, 0**; and **Soft Edge, 50**.

NOTE: You may have noticed that the Tool Settings are also available from the menu bar at the top of the PhotoPaint screen, as shown in Figure 1.9, but the roll-up Tool Settings has a little more information and may be easier to understand if you're not familiar with PhotoPaint.

Figure 1.9 Tool Settings on the toolbar at the top of the screen.

5. Hold down the **Alt** key, and **Alt+click** the Effects tool on two points of the triangle. This will connect the two clicks using the Effects tool. In Figure 1.10, I've anti-aliased the right edge of the triangle. You may want to save the variation of the Effects tool you've just created for future use.

Figure 1.10 Right side of the triangle has been anti-aliased.

SAVING FILES

You're probably eager to start getting your images up onto your Web site, but before you can, they must be saved properly. The most commonly used file formats for Web graphics are the GIF and JPG. You'll find much more information on these formats in Chapter 8, but in the meantime, we'll save this example as a GIF file. To do so, you must first index it, or reduce the colors in the image to 256 or fewer. GIF files are compressed, which means that they have smaller file sizes than uncompressed file formats. Therefore, they load more quickly on the Web.

If you try to save your file as a GIF when the file is still in RGB color mode, the GIF file format will not be listed. As just noted, you need to index the file to reduce the colors to 256 or fewer to save your file as a GIF. You can do this in Photoshop by using **Image/Mode/Indexed color**. From there, you'll see that the number of colors is listed for your image. For the images in this chapter, select **Palette, Web; Options, Dither, None**. Once you have indexed the colors for the image, you can save the file in GIF format.

To save your file as a GIF in PhotoPaint, apply **Image/Convert to/Palette 8 bit**. Select **Palette Type, Custom, Dither Type, None**. Since you've selected **Custom**, you'll see another screen prompting you to select a palette. Select the **Microsoft Internet Explorer** palette. (The Microsoft Internet Explorer and Netscape palettes listed here are actually the same color palette, with the colors arranged in different positions.) Then, save the file as a GIF. For now, save the GIF in 87a format.

Be aware that once you save your file as a GIF, you lose information from your file that cannot be replaced. GIF is called a *lossless* file format, because you've already lost the information once you convert from 24-bit color to 8-bit color.

If you think you'll need to revise, resize, or print the artwork you create, also save your file in a format that is not compressed or indexed, such as TIF, BMP, the Photoshop native file format (.PSD), or Corel PhotoPaint native file format (.CPT). In Figures 1.11–1.14, you'll see the difference between resizing a TIF file and resizing a GIF file. That way, when you go to make changes, you'll start out with the best possible version of your image. Also, once you have indexed the colors for an image, you won't be able to use filters on the image or use brushes with anti-aliased edges. (Learn more about indexing in Chapter 8.) If you've saved a file as GIF and want to use a filter on it, you'll need to convert the image back to RGB 24-bit color; or for the best possible quality image, return to the uncompressed file to make further changes or revisions.

Figure 1.11 The original TIF file.

Figure 1.12 The TIF file resized.

Figure 1.13 The GIF file.

Figure 1.14 The GIF file resized.

JPG is a full-color file format that is good for images with a lot of colors. However, every time you save a file and resave it as JPG, it will degrade the overall quality of the image, as you can see in Figures 1.15 and 1.16. This is why JPG is known as a lossy format: You lose information every time you select **File/Save As JPG**, even if you haven't otherwise made any changes to your image. The first time or two you save as JPG won't degrade the quality too much, but eventually you'll get this fuzzy-yet-crispy look to your images that is typical of an image that has been resaved as a JPG too many times. You'll also want to keep an uncompressed version of your JPG files in case you ever need to go back and revise them. Saving as a GIF or JPG is usually the last step in creating Web graphics, for the reasons just outlined.

Figure 1.15 The original JPG file.

Figure 1.16 The file resaved as a JPG several times.

What's in a Name?

Finally, it's a good time to start thinking about naming conventions for your files. For simplicity and consistency's sake, you'll want to use all lowercase letters when you name your files. In many computer applications, it doesn't matter if you use upper- or lowercase when naming files. HTML, however, is case-sensitive. If you name a file **HySTErIA.gif**, and your HTML code indicates **hysteria.gif**, your image will not appear on your Web page. To save yourself time and headaches, keep your file names short and lowercase. Another thing I've learned the hard way is not to use symbols or spaces within a file name.

Keep in mind that a GIF file must always end in .gif; a JPG file must always end in .jpg or .jpeg (for instance, logo.jpg); and HTML files must always end in .htm or .html. Some Web browsers will not display a file without the correct file extension.

Now that you know what anti-aliasing is, you'll no doubt use it all the time. It's not exciting or glamorous, but anti-aliasing will make your images appear cleaner and more professional.

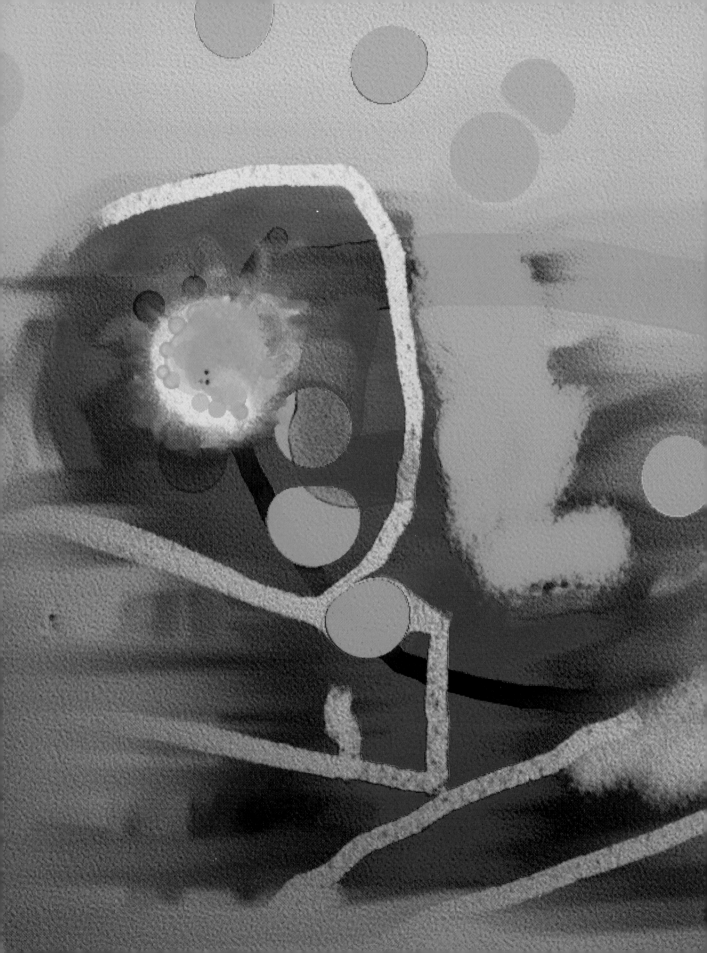

2

MAKING THOSE CLEVER LITTLE COLORED BALL ICONS

You've seen these friendly little icons on Web pages all over the place, sort of the Web version of the Smiley Face. And whether you find them helpful or annoying, creating them can be a great way to become comfortable with some of the basic tools in Photoshop and PhotoPaint. These colored ball icons may not be great art, but they provide good practice.

I'll show you two basic ways to craft these clever dollops of artwork, along with lots of recipes for variations. The first method uses traditional painting implements, including the fill and airbrush tools, with which we'll create a custom color gradient for the colored ball. The second method (for those of you who don't want to get your hands dirty) is done entirely with filters.

But before we begin, just a couple of quick notes about working at screen (monitor) resolution. You'll notice that I'm working with the images at a pixel level. In some of the screen shots, I've also used the rulers, set to pixels, to help orient you to how small I'm actually working. To make this more meaningful, change the units of measurement within the paint program you're using from inches to pixels. In Photoshop, go to **File/Preferences/Units/Ruler Units**; in PhotoPaint, go to **Tools/Options/General** and change the units to pixels. If you think it would be helpful to view rulers, simply use **Ctrl+R** (**Command+R** on the Mac in Photoshop) to view them.

Photoshop has added a new tool called the Navigator to view files. Select **Window/Show Navigator** to open the Navigator palette. By dragging the triangle below the preview of your image, called the zoom slider, you can quickly alter how much you're zoomed in or out from your image.

PhotoPaint has added a Navigator for images as well. If your image is sized so that it is only partially visible, look for the small square white icon in the lower-right corner. Click on this icon to pan around the entire image. Although it would be overkill and a waste of time to work this close for images that would be printed at 300 dpi or higher, you do need to work at a zoomed-in rate much of the time for images that will be displayed at 96 dpi or less on the Web.

As you begin to experiment, be aware that some of the tools in the paint programs are tweaked for use at higher resolutions. For example, some filters (such as the Color Halftone, Mezzotint, or Wind filters in Photoshop) will obliterate a file at 96 dpi. Luckily, Photoshop has added a **Fade Filter** command to the Filter menu, so you can lessen the impact of a very strong filter. Some paint tools will also need to be adjusted for working at a low resolution. An airbrush set to a large setting can more than cover the entire area of a Web icon, for instance. By adjusting tool sizes, you'll find a comfortable range for working at low resolutions. PhotoPaint has multiple undos, which can free you up to experiment more easily. You can even set the number of steps you'd like to be able to undo in the **Tools/Options/Memory** dialog box. Photoshop has only one level of undo.

Now, on with the show.

PHOTOSHOP

Making Colored Balls without Filters

1. Open a small file in Photoshop, 40 x 40 pixels at 96 dpi. Click and hold the **Marquee** tool to reveal the Elliptical Marquee tool. Create a circular selection by holding down the **Shift** key while you click and drag the **Elliptical Marquee** tool. Pressing the **Shift** key while you're creating the selection constrains the ellipse to a circle. Leave some room to include a drop shadow, as shown in Figure 2.1.

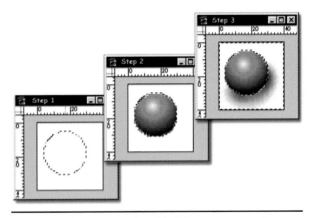

Figure 2.1 Creating a colored ball icon, steps 1 to 3.

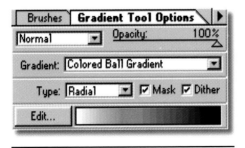

Figure 2.2 Gradient tool palette.

2. Double-click on the **Gradient** tool to open its Options palette. We'll be creating a custom gradient in order to give the colored ball a three-dimensional effect. Click the **Edit** option on the Gradient Tool Options palette, as shown in Figure 2.2.

C h a p t e r

2

3. Select the **Edit** button on the Gradient tool palette. This will open the Gradient Editor, as shown in Figure 2.3. Select **New**. Type **Colored Ball Gradient**, and select **OK**. Select the left square under the gradient bar, then click on the color swatch. Select white. Select the right square under the gradient bar, then click on the color swatch. Select black. Next, to add a new color to the gradient, click between the two squares below the gradient bar. Click on the color swatch and select red, as shown in Figure 2.3. If you wish to save this gradient for use later, select **Save**. Select **OK**. Make sure that **Radial** is selected for the type of gradient on the Gradient Option palette. Drag the Gradient tool from the upper-left corner to the lower-right corner of the circle to fill the selection with a smooth gradation.

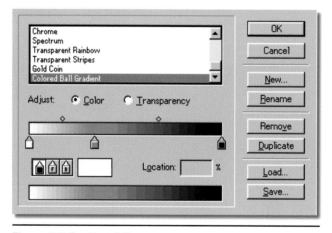

Figure 2.3 Gradient Editor.

4. From the menu bar, apply **Select/Inverse**. This will mask out the circle, allowing you to paint a drop shadow behind the circle. Use the Airbrush tool and dark gray as the color to paint a drop shadow along the edge of the circle. To save your image, select **Image/Mode/Indexed**. Then select **Palette/Adaptive/5 Bit** and **Dither/Diffusion**. Save your image as a GIF file, and it will be ready to be used on the Web.

    If this icon looks too large, you can resize the image, but do so *before* you index the file, as we discussed at the end of Chapter 1. To resize the image, select **Image/Image Size** and change the pixel dimensions. Then index the image as described previously.

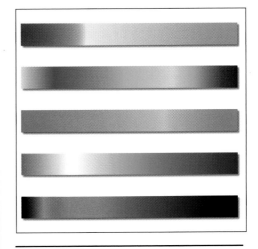

Figure 2.4   Custom gradients.

Making Colored Balls Using Filters

This method of creating a colored ball icon requires both the Alien Skin Drop Shadow filter and the Glass Lens filter from Kai's Power Tools. The Glass Lens filter is part of the Kai's Power Tools package, a set of useful commercial filters created by Metatools Software. Metatools has a Web site at http://www.meta-tools.com, where you can browse tutorials and download demo versions of their software. The Drop Shadow filter is part of Alien Skin Software's set of filters called Eye Candy. Alien Skin has a Web site at http://www.alienskin.com, where you can download demo versions of some of their filters. Neither of these sets of commercial filters is included with Photoshop. The Web site addresses for these and many other filters, fonts, tutorials, and much more are located in the Resources section at the back of this book.

1. As in the first example, open a small file in Photoshop, 40 x 40 pixels, or use **Ctrl+N** on Windows, or **Command+N** on the Mac. Use the Elliptical Selection tool to create a circular selection, as shown in Figure 2.5. Hold down the **Shift** key to constrain the ellipse to a circle. Use the Fill tool to fill the selection with a medium blue.

2. From the menu bar, apply **Filter/KPT 3.0/Glass Lens**. Select **Mode,Bright**; **Glue, Normal**; **Opacity,100**.

3. From the menu bar, apply **Filter/Eye Candy/Drop Shadow** to finish off your creation, setting the distance amount to about 4 pixels for the horizontal and vertical offset measurements, as shown in Figure 2.6 and set the direction amount to 315. Select black as the shadow color, and set the opacity to 60%. We used the Drop Shadow after the Glass Lens Bright filter because using the Drop Shadow removes the selection from the image, shown in Figure 2.5, step 3. To save your image, select **Image/Mode/Indexed**. Then select **Palette/Adaptive/ 5Bit** and **Dither, Diffusion**. Save your image as a GIF file.

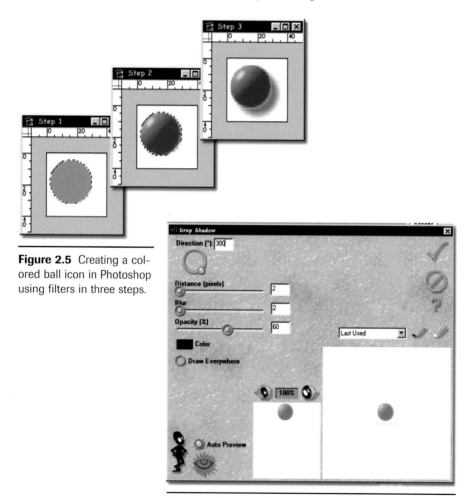

Figure 2.5 Creating a colored ball icon in Photoshop using filters in three steps.

Figure 2.6 The Eye Candy Drop Shadow filter.

PHOTOPAINT

Making Colored Ball Icons without Filters

One of the differences between Corel PhotoPaint and Photoshop is terminology. What PhotoPaint calls a *mask* roughly equates to a Photoshop *selection*. It's easy to become confused and frustrated trying to use a mask (or selection) tool. Masks and selections are really more similar to the tools photographers use than the tools artists traditionally use. A mask or selection can be as simple as a geometric shape (say, a circle) that allows you to paint within a circle, but it can also be as complex and as powerful as applying a filter using a grayscale photo to mask the image.

I'm going to start slow and "sneak up" on some of these masking tools to enable you to create some of those timeless, eternal little round ball icons using the masking tools:

1. Open a small file, 40 x 40 pixels, at 96 dpi. Click on the **Rectangle Mask** tool to reveal the flyout menu of masking tools. Select the **Circle Mask** tool. Hold down the **Control** key while you're creating the mask to constrain the ellipse to a circle. Make the circle a little smaller than the total image area so that you have room for the drop shadow.

2. Next, double-click on the **Fill** tool to open the Tool Settings roll-up (Figure 2.7). Select the **Fountain Fill** icon, and select **Edit**. You will want to select **Type, Radial**; **Center Offset**; **Horizontal, -15**; **Vertical, 15**. Select **Custom** for the type of color blend.

Figure 2.7 The Fill roll-up in Corel PhotoPaint.

We'll be creating a custom gradient that will provide both the shadow and highlight that make the colored ball appear three-dimensional. Above the color blend bar, you'll see two squares. Click on the left square, and select black from the swatches of color on the right. Click on the right square, and select white from the color swatches. Double-click between the two squares to add a third color to the color blend, and select red, as shown in Figure 2.8. If you wish to save this gradient so that you can use it again, type in a name for it in the Presets box, and select the **+** icon next to the Presets.

3. From the menu bar, select **Mask/Invert** so that you can paint next to, but not on, the ball. Select the **Paintbrush** tool, and double-click to open the Tool Settings roll-up. Select the **Airbrush** to paint a soft gray shadow. Select **Mask/None** (as shown in Figure 2.9, step 3). To save

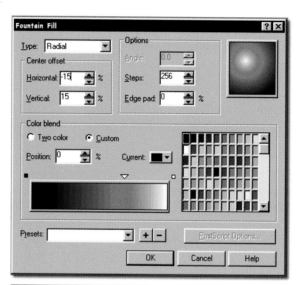

Figure 2.8 The Fountain Fill Edit dialog box in Corel PhotoPaint.

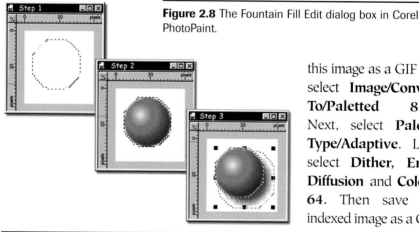

this image as a GIF file, select **Image/Convert To/Paletted 8Bit**. Next, select **Palette Type/Adaptive**. Last, select **Dither, Error Diffusion** and **Colors, 64**. Then save the indexed image as a GIF.

Figure 2.9 Creating the colored ball icon in Corel PhotoPaint.

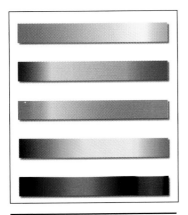

If this icon looks too large, you can resize it, but do so *before* you index the file. To resize the image, select **Image/Resample** and change the pixel dimensions. Then index the image as described earlier.

> **Extra Credit**
>
> Create and save your own custom gradients. Try to re-create some of the gradients shown in Figure 2.10. By using a consistent color gradient throughout a Web site for icons, headers, type, and so on, you can establish continuity.

Figure 2.10 Custom Fountain Fill examples.

Creating Colored Balls Using Filters

This method of creating a colored ball icon uses two filters that come with Corel PhotoPaint 7. To use filters, your image must be in grayscale or RGB color. Filters will be grayed out on the Effects menu if you try to use them on images where the color has been indexed.

The Spheroid Designer Filter is part of the Kai's Power Tools package, a set of useful filters created by Metatools Software. It's found on the Effects/KPT3.0 menu. Corel PhotoPaint contains some of the filters included in the Kai's Power Tools version 3. (You'll find many more pointers to filters and other software in the Resources section at the end of this book.) Corel has also included a Drop Shadow filter, located on the **Objects/Drop Shadow Filter** menu in PhotoPaint. If this option is grayed out, it means that your file does not have an object selected. If you have created a mask, you can convert your mask to an object simply by selecting **Object/Convert Mask to Object**. Then you should be able to apply the Drop Shadow filter to your image.

1. Open a small file, 40 x 40 pixels, at 96 dpi. Use the Circle Mask tool. Hold down the **Control** key while you're creating the mask to constrain the ellipse to a circle. Make the circle a little smaller than the image so you have room for the drop shadow, shown in Figure 2.11. Select the **Fill** tool, and double-click on it to open the Tool Settings roll-up. Click on **Uniform Fill**, and choose a light blue or a medium blue from the color palette at the right of the screen using the right mouse button. Fill the mask.

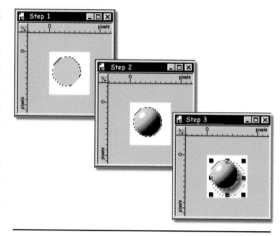

Figure 2.11 Creating a colored ball icon using filters in three steps.

2. Select **Effects/KPT3.0/KPT Spheroid Designer**, as shown in Figure 2.12. Click on the **Options** button, and select **Procedural+** to apply the filter to the existing image without changing its color.

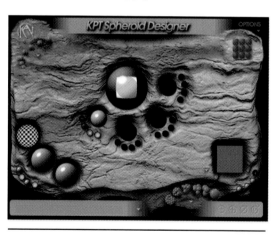

Figure 2.12 The Spheroid Designer.

3. Select **Object/Convert Mask to Object**. Select **Object/Drop Shadow**, with the settings **Horizontal, 4**; **Vertical, 4**; **Feather, 2**; **Direction, Inside**; **Opacity, 60**. To save this image as a GIF file, select **Image/Convert To/Paletted 8Bit**. Next select **Palette Type, Custom**; then select **Microsoft Internet Explorer** from the drop-down Color Table menu. Last, select **Dither, Error Diffusion**. Then save the indexed image as a GIF. The finished icon is shown in step 3 of Figure 2.11.

PHOTOSHOP RECIPES FOR COLORED BALL ICONS

All of the following files measured 40 x 40 pixels, were in RGB color, and used a circular selection with room for a drop shadow as demonstrated in this chapter.

A couple of quick shortcuts will help you as you work through these examples:

- To create a uniform set of selections, set your selection tool to a certain pixel size. Double-click on the **Elliptical Marquee** tool to open the Options palette; change the style to **Fixed Size**. Thereafter, each time you use the Elliptical Marquee tool, it will be set to the same size.

- To deselect a selection, use **Ctrl+D** (**Command+D** on the Mac). To undo the last step, use **Ctrl+Z** (**Command+Z** on the Mac).

A couple of notes about using filters in Photoshop 4.0. If a filter appears too strong, you can lessen the impact by selecting **Filter/Fade**. Also, many of the Photoshop filters rely on the foreground and background colors you have selected. If your filters are grayed out in the menu, make sure that your image is in RGB color by selecting **Image/Mode/RGB**. The following selections are suggestions to get you started. Have fun, and experiment!

Fill the selection with yellow. Apply **Filter/KPT 3.0/Glass Lens** with the mode set to **Bright**. Apply **Filter/Eye Candy/Drop Shadow** with the settings **Direction, 315; Distance, 4; Blur, 4; Opacity, 60;** and **Shadow Color, Black;** or use the airbrush to create a drop shadow as described in this chapter. Use the Paintbrush tool set to 1 or 2 pixels, and use black to paint the face as shown. Change the color to white and use the paintbrush to add highlights to the eyes.

Fill the selection with medium blue. Apply **Filter/Noise/Add Noise** with the amount set to **70** and distribution set to **Gaussian**. Apply **Filter/Eye Candy/Drop Shadow** with the settings **Distance, 4; Blur, 4; Opacity, 60;** and **Shadow Color, Black;** or use the airbrush to create a drop shadow as described in this chapter.

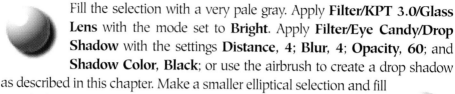

Chapter 2

Fill the selection with a very pale gray. Apply **Filter/KPT 3.0/Glass Lens** with the mode set to **Bright**. Apply **Filter/Eye Candy/Drop Shadow** with the settings **Distance, 4; Blur, 4; Opacity, 60**; and **Shadow Color, Black**; or use the airbrush to create a drop shadow as described in this chapter. Make a smaller elliptical selection and fill it with dark blue. From the menu bar, use **Select/Modify/Contract** with a setting of 3 pixels and fill with black. Apply **Filter/KPT 3.0/Glass Lens** with the mode set to **Bright**.

Fill the selection with light green, and draw dark green vertical stripes using the Paintbrush tool. You can constrain the Paintbrush tool to a straight line by holding down the **Shift** key as you draw. Use the Lasso Selection tool to draw a triangle on the right side of the circle, and fill with red. Apply **Filter/KPT 3.0/Glass Lens** with the mode set to **Bright**. Apply **Filter/Eye Candy/Drop Shadow** with the settings **Distance, 4; Blur, 4; Opacity, 60**; and **Shadow Color, Black**; or use the airbrush to create a drop shadow as described in this chapter.

Fill the selection with pale violet. Apply **Filter/Texture/Craquelure**. Next, apply **Filter/KPT 3.0/Glass Lens** with the mode set to **Bright**. Apply **Filter/Eye Candy/Drop Shadow** with the settings **Distance, 4; Blur, 4; Opacity, 60**; and **Shadow Color, Black**; or use the airbrush to create a drop shadow as described in this chapter.

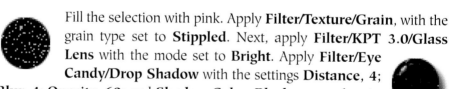

Fill the selection with pink. Apply **Filter/Texture/Grain**, with the grain type set to **Stippled**. Next, apply **Filter/KPT 3.0/Glass Lens** with the mode set to **Bright**. Apply **Filter/Eye Candy/Drop Shadow** with the settings **Distance, 4; Blur, 4; Opacity, 60**; and **Shadow Color, Black**; or use the airbrush to create a drop shadow as described in this chapter.

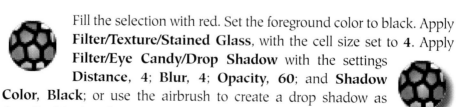

Fill the selection with red. Set the foreground color to black. Apply **Filter/Texture/Stained Glass**, with the cell size set to **4**. Apply **Filter/Eye Candy/Drop Shadow** with the settings **Distance, 4; Blur, 4; Opacity, 60**; and **Shadow Color, Black**; or use the airbrush to create a drop shadow as described in this chapter.

Fill the selection with green. Apply **Filter/Noise/Add Noise**, set to **70%**. Next apply **Filter/Brush Strokes/Dark Strokes**, changing the black intensity setting to **2**. Next, apply **Filter/KPT 3.0/Glass Lens** with the mode set to **Bright**. Apply **Filter/Eye Candy/Drop Shadow** with the settings **Distance, 4; Blur, 4; Opacity, 60**; and **Shadow Color, Black**; or use the airbrush to create a drop shadow as described in this chapter.

Fill the selection with light blue. Select **Filter/Render/Lighting Effects**. Select **Spotlight**, and drag the focus of the light so that it highlights the upper-left edge of the selection. Set the focus to **0**. Apply **Filter/Eye Candy/Drop Shadow** with the settings **Distance, 4; Blur, 4; Opacity, 60**; and **Shadow Color, Black**; or use the airbrush to create a drop shadow as described in this chapter.

Fill the selection with violet. Use the paintbrush to scribble different colors in the selection. Next apply **Filter/KPT 3.0/Glass Lens** with the mode set to **Bright**. Apply **Filter/Eye Candy/Drop Shadow** with the settings **Distance, 4; Blur, 4; Opacity, 60**; and **Shadow Color, Black**; or use the airbrush to create a drop shadow as described in this chapter.

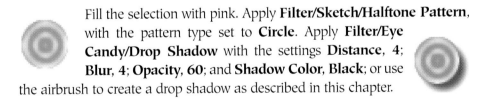

Fill the selection with yellow. Apply **Noise/Add Noise** with the amount set to **70%**. Next apply **Filter/Sketch/Chalk & Charcoal**. Apply **Filter/Eye Candy/Drop Shadow** with the settings **Distance, 4; Blur, 4; Opacity, 60**; and **Shadow Color, Black**; or use the airbrush to create a drop shadow as described in this chapter.

Fill the selection with pink. Apply **Filter/Sketch/Halftone Pattern**, with the pattern type set to **Circle**. Apply **Filter/Eye Candy/Drop Shadow** with the settings **Distance, 4; Blur, 4; Opacity, 60**; and **Shadow Color, Black**; or use the airbrush to create a drop shadow as described in this chapter.

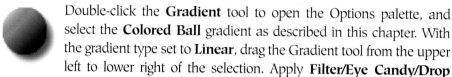

Double-click the **Gradient** tool to open the Options palette, and select the **Colored Ball** gradient as described in this chapter. With the gradient type set to **Linear**, drag the Gradient tool from the upper left to lower right of the selection. Apply **Filter/Eye Candy/Drop Shadow** with the settings **Distance, 4**; **Blur, 4**; **Opacity, 60**; and **Shadow Color, Black**; or use the airbrush to create a drop shadow as described in this chapter. Then create a smaller circular selection and apply the gradient from the lower right to upper left.

Fill the selection with red. Apply **Filter/Sketch/Photocopy**. Change the foreground color to black, and apply **Edit/Stroke**, set to **2 pixels** and **Inside**. Apply **Filter/Eye Candy/Drop Shadow** with the settings **Distance, 4**; **Opacity, 60**; and **Shadow Color, Black**; or use the airbrush to create a drop shadow as described in this chapter.

Fill the selection with pink. Apply **Sketch/Halftone Pattern**, with the pattern type set to **Line**. Apply **Filter/Distort/Twirl** set to **160**. Next apply **Filter/KPT 3.0/Glass Lens** with the mode set to **Bright**. Apply **Filter/Eye Candy/Drop Shadow** with the settings **Distance, 4**; **Blur, 4**; **Opacity, 60**; and **Shadow Color, Black**; or use the airbrush to create a drop shadow as described in this chapter.

Extra Credit

Can't get enough icons? Follow these same step-by-step recipes, but in the first step, begin with a square or rectangular selection, created with the Marquee tool or with an irregular selection created with the Lasso tool.

COREL PHOTOPAINT RECIPES FOR COLORED BALL ICONS

All of the following files started with a new file 40 x 40 pixels in size, in RGB color, and used a circular mask with room for a drop shadow, as demonstrated in this chapter.

A couple of quick shortcuts will help you as you work through these examples:

- To create a uniform set of masks, set your Masking tool to a certain pixel size. Double-click on the **Circular Mask** tool to open the Tool Settings roll-up; change the style to **Fixed Size**. Thereafter, each time you use the Circular Mask tool, it will be set to the same size.

- To deselect a mask, use **Ctrl+D**. To undo the last step, use **Ctrl+Z**. To undo a series of actions, select **Edit/Undo List**. To change the number of undos, select **Tools/Options/Memory/Undo Levels**.

A couple of notes about using filters (also called *Effects*) in PhotoPaint 7. All of the instructions given for the examples use the default settings for the filters unless otherwise specified. You can reset the filter settings to their defaults for most filters by selecting the filter and then the **Reset** icon. Some of the filters rely on the foreground and background colors you have selected for the effect you create. If your filters are grayed out in the menu, make sure that your image is in RGB color by selecting **Image/Convert To/RGB Color**. The following examples are suggestions to get you started and comfortable with the tools in PhotoPaint. Have fun, and experiment!

Fill the mask with pale violet. Apply **Effects/Add Noise**. Apply **Effects/KPT3.0/Spheroid Designer**, with the options set to Procedural+. Next select **Object/Create From Mask**. Select **Object/Drop Shadow**, with the settings **Horizontal, 4**; **Vertical, 4**; **Feather, 2**; **Direction, Inside**; **Opacity, 60**.

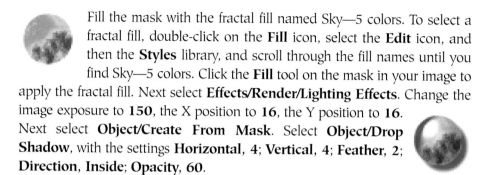

Fill the mask with the fractal fill named Sky—5 colors. To select a fractal fill, double-click on the **Fill** icon, select the **Edit** icon, and then the **Styles** library, and scroll through the fill names until you find Sky—5 colors. Click the **Fill** tool on the mask in your image to apply the fractal fill. Next select **Effects/Render/Lighting Effects**. Change the image exposure to **150**, the X position to **16**, the Y position to **16**. Next select **Object/Create From Mask**. Select **Object/Drop Shadow**, with the settings **Horizontal, 4**; **Vertical, 4**; **Feather, 2**; **Direction, Inside**; **Opacity, 60**.

Fill with a two-color turquoise-to-violet radial fountain fill using the Fill tool. Apply **Effects/3D/Emboss**, using **Original Color**; **Depth, 7**; **Level, 100**; **Direction, 0**. Use paint color. Next select **Image/Flip/Horizontal**, then **Object/Create From Mask**. Select **Object/Drop Shadow**, with the settings **Horizontal, 4**; **Vertical, 4**; **Feather, 2**; **Direction, Inside**; **Opacity, 60**.

Fill the mask with purple. Select **Effects/KPT3.0/Spheroid Designer**. Set the options to **Procedural+**, and click the **Bump Map** menu, the small triangle to the left of the gray swatch (the Bump Pan window) at the lower-right corner of the Spheroid Designer interface. Select the **Golfoid** preset from the Bump Map menu. You'll want to resize the bump map by selecting the **Bump Zoom** icon, which is located below the Bump Pan window. Select the **Bump Zoom** icon and drag your mouse to the left until the bump map has been resized to about 80%. Next select **Object/Create From Mask**. Select **Object/Drop Shadow**, with the settings **Horizontal, 4**; **Vertical, 4**; **Feather, 2**; **Direction, Inside**; **Opacity, 60**.

Center the circular mask in the image before beginning this example. Fill the circular mask with a red-to-black radial fountain fill. Next select **Object/Create From Mask**. Select **Object/Drop Shadow**, with the settings **Horizontal, 0**; **Vertical, 0**; **Feather, 8**; **Direction, Outside**; **Opacity, 100**; **Custom Color, red**.

Fill the mask with a two-color radial fountain fill, using red for both the beginning and ending colors of the fill. Select the **Clockwise Color Blend** icon in the Fountain Fill dialog box to achieve the rainbow gradient. Apply **Effects/KPT3.0/Spheroid Designer**, with the options set to **Procedural+**. Next select **Object/Create From Mask**. Select **Object/Drop Shadow**, with the settings **Horizontal, 4**; **Vertical, 4**; **Feather, 2**; **Direction, Inside**; **Opacity, 60**.

Fill the mask with the fractal fill named 5 Color Block. Apply **Effects/3D/Map to Object**, with the mapping mode set to **Spherical** and the adjust amount set to **70**. Next select **Object/Create From Mask**. Select **Object/Drop Shadow**, with the settings **Horizontal, 4**; **Vertical, 4**; **Feather, 2**; **Direction, Inside**; **Opacity, 60**.

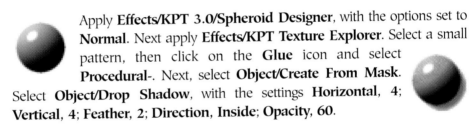

Apply **Effects/KPT 3.0/Spheroid Designer**, with the options set to **Normal**. Next apply **Effects/KPT Texture Explorer**. Select a small pattern, then click on the **Glue** icon and select **Procedural-**. Next, select **Object/Create From Mask**. Select **Object/Drop Shadow**, with the settings **Horizontal, 4**; **Vertical, 4**; **Feather, 2**; **Direction, Inside**; **Opacity, 60**.

Fill the mask with a linear fountain fill. In the Fountain Fill dialog box, select **2 Color**, and create a red-to-red gradient, and select the **Counterclockwise Color Blend** icon. Set the steps for the gradient to **6**. Fill the mask, then apply **Effects/3D/Map to Object**, with the mapping mode set to **Spherical** and the adjust amount set to **30**. Select **Mask/Shape/Reduce by 1 pixel**. Next select **Object/Create From Mask**. Select **Object/Drop Shadow**, with the settings **Horizontal, 4**; **Vertical, 4**; **Feather, 2**; **Direction, Inside**; **Opacity, 60**.

Fill the mask with a linear fountain fill. In the Fountain Fill dialog box, select **2 color**, create a light blue–to–white gradient, and set the number of steps to **2**. Fill the mask, then apply **Effects/Artistic/ Vignette, Color, Black; Shape, Circle; Offset, 90; Fade, 80**. Next, select **Object/Create From Mask**. Select **Object/ Drop Shadow**, with the settings **Horizontal, 4; Vertical, 4; Feather, 2; Direction, Inside; Opacity, 60**.

Center the mask in the middle of the image. Fill the mask with pale green. Select **Mask/Invert (Ctrl+I)**. Then select **Mask/Feather; Width, 2; Direction, Middle; Edges, Curved**. Apply **Effects/Fancy/The Boss**.

Fill the entire image with red. Center the mask in the image. Select **Mask/Invert (Ctrl+I)**. Apply **Effects/KPT3.0/Spheroid Designer**, with the options set to **Procedural+**. Select **Mask/Invert (Ctrl+I)**. Select **Mask/Shape/Reduce**, and set the amount to **2 pixels**. Apply **Effects/KPT3.0/Spheroid Designer**, with the options set to **Procedural+**; or use **Ctrl+F** to apply the previous filter.

Center the mask in the image. Fill with a light–to–dark blue radial fountain fill. Select **Mask/Invert (Ctrl+I)**. Apply **Effects/KPT 3.0/Spheroid Designer**, with the options set to **Procedural+**.

Fill the mask with a rust color. Apply **Effects/KPT3.0/Spheroid Designer**, with the options set to **Difference**. Next, select **Object/Create From Mask**. Select **Object/Drop Shadow**, with the settings **Horizontal, 4; Vertical, 4; Feather, 2; Direction, Inside; Opacity, 60**.

Fill the entire image with a medium gray. Center the mask in the image. Select **Mask/Invert (Ctrl+I)**. Apply **Effects/Fancy/The Boss**. Apply **Effects/KPT3.0/Spheroid Designer**, with the options set to **Procedural+**. Select **Mask/Invert (Ctrl+I)**. Select **Mask/Shape/Reduce**, and set the amount to **2 pixels**. Fill this mask with a medium blue. Apply **Effects/KPT3.0/Spheroid Designer**, with the options set to **Procedural+**; or use **Ctrl+F** to apply the previous filter.

Extra Credit

Want more practice? Use these same step-by-step recipes, but in the first step, begin with a square or rectangular mask, created with the Rectangle Mask tool or with an irregular selection created with the Lasso Mask tool.

3

CREATING ICONS WITH BEVELED EDGES, OR DESIGNING ICONS LIKE A PRO

Whether an icon on a Web page is used for navigation or as a page decoration, its most important feature is clarity. If the person viewing the icon has to think about what the icon means, it's a poorly designed icon. Think back over your experience in using software, and I'm sure you can remember at least a few frustrating, ambiguous icons.

More new users launch themselves on the Web every day, and for many of them, browsing the Web will be one of their first experiences using a computer. By the time a reader gets to your Web page, he or she has been inundated with hundreds of tiny pictures. Consequently, the visitor doesn't want to have to figure out if the icon means reload, home, previous page, or don't forget to write home. The best measure of success for a Web site is not how many "what a cool Web site" e-mails you get (although those are always nice), but how many visitors to your site can find the information they came there to get.

Most large software companies use focus groups to test the ease of use of their software before they ever release it. A focus group is made up of average people, and their responses and actions are recorded as they use the software under scrutiny. Setting up a focus group normally costs thousands of dollars, but you can create your own for your Web site free of charge. Select a few people, such as friends, coworkers, or relatives, to test your Web pages before you announce your site. Try to find at least one novice computer user to test your site if you can. Then ask each person to try to find several important features of your site, including your e-mail address. Watching someone use your Web site can tell you a lot about how easy or difficult you've made the navigation.

The point of icons is not to make the viewer think. Ideally, an icon should have the same immediate association for every visitor to your Web site. This is a lot of pressure for a tiny picture to carry, so consider using a picture combined with text to make navigation clear and easy.

For icons that are used as simple page decoration—for example, in place of bullets—keep them simple. Remember that basic page design principles apply to Web pages, too. Use the artwork you are creating to guide the viewer's eye to the important points on the page. Icons are tiny bits of color and texture that can bring life to an otherwise static text page.

Great artists have traditionally used a bit of contrasting color in a composition to draw the viewer's eye through the artwork, as in Figures 3.1 and 3.2, reproductions of a Degas painting. Degas used little touches of red in an otherwise monochromatic painting.

Figure 3.1 A reproduction of Degas.

Figure 3.2 Notice how little bits of contrasting color draw your eyes through the painting.

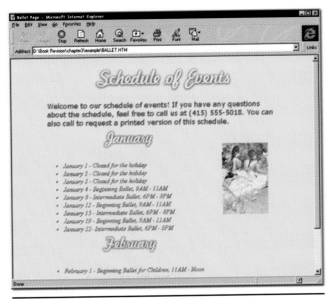

Figure 3.3 A Web page without icons.

You can use this technique to draw your Web site visitor's eye through your page, and enliven an otherwise dull page with the addition of little splashes of contrasting color. In Figures 3.3 and 3.4, you'll recognize the subtle difference that a few icons can make.

How big should an icon be? Windows icons on the desktop are generally 32 x 32 pixels. Toolbar icons that you see in applications like Word and Corel are usually 24 x 24 pixels. If you plan on adding text or backgrounds or drop shadows to your icons, you'll probably want to work a little larger than 32 x 32 pixels.

One way to streamline your work on a Web site is to decide ahead of time the size of your graphics. Maintaining a consistent size can help to organize and unify the design of each page. For instance, you might decide that all icons and icon bars will be 40 pixels in height, and all headers will be 400 x 100 pixels.

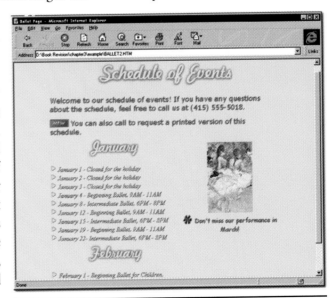

Figure 3.4 The same page after the addition of two icons.

In the following tutorials, you'll create two different types of icons. One is a simple beveled icon with a picture, and the other is an icon with a textured background and beveled edge and text. After the tutorial you'll find recipes for more than a dozen other three-dimensional icons in a variety of shapes, colors, and textures. This chapter also teaches you more about using paint tools and filters in Photoshop and PhotoPaint.

PHOTOSHOP

Creating a Simple Icon

1. Open a new file, 40 x 40 pixels, 96 pixels/inch, RGB mode. Using the Paint Bucket tool, fill the image with light gray, as shown in Figure 3.5.

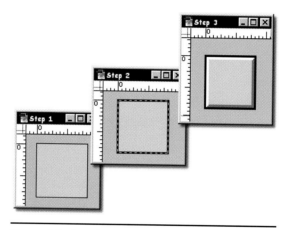

Figure 3.5 Creating a simple icon in Photoshop.

2. Set the foreground color to black. Choose **Select All** (or **Ctrl+A** on Windows, **Command+A** on the Mac). Select **Edit/Stroke**; **Width, 1**; **Location, Center**. This will create a black outline for the icon.

3. Double-click on the **Pencil** tool to bring up the Pencil Options dialog box. Select the smallest brush size (1 pixel) and set the foreground color to white. Hold down the **Shift** key and draw a 3-pixel-wide white line at the top and left edges. This will constrain your drawing to a straight line. Change the foreground color to dark gray. Draw a 3-pixel-wide dark gray line at the bottom and right edges. The gray and white edges should meet at 45° angles.

4.   Now draw the arrow using the Pencil tool. Draw the bottom edge of the arrow with a 1-pixel white line, as shown in Figure 3.6.

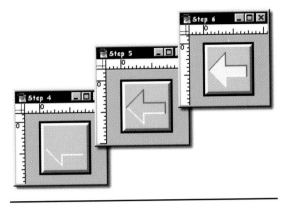

Figure 3.6 Adding an arrow to the icon.

5.   Draw the top portion of the arrow with the Pencil tool using a dark gray 1-pixel line.

6.   Fill the arrow with a little lighter gray than you used to fill the icon. You have now designed your first bevel-edged icon.

Creating a Textured Icon

1.   Open a new file, 100 pixels wide by 40 pixels tall. Fill the image with light blue, as shown in Figure 3.7, step 1.

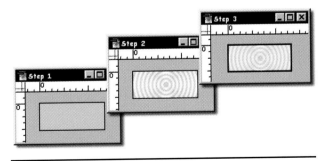

Figure 3.7 Creating a textured icon in Photoshop.

2. Use the **Filter/Sketch/Halftone Pattern**, with the pattern type set to **Circle**.

3. Apply **Filter/Blur/Blur More**. Blurring the background you have created will make the type stand out, and thus easier to read.

4. Set the foreground color to black. Choose **Select All** (or **Ctrl+A** on Windows, **Command+A** on the Mac). Select **Edit/Stroke**; **Width, 1; Location, Center**. This will create a black outline for the icon as shown in Figure 3.8.

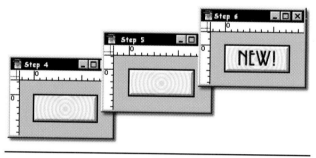

Figure 3.8 Adding a beveled edge.

5. Double-click on the **Pencil** tool, which will open the Pencil Options palette. Change the mode from Normal to **Multiply,** and change the opacity to **70%.** This will allow some of the texture to show through the shadow you'll draw on the edge of the icon. Using a dark gray, draw a 3-pixel border at the bottom and right edges of the icon. Change the foreground color to white, and set the mode to **Screen** on the Pencil Options palette. Leave the opacity at 70%, and draw a 3-pixel border at the top and left edges of the icon.

6. As a final step, add some text to your icon using the Type tool, as shown in Figure 3.8, step 6. Don't forget to anti-alias your text!

Photoshop and the Eye Candy Filters

Alien Skin makes a set of commercially available filters called Eye Candy that runs from within Photoshop, PhotoPaint, or any paint program that supports Photoshop-style plug-in filters. You can find out more about Alien Skin's filters at http://www.alienskin.com. You'll find other software and shareware filter resources in the Resources section of this book. All of the filters are useful, but for making icons, the Inner Bevel filter works especially well; it will add a shadow and a highlight to your image, giving it a 3D bevel in two steps, described next:

1. Repeat steps 1 through 3 from the preceding textured icon project.
2. Select **Filters/Eye Candy/Inner Bevel**. Apply **Bevel Width**, **6**; **Shadow Depth**, **30**; **Smoothness**, **1**; **Bevel Shape**, **Mesa**. Your finished icon will look like Figure 3.9.

Figure 3.9 Using a filter to create an icon.

PHOTOPAINT

Creating a Simple Icon

1. Start with a new file, using RGB 24-bit color, a size of 40 x 40 pixels, and the dpi set to 96. Fill the image with light gray, as shown in Figure 3.10.

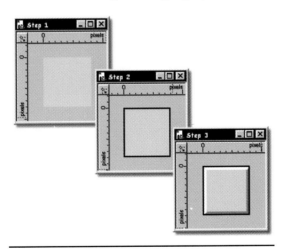

Figure 3.10 Creating a simple icon in PhotoPaint.

2. Double-click the **Line** tool (located on the Rectangle Tool flyout) to open the Tool Settings roll-up. Set the width to 1 pixel, and deselect the **Anti-aliasing** option. You want to create a hard-edged line in this example. Using the Line tool, draw a black line around the outer edge of the image. You can constrain the Line tool to a 90° angle by holding down the **Control** key while you click at the corners of the image. Double-click with the **Line** tool to finish the black line.

3.   Use the Line tool to draw a 3-pixel-wide gray border at the bottom and right edges of the image. Draw a 3-pixel-wide white border at the top and left edges of the image as seen in step 3 of Figure 3.10.

4.   Use the Rectangle Mask tool to create a rectangle in the center of the icon. Fill the mask with white.

5.   Select **Object/Create From Mask**. Next, select **Object/Drop Shadow**, with the settings **Horizontal, 1; Vertical, 1; Feather, 2; Direction, Inside; Opacity, 60**. Select **Objects/Combine/Combine All Objects with Background**.

6.   Finish the envelope by drawing gray lines to simulate text and a blue square using the Line tool, as shown in step 6 of Figure 3.11.

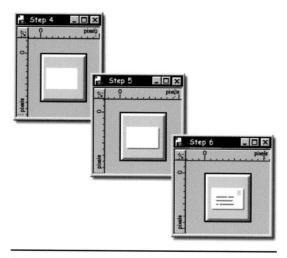

Figure 3.11 Adding a picture to the icon.

Creating a Textured Icon

1.   Start with a new file, using 24-bit color, a size of 100 x 40 pixels, and the dpi set to 96. Fill the image with a pale green color, as shown in Figure 3.12, step 1.

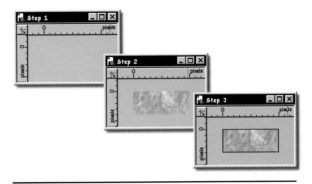

Figure 3.12 Creating a textured icon in Corel PhotoPaint.

2. Apply **Effects/Fancy/Alchemy**, with the style set to **Trees.** This creates a nice soft texture for the background of the icon, and the crispness of the type will stand out in contrast and thus be easier to read.

3. Using the Line tool, draw a 1-pixel black line around the outer edge of the image, as shown in Figure 3.13.

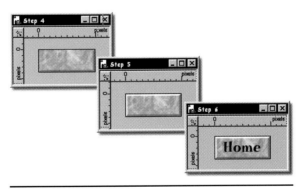

Figure 3.13 Adding a beveled edge.

4. Set the transparency for the Line tool to **10** and the mode to **Multiply** to allow some of the texture to appear on the bevel. Change the paint color to dark green. Draw a 3-pixel line at the bottom and right sides of the image. Change the paint color to white, and change the mode back to **Normal.** Draw a 3-pixel white edge at the left and top of the image as seen in step 5 of Figure 3.13.

5. Add some text to the icon using the Text tool . Don't forget to anti-alias your text! After you've used the Text tool, apply **Object/Combine/ All Objects with Background**.

Your finished icon will look like step 6 in Figure 3.13.

PhotoPaint and Alien Skin Filters

Several of the Alien Skin filters are built into PhotoPaint. We'll be using one filter named The Boss, which is especially effective for creating beveled edges. The Boss filter creates a shadow and a highlight on the image, giving it a three-dimensional look.

Repeat steps 1 to 3 in the previous exercise to create the textured icon. Then apply **Mask/All (Ctrl+A)**, **Mask/Shape/Reduce**, set to 5 pixels. Select **Mask/Invert (Ctrl+I)** to create a selection around the edge of the icon. Next, apply **Effects/ Fancy/The Boss**, with the settings **Width, 10; Smoothness, 30; Height, 15; Drop Off, Mesa**. The result is shown in Figure 3.14.

Figure 3.14 Using a filter to create a textured icon in PhotoPaint.

PHOTOSHOP RECIPES FOR THREE-DIMENSIONAL ICONS

All of the recipe files started as 40 x 40 pixels in size, in RGB color. Use these shortcuts as you work through these examples:

- To deselect a selection, use **Ctrl+D (Command+D** on the Mac). To undo the last step, use **Ctrl+Z (Command+Z** on the Mac).
- A few of these examples use the Type tool, which automatically creates a new layer in the image. In order to save a file with more than one layer in a file format other than the native Photoshop file format (**PSD**), you have to merge the layers into a single layer by selecting **Layers/Merge Down (Ctrl+E** on Windows, **Command+E** on the Mac).

If a filter appears too strong in Photoshop 4.0, you can lessen the impact by selecting **Filter/Fade**. Also, many of the Photoshop filters rely on the foreground and background colors you have selected. If your filters are grayed out in the menu, make sure that your image is in RGB color by selecting **Image/Mode/RGB**.

Fill the image with light gray. **Select All (Ctrl+A** or **Command+A)** and change the foreground color to black. Select **Edit/Stroke; Width, 1 pixel; Location, Center.** Using the Pencil tool as described in this chapter, create a 2-pixel dark gray bor-der at the top and left edges of the image, and a 2-pixel white border at the bottom and right edges of the image. This type of shading on an icon is generally used to indicate a depressed, or clicked, state.

Start with an image 100 x 40 pixels. Create an elliptical selection and fill with lavender. Change the foreground color to purple. Select **Edit/Stroke; Width, 2 pixels; Location, Inside.** Apply **Filter/Render/Lighting Effects** using the Soft Omni preset. Reset the focus of the light to the upper-left side of the image by dragging the light in the preview window. Create a drop shadow by select-ing **Filter/Eye Candy/Drop Shadow**. Add text using the Type tool. Apply **Layers/Merge Down (Ctrl+E** on Windows, **Command+E** on the Mac).

Fill the selection with pale yellow. **Select All (Ctrl+A,** or **Command+A** on the Mac). Change the foreground color to brown. Select **Edit/Stroke; Width, 2 pixels; Location, Inside.** Use the Type tool to add text. Apply **Layers/Merge Down (Ctrl+E** on Windows, **Command+E** on the Mac). Apply **Filter/Render/Lighting Effects** using the Soft Omni preset. Reset the focus of the light to the upper-left side of the image by dragging the light in the preview window.

Fill the image with black. Change the foreground color to red and use the Type tool to add type. Apply **Layers/Merge Down (Ctrl+E** on Windows, **Command+E** on the Mac). Apply **Filter/Artistic/Plastic Wrap**, with **Highlight Strength, 12; Detail, 12; Smoothness, 5.**

Fill the selection with pale blue. **Select All (Ctrl+A** on Windows or **Command+A** on the Mac). Change the foreground color to a medium blue. Select **Edit/Stroke; Width, 2 pixels; Location, Inside.** Apply **Filter/Artistic/Rough Pastels** with the texture set to **Sandstone.** Use the Type tool to add text. Apply **Layers/Merge Down (Ctrl+E** on Windows, **Command+E** on the Mac).

Create a pale pink–to–magenta linear gradient using the Gradient tool. Drag the Gradient tool from the upper-left to lower-right corner of the image. Create a square selection a little smaller than the original image. Fill this selection with the same gradient applied in the opposite direction.

Fill the image with medium green. Change the foreground color to black. Select **Edit/Stroke**; **Width, 2 pixels; Location, Inside.** Change the foreground color to white and add a symbol from a font using the Type tool. The symbol in this example came from the Zapf Dingbats font. Apply **Layers/Merge Down (Ctrl+E** on Windows, **Command+E** on the Mac). Apply **Filter/Artistic/Poster Edges**, with **Edge Thickness, 3; Edge Intensity, 10; Posterization, 5.**

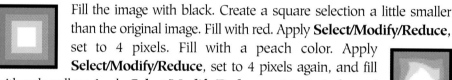

Fill the image with black. Create a square selection a little smaller than the original image. Fill with red. Apply **Select/Modify/Reduce**, set to 4 pixels. Fill with a peach color. Apply **Select/Modify/Reduce**, set to 4 pixels again, and fill with pale yellow. Apply **Select/Modify/Reduce**, set to 4 pixels, and fill with white. Apply **Filter/Distort/Twist**, with the angle set to **120.**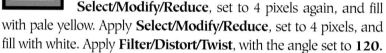

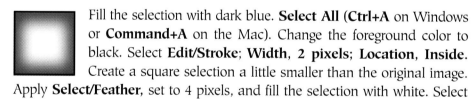

Fill the selection with dark blue. **Select All (Ctrl+A** on Windows or **Command+A** on the Mac). Change the foreground color to black. Select **Edit/Stroke**; **Width, 2 pixels; Location, Inside.** Create a square selection a little smaller than the original image. Apply **Select/Feather,** set to 4 pixels, and fill the selection with white. Select the original fill color (dark blue) and add a symbol from a font using the Type tool. The symbol in this recipe came from the Zapf Dingbats font. Apply **Layers/Merge Down (Ctrl+E** on Windows, **Command+E** on the Mac).

Change the foreground color to black. Select **Edit/Stroke; Width, 2 pixels; Location, Inside.** Select the right half of the image using the Marquee tool and apply **Image/Adjust/Invert (Ctrl+I** on Windows, **Command+I** on the Mac). Change the foreground color to red and add a symbol from a font using the Type tool. The symbol here came from the Zapf Dingbats font. Apply **Layers/Merge Down (Ctrl+E** on Windows, **Command+E** on the Mac).

Fill the image with purple. Change the foreground color to aqua. Select **Edit/Stroke**; **Width, 2 pixels; Location, Inside.** Apply **Render/Lighting** using the Soft Omni preset. Select **Image/ Rotate Canvas/Arbitrary**, with a setting of 45 degrees clockwise. Photoshop will use your background color to fill the areas around the square. I used white in the example. Change the foreground color to aqua and add a symbol from a font using the Text tool; the one here came from the Zapf Dingbats font. Apply **Layers/Merge Down (Ctrl+E** on Windows, **Command+E** on the Mac).

 Change the foreground color to black. Select **Edit/Stroke**; **Width, 2 pixels; Location, Inside.** Add a symbol from a font using the Type tool. This symbol came from the Zapf Dingbats font. Apply **Layers/Merge Down (Ctrl+E** on Windows, **Command+E** on the Mac). Change the foreground color to white and the background color to dark green. Apply **Filter/Artistic/Neon Glow**. Change the glow color to pale green and **Glow Size, -8; Glow Brightness, 20.**

 Create a circular selection using the Elliptical Marquee tool. Apply **Select/Modify/Contract by 2 pixels**. Fill with yellow. Apply **Select/Modify/Contract by 2 pixels**. Fill with red. Repeat this until you reach the center of the image.

Use the Lasso tool to create a triangle by **Alt**+clicking (**Control**+ clicking on the Mac) in three places. Fill the triangular selection with black. Apply **Select/Modify/Contract by 4 pixels**. Apply **Select/Feather at 2 pixels**, and fill the selection with red.

 Open the image created in this chapter (Creating a Textured Icon). Select **Image/Adjust/Hue-Saturation**, and drag the Hue slider until you find a different color for the icon. You can see how this technique would enable you to create a series of icons in an array of colors very quickly and easily.

Extra Credit

Having too much fun to stop now? Prepare these recipes again, but begin each recipe with type or a dingbat as the selection instead of a square.

COREL PHOTOPAINT RECIPES FOR THREE-DIMENSIONAL ICONS

All of the following files started as 40 x 40 pixels in size, in RGB color, as demonstrated in this chapter.

Take these shortcuts as you work through these examples:

- To deselect a mask, use **Ctrl+D**.
- To undo the last step, use **Ctrl+Z**.
- To undo a series of actions, select **Edit/Undo List**.
- To change the number of undos, select **Tools/Options/Memory/ Undo Levels**.

All of the instructions given for the PhotoPaint 7 examples use the default settings for the filters (also called Effects) unless otherwise specified.

Fill the image with red. Apply **Mask/Select All (Ctrl+A)**. Apply **Effects/Fancy/The Boss**, with the settings **Width, 6; Smoothness, 70; Height, 15; Dropoff, Mesa**. Change the paint color to white and add the symbol using the Text tool. This symbol came from the Zapf Dingbats typeface. Use the Object Picker tool to move the type into the center of the image. Next, apply **Mask/Create From Object**. Then apply **Effects/Fancy/The Boss**, with the settings **Width, 6; Smoothness, 70; Height, 15; Dropoff, Mesa**. Select **Object/Combine/All Objects with Background**.

Fill the image with a fountain fill with the settings **Type, Square; Steps, 5; Two Color; From, Orange; To, Orange; Clockwise Blend**. Apply **Mask/Select All (Ctrl+A)**. Select **Mask/Shape/Reduce** with a setting of 4 pixels. Apply **Effects/Fancy/The Boss**.

Fill the image with blue. Change the paint color to white and add the symbol using the Text tool. This symbol came from the Zapf Dingbats typeface. Select **Mask/Create From Object (Ctrl+M)**. Apply **Effects/Fancy/The Boss**, with the settings **Width, 6; Smoothness, 70; Height, 15; Dropoff, Mesa**. Select **Mask/Invert**. Apply **Effects/3D/Map to Object**, with the settings **Mapping Mode, Spherical; Percentage, 30**. Select **Object/Combine/All Objects with Background**.

Fill the image with black. Change the paint color to white and add the symbol using the Text tool. This symbol came from the Zapf Dingbats typeface. Select **Mask/Create From Object (Ctrl+M)**. Select **Mask/Shape/Reduce** with the setting of 1 pixel. Apply **Effects/KPT3.0/Spheroid Designer**, with the options set to **Procedural+**. Apply **Effects/Fancy/The Boss**. Select **Object/Combine/All Objects with Background**.

Fill the image with a fractal fill named Borealis Mountain found in the Texture Library named Samples. Apply **Effects/Artistic/Vignette**, with the settings **Color, Black; Shape, Square; Offset, 100; Fade, 32.** Change the paint color to white and add the symbol using the Text tool. This symbol came from the Zapf Dingbats typeface. Select **Object/Combine/All Objects with Background**.

Start with an image 100 x 40 pixels. Create an elliptical mask using the Circle Mask tool. Fill the mask with lavender. Apply **Effects/KPT3.0/Spheroid Designer**, with the options set to **Procedural-**. Change the paint color to purple, and add the text using the Text tool. Select **Object/Combine/All Objects with Background**.

Fill the image with blue. Select **Apply Effects/KPT3.0/Spheroid Designer**, with the options set to **Procedural-**. Change the paint color to light blue, and add the text using the Text tool. Apply **Object/Drop Shadow**, with the settings **Horizontal, 2; Vertical, 2; Blur, 2; Opacity, 60; Color, Black.** Select **Object/Combine/All Objects with Background**.

Fill the image with red. Change the paint color to light blue, and add the text using the Text tool. Apply **Object/Drop Shadow**, with the settings **Horizontal, 2; Vertical, 2; Blur, 2; Opacity, 60; Color, Black.** Select **Object/Combine/All Objects with Background**. Apply **Effects/Artistic/Vignette**, with the settings **Color, Black; Shape, Circle; Offset, 100; Fade, 50.**

Fill the image with green. Change the paint color to white, and add the text using the Text tool. Apply **Object/Combine/All Objects with Background**. Apply **Effects/3D/Page Curl**, with the background color set to black. Apply **Image/Rotate/90** **degrees Clockwise**. Repeat the Page Curl filter (**Ctrl+F**), and **Image/Rotate/90 degrees Clockwise** three times. Apply **Image/Rotate/90 degrees** a final time to restore the image to its original position.

 Fill the image with black. Apply **Mask/Select All (Ctrl+A)**. Apply **Mask/Shape/Reduce** with a setting of 4 pixels. Fill the mask with a fountain fill with the settings **Conical; Steps, 5; Two Color; From, Orange; To, Purple**. Change the paint color to black, and add the text using the Text tool. This symbol came from the Zapf Dingbats typeface. Apply **Object/Drop Shadow**, with the settings **Horizontal, 0; Vertical, 0; Feather, 5; Opacity, 100; Custom Color, White**.

 Fill the mask with a fountain fill with the settings **Linear; Steps, 256; Angle, 130; Two Color; From, Turquoise; To, Purple**. Apply **Mask/Select All (Ctrl+A)**. Apply **Mask/Shape/Reduce** with a setting of 4 pixels. Apply the same fountain fill, but change the angle to **-50**. Change the paint color to turquoise, and add the text using the Text tool. This symbol came from the Zapf Dingbats typeface. Apply **Object/Drop Shadow**, with the settings **Horizontal, 2; Vertical, 2; Blur, 2; Opacity, 60; Color, Black**. Apply **Object/ Combine/All Objects with Background**.

 Apply a fountain fill with the settings **Conical; Angle, 0; Steps, 3; Two Color; From, Light Blue; To, Light Blue**. Apply **Mask/Select All (Ctrl+A)**. Apply **Mask/Shape/ Reduce** with a setting of 4 pixels. Change the angle of the fountain fill to **90** and fill the mask.

Fill the image with the fractal fill named Threads, Rainbow found in the Texture Library named Styles. Apply **Effects/Artistic/ Vignette** with the settings **Color, Black; Shape, Square; Offset, 100; Fade, 24.** Change the paint color to white, and add the text using the Text tool. Apply **Object/Drop Shadow,** with the settings **Horizontal, 0; Vertical, 0; Feather, 5; Opacity, 100; Custom Color, Light Blue.**

 Fill the image with the fractal fill named Texture Blend Vertical found in the Texture Library named Styles. Change the paint color to white, and add the text using the Text tool. Apply **Object/Combine/All Objects with Background.** Apply **Effects/Render/Lighting,** using the Floodlight preset.

 Open the image created in this chapter (Creating a Textured Icon). Select **Image/Adjust/Hue-Saturation-Lightness,** and drag the Hue slider until you find a different color for the icon. You can see how this technique  would enable you to create a series of icons in an array of colors very quickly and easily.

Extra Credit

Having too much fun to stop now? Prepare these recipes again, but begin each recipe with type or a dingbat as the selection instead of a square selection.

---

4 CREATING SEAMLESS PATTERN TILES TO ELIMINATE THOSE VISIBLE PANTY LINES OF GRAPHICS

A background pattern is a great way to repeat a theme for your Web site or to introduce subtle elements of texture and color. I especially love making "seamless" pattern tiles; they're easy once you learn the tricks, and you can make a gorgeous background in a matter of minutes. Plus, working in a small format gives you a great excuse to experiment with colors and filters and textures.

What do I mean by seamless? If you're creating a background pattern tile that will be repeated, the edges where the pattern meets are usually very noticeable, as in Figure 4.1. These seams are annoying and distracting, making it difficult to focus on the other elements of the Web page. Learn how to smooth those pesky seams, as shown in Figure 4.2, and you're on your way to creating a more professional and legible Web site.

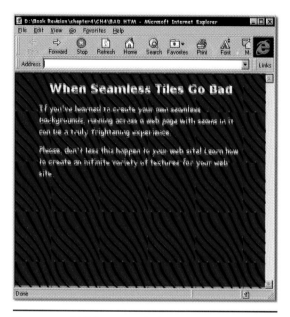

Figure 4.1 A Web page with (gasp!) visible seam lines.

Seamless pattern tiles are useful for a lot more than just background patterns for Web pages. They can be used as backgrounds for individual frames on a Web page, or even table rows or table cells that will display for Internet Explorer (but not Netscape). You can also use seamless pattern tiles as fills for text and icons, or to create bump maps and surfaces for 3D objects in 3D rendering programs. You can also use seamless patterns in desktop publishing programs to create borders and backgrounds for printed pieces.

There are a number of ways to eliminate or avoid those pesky seams. Following the tutorials, you'll find a number of recipes for seamless pattern tiles. I warn you, though, creating pattern tiles can be addictive and there is no known cure. But don't get so caught up in these backgrounds that you forget the text. Remember, it must be legible over the top of your pattern. I discuss decreasing the contrast in images in detail in Chapter 5, so for now just be aware of this design dilemma.

Figure 4.2 The same Web page with a seamless background.

This chapter covers creating a seamless pattern tile "by hand," or without filters, in both Photoshop and Corel PhotoPaint. We also discuss using filters to create seamless pattern tiles, offering you an endless variety of possibilities.

In Figure 4.3, the actual background image is only 30 pixels tall but 1200 pixels wide. Why? So that the image will be wider than most computer screens and the left-hand side of the image will appear only once for most viewers. The actual background image is shown in Figure 4.4, with a second example in Figures 4.5 and 4.6. In addition to creating horizontal rectangles, you can create vertical rectangles, in which the text is prevented from covering these left-border images by being placed in a table.

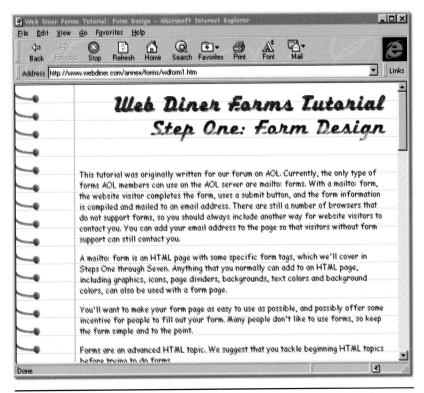

Figure 4.3 A background created from a long rectangle.

Figure 4.4 The background graphic for the Web page in Figure 4.3.

There are a number of fun things to experiment with when you create seamless pattern tiles. For instance, the Noise filter, followed by the Emboss filter, can result in some nice paper effects. A little noise can also obscure obvious pixelation or other minor defects in your image. Blurring can help obscure defects as well.

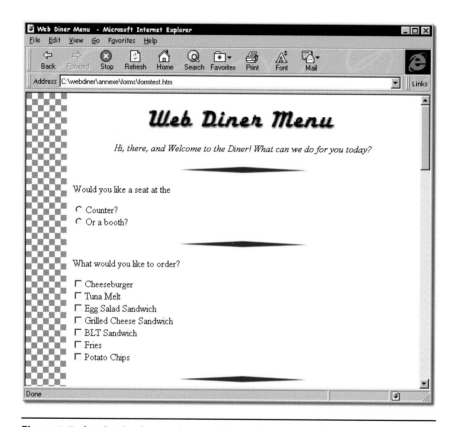

Figure 4.5 Another background created from a long rectangle.

Figure 4.6 The background graphic for Figure 4.5.

PHOTOSHOP

Creating a Seamless Pattern Tile

The following steps will show you how to create a seamless pattern tile without using filters in Photoshop:

1. Start with a new file, 100 x 100 pixels, RGB color. Select pale yellow as a foreground color and dark red as a background color. The filter we'll be using uses foreground and background colors to create its effect. Apply **Filter/Sketch/Halftone Pattern**, with the pattern type set to **Circle**. The result will look like step 1 in Figure 4.7.

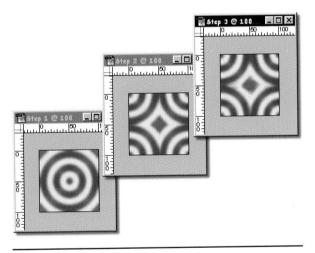

Figure 4.7 Creating a seamless pattern tile in Photoshop.

2. There are probably seams in the image you've just created. To check, use **Filter/Other/Offset**, with the **Wrap Around** radio button checked. The horizontal and vertical offset amounts are 50 and 50 (see Figure 4.8). This way, the seam will appear through the middle of the image, where it will be easier to see and clean up.

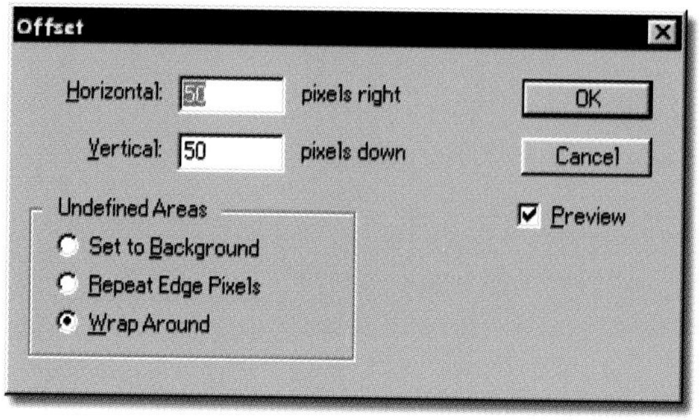

Figure 4.8 Offset filter dialog box.

3.   There are now a number of ways to smooth that ugly seam. Many people use the Rubber Stamp tool, but I prefer to use the Smudge tool. It's a lot like finger painting. Just drag the Smudge tool, set to a small or medium brush size, across the center seam a couple of times. You can constrain the tool (as you can many other Photoshop tools) to a straight line by pressing the **Shift** key while you click the **Smudge** tool at either end of the straight line you're creating.

Another way to clean up those seams is to grab a piece of the image and copy it and paste it over the seam. Use the Lasso selection tool to make a small, irregular selection. Apply **Select/Feather at 2 pixels**. Apply **Edit/Copy** (**Control+C** on Windows, **Command+C** on the Mac), **Edit/Paste** (**Control+V** on Windows, **Command+V** on the Mac), and drag or nudge (using the arrow keys) the patch over a seam. Continue patching until all the seams are covered. You'll need to apply **Layers/Merge Down** before you can save the finished file.

A third method is to use a paint tool. Since the pattern tile in this sample is made up of a very soft texture, you can use the Airbrush tool set to a small brush size and low opacity setting.

4.   Now fill a larger selection to check how your image will look when it is tiled and used as a background. Open a new file (**Control+N** on Windows, **Command+N** on the Mac) set to 300 x 300 pixels. This is large enough to show the pattern tiled. Return to the seamless tile you've created. Apply **Select All** (**Control+A** on Windows, **Command+A** on the Mac), **Edit/Define Pattern**.

5. Next, select the new file, and apply **Edit/Fill**. Within the Fill dialog box, select **Use, Pattern**; **Opacity, 100%**; and **Mode, Normal**. The results will appear as shown in Figure 4.9. If you see any obvious seams when the tile is repeated, you can clean them up in the original file, using the Smudge tool or the patch method. Save this file as a TIF file, because we'll be using it in Chapter 5 to demonstrate how to reduce contrast in backgrounds for Web pages.

Figure 4.9 Applying a pattern as a fill.

Photoshop's Cloud Magic

The Clouds and Difference Clouds filters in Photoshop will enable you to create a seamless pattern any time they are applied to an image whose measurements are some multiple of 128 pixels. Here's how:

1. Start with a new file, 128 x 128 pixels, in RGB color. Select white as a foreground color and purple as a background color. The filter we'll be using uses foreground and background colors to create its effect.

2. Apply **Filter/Render/Clouds**. To check the image for seams, open a new file (**Control+N** on Windows, **Command+A** on the Mac), set to 300 x 300 pixels.

3. Select the original cloud image. Apply **Select All** (**Control+A** on Windows, **Command+A** on the Mac), **Edit/Define Pattern**.

4. Select the new file, and apply **Edit/Fill**. Within the Fill dialog box, select **Use, Pattern**; **Opacity, 100%**; and **Mode, Normal**.

The resulting image will be a seamless pattern tile, as seen in Figure 4.10.

Chapter

4

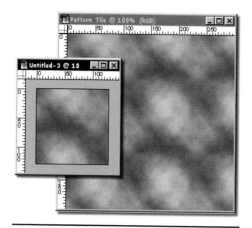

Figure 4.10 The seamless cloud background.

Extra Credit

The Clouds filter is a great place to explore the use of different textures using the filters that come with Photoshop. Start with the Clouds filter; duplicate the image by selecting **Image/Duplicate**, then apply some of the artistic, noise, or texture filters. Too tame? Try applying **Image/Adjust/Invert** (**Control+I** on Windows, **Command+I** on the Mac) to create a dramatic change in the contrast and color in your image. Figure 4.11 shows some examples.

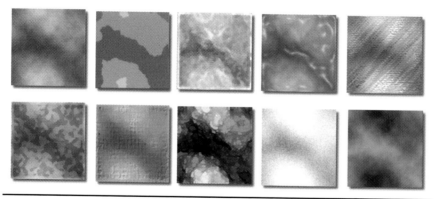

Figure 4.11 The seamless cloud background and nine variations. From the upper left: the original image, **Artistic/Cutout** filter applied, **Artistic/Paint Daubs** filter applied, **Artistic/Plastic Wrap** filter applied, **Artistic/Rough Pastels** filter applied. Second row: **Artistic/Sponge** filter applied, **Artistic/Underpainting** filter applied, **Artistic/Watercolor** filter applied, **Distort/Diffuse Glow** filter applied, and **Image/Adjust/Invert** applied.

Using Kai's Power Tools Filters

Kai's Power Tools (KPT) is a set of commercially available filters. They offer an extensive array of filters that are very useful for digital artists. You can find out about other commercial and shareware filters and background graphic archives in the Resources section of this book. To use Kai's Power Tools filters:

1. Start with an image 100 x 100 pixels in RGB mode. Select **Filters/KPT3/ Texture Explorer**. The textures created by the Texture Explorer in KPT 3.0 are not seamless. Click around the Texture Explorer until you find a texture you like. Apply the texture to your image.

2. Create a selection that is smaller than the image itself, as shown in Figure 4.12. Select **Filters/KPT3/Seamless Welder**. Next, select **Image/Crop** to crop to the edges of the selection. Now your texture is seamless.

The Seamless Welder creates a seamless tile by repeating areas of the image at the outermost edge of the selection. This can create a slightly fuzzy or blurred look to your image, which may or may not be desirable, depending on the type of image you're working on. If, for instance, your background was made up of words, this wouldn't work well, but it's fine for most abstract types of textures.

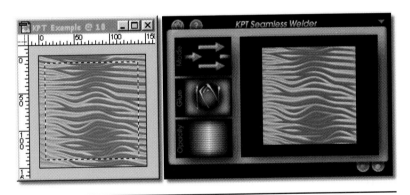

Figure 4.12 Creating a seamless background using KPT 3.0.

If you own KPT version 3.0, you also have KPT version 2.0. On the KPT 3.0 CD, look in a folder labeled Classics and you'll find version 2.0. One of the nice features of KPT 2.0 was that it was simple to create seamless pattern tiles in the Texture Explorer.

1. Create a new file, 96 x 96 pixels. The size of the image is important when you're creating a seamless pattern tile with Texture Explorer version 2.

2. Select **Filters/KPT2/Texture Explorer 2**. Use your mouse to click and hold on the largest texture swatch. You'll see a pop-up menu, as shown in Figure 4.13.

3. Select a tile size of 96 x 96 pixels. Find a texture you like and select **OK**.

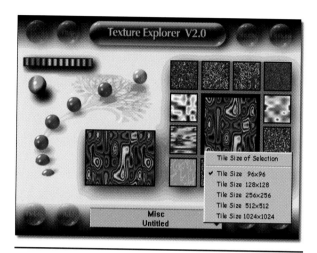

Figure 4.13 Creating a seamless pattern tile with KPT version 2.

Seamless Patterns from Scanned Objects

Using a flatbed scanner, you can use virtually any object that will fit onto the scanner as a background for your Web page. Figure 4.14 shows just a few of the amazing possibilities that ordinary objects offer for creative backgrounds.

Figure 4.14 Unique backgrounds created with a scanner.

The objects used in Figure 4.14 include, from left to right, a bit of fabric, a handful of plastic "jewels" from a craft supply store, a swatch of handmade paper, a paper doily, breakfast cereal, and an artichoke. Think of all the creative backgrounds you can generate from household and found objects.

This tutorial does require the use of a flatbed scanner. Obviously, you couldn't feed half an artichoke or a handful of dry pasta through a handheld or single-sheet-fed scanner. I also suggest, if you'll be scanning messy or rough objects, you protect the glass on your scanner by covering it with a sheet of clear acetate, available at art stores. You can also enclose the objects you'll be scanning in a plastic bag. This tutorial will show you how to scan, make a simple adjustment, and create a seamless background from some colorful candy. We'll be covering more aspects of scanning in Chapter 6.

1. Select **File/Import**, and select your scanner (your scanner drivers, obviously, must be installed prior to this step). Scan a little larger than the image will show up on your Web page, at about 120 dpi. Your scan will probably be dark gray in tone and have small artifacts (what I call glitches) visible, but that's okay.

2. Fix the overall cast of the image first. This image scanned in too dark, as shown in step 1 of Figure 4.15. By selecting **Image/Adjust/Levels** and dragging the right (or white) input slider toward the center, you'll lighten the highlights and midtones in the image, as seen in step 2 of Figure 4.15.

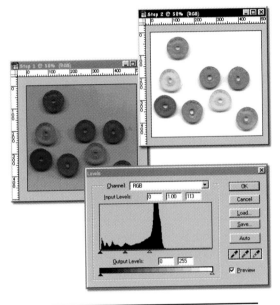

3. Select **Image/Offset** with the horizontal and vertical amounts set to about half of your file size. Make sure that the **Wrap Around** radio button is selected

4. There's a gap in the image, so I selected one of the bits of candy and feathered the selection (**Select/Feather**), then copied (**Control+C** on Windows, **Command+C** on the Mac) the selection and pasted the selection (**Control+V** on Windows, **Command+V** on the Mac) to cover the blank area (see Figure 4.16).

Figure 4.15 Creating a seamless pattern from a scanned image.

5. Paint out any glitches in your image using the paintbrush, and resize the image by selecting **Image/Image Size** and changing the pixel size.

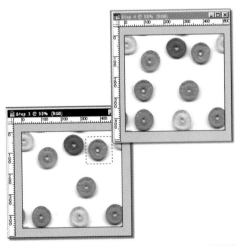

Figure 4.16 Creating a seamless pattern from a scanned image.

PHOTOPAINT

Creating a Seamless Pattern Tile

The following steps show you how to create a seamless pattern without using filters in PhotoPaint:

1. Start with a new file, 100 x 100 pixels, 24-bit RGB color. Double-click on the **Fill** tool to open the Fill roll-up. Select the **Texture Fill** icon, and select the **Edit** icon. Next, select the **Samples** library, then the **Banded Malachite** fill as shown in Figure 4.17. Click the **Fill** tool on the image to apply the texture fill to the image. Texture fills are not automatically seamless.

2. Now apply the **Offset** filter so that you can clean up any unsightly edges. Apply **Effects/2D/Offset**, with the horizontal and vertical values set to 50 and the **Wrap Around** radio button selected. The outer edges of the image will be wrapped to the center, where any seams will be clearly visible and therefore easier to eliminate.

3. Start to clean up the edges by double-clicking the **Effect** tool to open the Tool Settings roll-up. Select **Smudge**, **4 pixel size; Transparency, 5; Soft Edge, 0**. (You may want to save this smudge brush for later use on other Web projects.) Select the **Save Brush** button and name the brush you've created. Next, smudge the vertical edge by using the **Smudge** brush. If the pattern you're trying to make seamless is obvious, it helps to follow the pattern with the smudge.

4. There are a number of ways to clean up edges. Use the **Lasso Mask** tool to select an irregular area. Double-click the tool to finish the selection. Apply **Mask/Feather; Width, 2; Direction, Inside**. Next, select **Edit/Copy (Control+C)** and **Edit/Paste/As Object (Control+V)**. Drag the copy into position to cover the horizontal edge, as shown in step 3 of Figure 4.17. In addition, you could use the **Brush** tool or the **Clone** tool to cover up the edges.

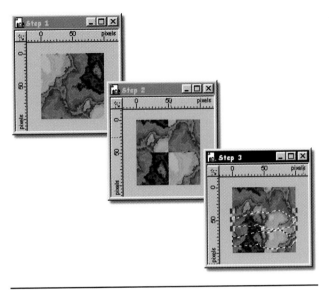

5. Save the tile you've created as a TIF, so that we can use it to practice lightening images to use as backgrounds in Chapter 5. If you've used the Lasso Mask tool, you'll have created some floating objects that will need to be merged before you can save the image as a TIF. Select **Objects/Combine/Combine All Objects with Background**. Then save as a TIF.

Figure 4.17 Creating a seamless pattern tile in PhotoPaint.

6. To see how the pattern tile you have just created will look when it's repeated, open a new file, 300 x 300 pixels. Double-click on the **Fill** tool to open the Fill roll-up. Select the **Bitmap Fill** icon. Select **Edit**, then **Load**, and select the tile you've just saved (Figure 4.18).

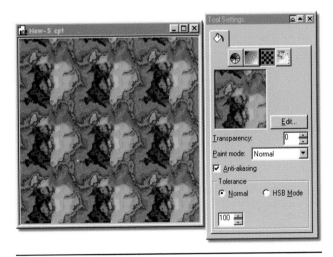

Figure 4.18 Checking the seamless pattern tile.

PhotoPaint's Built-In Seamless Tiles

PhotoPaint comes with dozens of textures that are already seamless, but you have to know how to use them. On CD number 2, they're located in a Tiles directory. Within this directory are tiles divided into Design, Food, Marble, Metal, Nature, Paper, Stone, Texture, and Wood categories. To use these as seamless pattern tiles, double-click on the **Fill** tool, which will open the Fill roll-up. Select the **Edit** icon, and you'll see the Bitmap Fill dialog box, as shown in Figure 4.19. Load the patterns from the CD by selecting the **Load** icon. You'll be presented with the tiles in small, medium, and large formats. For backgrounds, select the medium version of the file. Browse through the files until you find one that you like, then select **OK**.

Next, be sure to select the **Scale pattern to fit** checkbox. The pattern will be resized to automatically fit the image you are filling. Click the **Fill** tool on your image. In Figure 4.20, you can see the wide variety of patterns that are included.

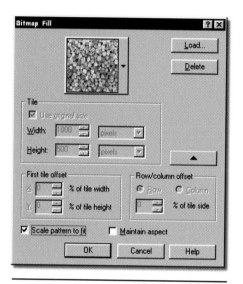

Figure 4.19 Selecting **Scale pattern to fit** ensures a seamless pattern.

Figure 4.20 A wide variety of textures are available in PhotoPaint.

PhotoPaint's Coolest Tool, Terrazzo

PhotoPaint excels in creating seamless pattern tiles, thanks to its built-in Terrazzo filter. If you're familiar with quilt patterns, you'll understand the way Terrazzo creates a seamless pattern tile. It takes a geometric shape and repeats it, similar to the way that quilt patterns repeat. From one file, you can make dozens of unique seamless pattern tiles. But enough talking, let's play!

Start with an image, which can be a photo, a drawing, or just about anything you want (Figure 4.21). Once you've opened your image, apply **Effects/Artistic/Terrazzo**.

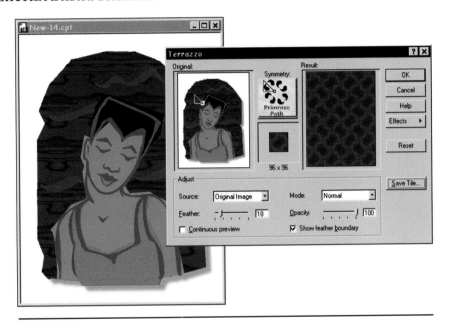

Figure 4.21 Terrazzo dialog box.

Drag the selection tool within the Terrazzo dialog box to select the area you would like to see tiled. Click on the **Symmetry** icon, and you'll have a number of choices for how you would like the selection repeated. The patterns for the geometrical repetition are named after quilt patterns, such as Honey Bees and Card Tricks.

You can play with the Feather slider, too, to soften the transitions. When you find a pattern you like, just use the **Save Tile** button.

As an example of the versatility of Terrazzo, Figure 4.22 shows a variety of patterns created from the previous image. There are more than 70 filters included with PhotoPaint version 7, which means you can create an endless number of unique patterns simply by applying a filter or two to an image, then use Terrazzo to create a seamless pattern tile.

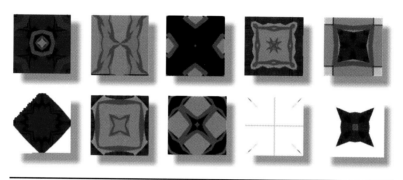

Figure 4.22 Seamless patterns created using Terrazzo.

PhotoPaint's Image Sprayer

There's a nifty new tool in Corel PhotoPaint 7 called the Image Sprayer. This tool applies images that follow the trail of your brushstroke across an image. The images that the Image Sprayer uses are stored in an Image List. In this example, you'll discover how surprisingly easy it is to build a custom Image List and use it to create a seamless tile.

1. Start with a new file, 200 x 200 pixels in 24-bit RGB color. First, create your objects using the Text tool and a dingbat (or symbol) typeface. In the example shown in Figure 4.23, I've used the Zapf Dingbat typeface, which is included with CorelDRAW 7, and I varied the size and color of the symbols. As you create each symbol PhotoPaint automatically makes it an object.

2. Once the assortment of symbols is created, select **View/Objects** to view the Object roll-up. Select all the objects by **Shift+clicking** on each object icon. Or use the **Object Picker** tool to marquee the entire image, thus selecting all the objects. Once you have selected all the objects, select **Object/Drop Shadow**, with the settings **Horizontal, 4; Vertical, 4; Feather, 2; Direction, Inside; Opacity, 60.** Each object will then have its own drop shadow, as shown in Figure 4.23.

3. Double-click the **Image Sprayer** tool to open its Tool roll-up. Click on the flyout menu and select **Save Objects as Image List**. You now have a custom Image List that you can use for any project.

4. To create your seamless pattern tile, start with a new file, 100 x 100 pixels in 24-bit RGB color.

5. Select the **Image Sprayer** tool and cover the entire image, as shown in Figure 4.24. Next select **Effects/2D/Offset** with the horizontal and vertical values set to 50 and the **Wrap Around** radio button selected. Clean up the visible seam by clicking the **Image Sprayer** to cover any visible edges.

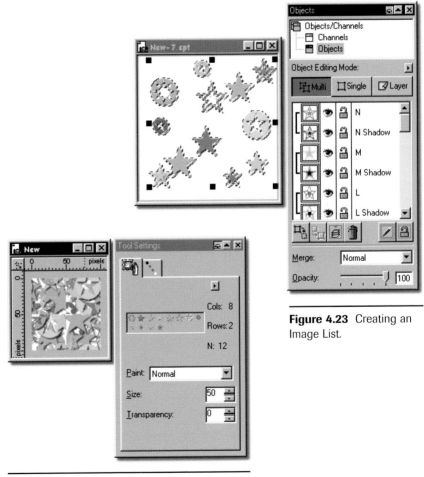

Figure 4.23 Creating an Image List.

Figure 4.24 Creating a seamless tile with the Image Sprayer.

The examples in Figure 4.25 were all created with the Image Sprayer. The first example is the stars seamless tile used throughout this section. As you can see, using the Image Sprayer creates a very full, busy background. You can also create stripes of images across the tile for a simpler, more geometrical appearance by holding down the **Control** key while you use the **Image Sprayer** as I did in the second example, which uses the same Image List, but I changed the Size setting on the Image Sprayer Tools roll-up before I used the Image Sprayer.

The third example in Figure 4.25 was created by using the Arrows typeface included with CorelDRAW 7, found on CD number 1 in the Fonts/Symbols directory. A number of arrows were created in a variety of colors and sizes, then all were selected using the **Object Picker** tool. Next **Mask/Create From Object**, then **Mask/Invert** were selected. **Effects/Fancy/The Boss** was used with the bevel set to 8. As a final step, **Object/Drop Shadow** was selected, with the settings **Horizontal, 4; Vertical, 4; Feather, 2; Direction, Inside; Opacity, 60.**

The alphabet example was fun to create. Each letter was created individually using the Text tool, with white as the paint color. A different typeface was used for each letter. All the objects were selected, and **Object/Drop Shadow** was applied with the settings **Horizontal, 0; Vertical, 0; Feather, 4; Direction, Middle; Opacity, 100; Color, Custom,** with a dark blue color.

The food example in Figure 4.25 was created using some of the objects included on the CorelDRAW CD number 2, in the Objects directory. The objects were resampled down to 85 x 85 pixels using the **Image/Resample** option with **Anti-aliasing** selected. Next, **Object/Drop Shadow** was applied with the settings **Horizontal, 4; Vertical, 4; Feather, 2; Direction, Inside; Opacity, 60.**

The last example was created by selecting clip art from CorelDRAW CD number 3. The clip art was pasted into a new larger blank image, then transformed into objects by selecting the background with the **Magic Wand** tool. Then **Mask/Invert** was applied and **Object/Create From Mask**. **Effects/Fancy/The Boss** was used with the bevel set to 8. The final step was to select **Object/Drop Shadow**, with the settings **Horizontal, 4; Vertical, 4; Feather, 2; Direction, Inside; Opacity, 60.**

You can create many different effects easily using the **Image Sprayer**. The Image Lists for the stars, arrows, letters, and signs in Figure 4.25 can be downloaded from http://www.mccannas.com/book/imglist. In addition, Corel includes more Image Lists on CD number 2 of the CorelDRAW 7 package, where you'll find a directory titled ImgLists. You can load these from within PhotoPaint by double-clicking on the **Image Sprayer** tool to open the Tool palette. Then select the little arrow on the palette and select **Load** from the menu.

Figure 4.25 More examples of seamless tiles created with the Image Sprayer.

PHOTOSHOP RECIPES FOR SEAMLESS PATTERNS

All of the following recipes for patterns start with an RGB file 100 x 100 pixels. Use **Filter/Other/Offset** to check that the edges are seamless when you're done. If they're not, clean them up as described in the first Photoshop tutorial in this chapter.

  Fill with light blue. Apply **Filter/Noise/Add Noise**; **Amount, 60; Distribution, Uniform**. Apply **Filter/Pixelate/Facet**.

  Fill with violet. Change the foreground color to magenta. Use a small paintbrush to scribble. Apply **Filter/Other/Offset**. Apply **Filter/Stylize/Diffuse**.

 Fill with pale yellow. Change the foreground color to ochre. Scribble with a small paintbrush. Apply **Filter/Other/Offset**. Next apply **Filter/Noise/Dust and Scratches; Radius, 4 pixels; Threshold, 0.** Apply **Filter/Noise/Add Noise; Amount, 30.**

 Fill with light gray. Apply **Filter/Noise/Add Noise**. Change the foreground color to a medium gray, and use the Type tool to add "Cool" at 36 points. Apply **Select All (Ctrl+A)**. Apply **Filter/Other/Offset**, and add "stuff!" at 36 points.

 Fill with light gray. Apply **Filter/Noise/Add Noise**. Apply **Filter/Blur/Radial Blur; Blur Amount, 10; Blur Method, Spin; Quality, Good.**

 Fill with light blue. Apply **Filter/Noise/Add Noise**. Apply **Noise/Median; Radius, 2**. Apply **Filter/Other/Offset**. Apply **Noise/Median; Radius, 2**.

Draw vertical stripes using a small paintbrush. You can constrain the paintbrush to a straight line by using the **Shift** key. The stripes don't need to be perfect. Apply **Filter/Distort/Ripple**; **Size, Small**; **Amount, 230**.

Using the rippled stripe tile (from the preceding recipe), apply **Filter/Stylize/Emboss**; **Angle, 135**; **Height, 3 pixels**; **Amount, 100%**. Apply **Filter/Stylize/Diffuse**; **Mode, Normal**.

Beginning with a striped tile, apply **Filter/Noise/Add Noise**; **Amount, 130**. Next apply **Filter/Noise/Dust and Scratches**; **Radius, 4**; **Threshold, 0**.

Fill the image with yellow. Paint magenta stripes using the Paintbrush tool. Apply **Filter/Blur/Radial Blur**; **Amount, 72**; **Blur Method, Spin**; **Quality, Good**. Apply **Filter/Other/Offset**; **Horizontal Offset, 48 pixels**; **Vertical Offset, 48 pixels**; **Wrap Around**. Clean up the edges with the Smudge tool as described earlier in this chapter.

Fill the image with the gradient fill named Copper using the Gradient tool. As you apply the fill, hold down the **Shift** key to constrain the fill to a 90° angle. Apply **Filter/Noise/Add Noise**, with **Monochromatic** selected. Next apply **Filter/Blur/Motion Blur**, with **Angle, 0**; **Distance, 20**.

Apply **Filter/Texture/Patchwork**. Then apply **Filter/Stylize/Glowing Edges**.

Fill the image with a cream color. Apply **Filter/Texture/Texturizer** and select **Burlap**. Apply **Filter/Artistic/Colored Pencil**.

Fill the image with a pale pink. Apply **Pixelate/ Crystalize/Pointillize**. Next apply **Filter/Distort/ Ripple** with the amount set to **400** and the size to **Medium**.

Fill the image with pale green. Apply **Filter/Noise/ Add Noise** with **Monochromatic** selected. Next apply **Filter/Distort/Ripple** with the amount set to **400** and the size to **Medium**.

Extra Credit

Create a left-edged seamless pattern for your Web site. Start with a file 2000 x 30 pixels. Fill the image with a pale yellow. Turn on the rulers (**Ctrl+R** on Windows, **Command+R** on Mac) and use the Marquee tool to select the first 100 or so pixels of your image. Fill the first 100 pixels with another color or texture. If you used this as a background, you would use a table to keep your text from running over the first 100 pixels. Your image will look like the example below.

PHOTOPAINT RECIPES FOR SEAMLESS PATTERNS

All of the following recipes for patterns start with a 24-bit RGB file 100 x 100 pixels. Use **Effects/2D/Offset** to check that the edges are seamless when you're done. If they're not, clean up the edges as described in the first PhotoPaint tutorial in this chapter.

 Double-click on the **Fill** tool to open the Fill Tool Settings roll-up. Select **Bitmap Fill/Edit**. Click on the colored tile to scroll through more tile examples. Select the tile shown on the left. Check the **Scale pattern to fit** checkbox. Apply **Effects/2D/Edge Detect; Background Color, White; Sensitivity, 2**. Last, apply **Effects/Jaggy Despeckle**.

 Double-click on the **Fill** tool to open the Fill Tool Settings roll-up. Select **Bitmap Fill/Edit/Import**. Using the CD labeled Disk 1 from Corel 7, select **Tiles/Nature/Nature06m.cpt**. Check the **Scale pattern to fit** checkbox. Apply **Effects/Noise/Add Noise using Color Noise**.

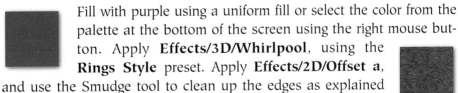

Fill with brown using a uniform fill or select the color from the palette at the bottom of the screen using the right mouse button. Apply **Effects/Artistic/Canvas**. Load the file **stuccoc.pcx** from the Canvas dialog box. Apply using the defaults.

Fill with purple using a uniform fill or select the color from the palette at the bottom of the screen using the right mouse button. Apply **Effects/3D/Whirlpool**, using the **Rings Style** preset. Apply **Effects/2D/Offset a**, and use the Smudge tool to clean up the edges as explained earlier in this chapter.

Fill with yellow using a uniform fill or select the color from the palette at the bottom of the screen using the right mouse button. Apply **Effects/Noise/Add Noise**. Select **Color Noise; Level, 50; Density, 50; Uniform**. Apply **Effects/2D/Pixelate, Pixelate Mode, Rectangular; Width, 10; Height, 10; Opacity 70%**.

 Fill with pale blue using a uniform fill or select the color from the palette at the bottom of the screen using the right mouse button. Apply **Effects/Fancy/Alchemy**. Apply the **Pointillist Style**.

 Fill with green using a uniform fill or select the color from the palette at the bottom of the screen using the right mouse button. Apply **Effects/Artistic/Vignette; Vignette Mode, Black; Offset, 0; Fade, 75**. Next apply **Effects/Fancy/Alchemy; Style, Planet Paint**.

 Double-click on the **Fill** tool to open the Fill Tool Settings roll-up. Select **Bitmap Fill/Edit/Import**. Using CD number 2 from Corel 7, select **Tiles/Food/Food15m.cpt**. Check the **Scale pattern to fit** checkbox. Next, apply **Effects/Color Transform/Solarize; Level, 120**.

 Apply **Effects/Fancy/Julia Explorer/Presets/Rainbow Twist**. The resulting pattern is not seamlessly tiled, so apply **Effects/2D/Offset at 50%**. Next apply **Effects/3D/Zigzag; Period, 50; Strength, 50; Damping, 50**. The resulting tile is seamless.

 Fill with orange using a uniform fill or select the color from the palette at the bottom of the screen using the right mouse button. Apply **Effects/Fancy/Alchemy; Style, Oil Canvas Blur**. Next apply **Effects/3D/Emboss using Original Color; Depth, 2; Direction, lower right**.

 Apply **Effects/Fancy/Alchemy**, with the style named **Woven Mat**. Next apply **Effects/Render/Lighting Effects** with the **Texturize Style**.

Apply **Effects/Fancy/Alchemy**, with the style named **Spatula Horizontal**. Set the paper color to a pale blue. Next, apply **Effects/3D/Emboss**, and select **Paper Color** for the emboss color.

Apply **Effects/Noise/Add Noise** using the default settings. Next apply **Effects/Render/Lighting Effects**, with the **Texturize Style** selected.

Select **Effects/Noise/Add Noise**. Deselect the **Color Noise** checkbox, and set the adjust noise to **Level 80; Density, 80**. Apply **Effects/Blur/Motion Blur; speed 50;** and the off image sampling set to **Ignore Pixels Outside Image**. Last apply **Effects/Photo Lab-CSI Grad Tone** with the **Snake** preset.

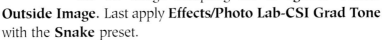

Fill the image with yellow orange. Select **Effects/Noise/Add Noise**. Deselect the **Color Noise** checkbox, and set the adjust noise to **Level 80; Density 80**. Apply **Effects/Blur/ Motion Blur; speed 50;** and the off-image sampling set to **Ignore Pixels Outside Image**. Apply **Effects/Render/ Lighting Effects** with the **Texturize Style**.

Extra Credit

Create a left-edged seamless pattern for your Web site. Start with a file 2000 x 30 pixels. Change your color palette by selecting **View/Color Palette**. Select either **Netscape Navigator** or **Microsoft Internet Explorer.** (They have the same palette with the colors in a different order.) Select a pale yellow for a fill by right-clicking on the swatch in the color palette. Turn on the rulers (**Ctrl+R**) and use the Rectangle Mask tool to select the first 100 or so pixels of your image. Fill the first 100 pixels with another color from the color palette. If you use this as a background, use a table to keep your text from running over the first 100 pixels. Your pattern will look like the example below.

---

c h a p t e r

4

PART 2
INTERMEDIATE
WEB GRAPHICS

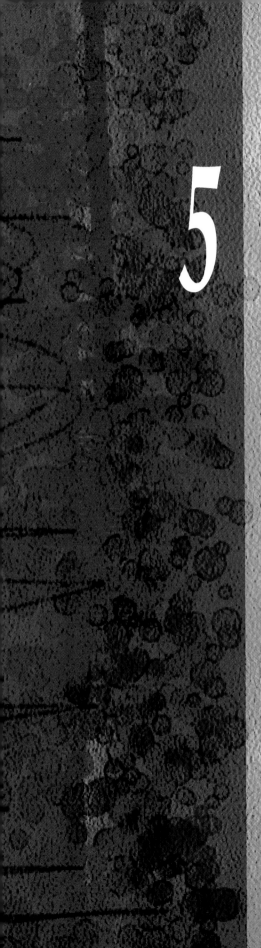

5

USING COLOR AND BRINGING CONTRAST DOWN, OR HOW TO PREVENT READER MIGRAINES

A visitor to my Web site told me that he was grateful to find my Photoshop tips because his graphics had ended up on Mirsky's Worst of the Web (http://mirsky.com/wow/). Although public humiliation can be a great motivation for improvement, I'm assuming you'd rather avoid the pitfalls in the first place. Therefore, this chapter concentrates on how to troubleshoot design problems on a Web page, which naturally raises the issues of using color for emphasis, mood, and unity.

We'll start by thinking about overall page design, and specifically color in page design and how color is rendered by specific browsers. Although we won't be discussing HTML in great depth, we will discuss it in the context of graphic placement and layout.

Some of the questions we will answer in this chapter include why some colors will dither under certain circumstances while others will not and how to choose a color scheme when you have no idea where to start. Two graphic tutorials at the end of this chapter demonstrate how to adjust the color and contrast in those fun backgrounds we created in the previous chapter.

USING COLOR FOR EMPHASIS

Color can be a wonderful tool or a deadly weapon. In my first two years in art school, we were allowed to work only in black and white, the theory being that we weren't educated enough to deal with color and that we were better off learning the basics of drawing and painting in black and white. Although it was frustrating at the time, it proved to be a good way to learn. Working in black and white forces you to focus on the design of the artwork.

Figure 5.1 An unreadable Web page.

Unfortunately, nobody is learning Web graphics this way. You have the full range of color available from the moment you open Photoshop or PhotoPaint. But just because you have 16 million colors doesn't mean that you should use them all on the same Web page. Color can be used to organize and emphasize, but it can also confuse and distract.

If you have a Web page that just isn't working for some reason, check the following elements in the design of the page.

Go Gray

Look at the page in grayscale, so that you aren't distracted by color. If your page works well in grayscale, it will usually work well in color, too. Any problems with light and dark contrast and legibility will become instantly apparent.

Figure 5.2 Looking at the Web page in grayscale.

In Figures 5.1 and 5.2, you can see that the only part of the page that is legible at all is the heading "Adrian's Amazing Bean Dip." The background pattern is so busy and so dark that you can't read the smaller text at all.

You can convert your Web page to grayscale by taking a screenshot of it. This is a simple procedure, but few people seem to know how to do it, making it one of the Great Secrets of the Computer. But I'll reveal that secret here:

- In Windows, with your Web page visible, press the **Print Scrn** key. This copies a picture of your screen to the Windows clipboard. Open a paint program. In Photoshop, select **File/New**, **Edit/Paste**. In PhotoPaint, use **Edit/Paste As New Document**. Now convert your screenshot to grayscale. In Photoshop, apply **Image/Mode/ Grayscale**; in PhotoPaint, use **Image/Convert To/Grayscale**.

- On the Mac, select **Command+Shift+3**. This will create a file named **Picture 1** in your main hard drive directory. Open this in Photoshop, and apply **Image/Mode/Grayscale** to view the image without the distraction of color.

There are also many utilities that enable you to create multiple screen-shots, or screenshots in a particular size or format. Corel includes one in the CorelDRAW package called Capture. You can search at http://www.shareware.com for other screenshot utilities as well.

After you have converted your image to grayscale, check to see what draws your eye first. Probably the area of the page that has the most contrast. Ask yourself: Is this the most important element? Would the page benefit from more contrast? Less con-trast? Are the elements (text, buttons, etc.) organized logically? Is it easy to find impor-tant information?

In the Amazing Bean Dip example in Figure 5.3, the only change made was to lighten the back-ground, thus making the text legible. The title is the first item to draw your attention, followed by a now easy-to-read recipe.

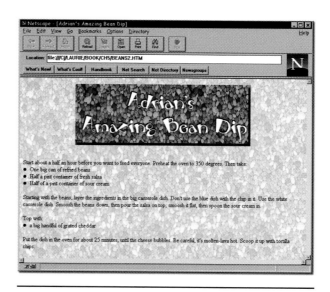

Figure 5.3 Changing the contrast of the background.

Limit Your Palette

If you're confused about using color, and even if you aren't, always err on the side of a limited palette. What's a limited palette? It's one in which all of the colors that you use in your graphics will be related. For example, maybe you'll want to limit your colors to blues, greenish blues, aquamarines, navy blues, blue violets, and violets, along with pale blues and deep dark blues.

Working in a limited color palette can help you design more profession-al pages in the following ways:

- Using a dominant color establishes a mood and can visually tie dissimilar elements together.

- When you use a limited palette, you'll be saving your graphics in the GIF file format, and you'll be able to index to a smaller number of colors, thus creating a smaller file that will load more quickly. When you save in the GIF file format, you can specify how many colors you want to reduce the graphic to. The fewer the number of colors in a graphic, the smaller the file size.

- You can use color for organization. A dominant color can indicate to viewers that all your pages are linked. Or you could use a different dominant color on separate pages to establish clearly their separate identities. For example, if you're designing a Web cooking site, the page titled Appetizers could be red, your Main Dish page could be violet, and so on. That way, visitors would have a clearer sense of where they are within your site.

- When you design your page with a dominant color and then add a contrasting color, it will really draw attention.

Figure 5.4 shows a representation of the color wheel. Obviously, it doesn't display the full spectrum of colors, but it can give you a place to start for your Web page color selection. Choose a color, say, navy blue, then start with a limited palette of blues. Your Web page background might be white, but your graphics could range in color from palest blues to deep rich navy. Colors directly across from one another on the color wheel are complementary; those are the colors you use for accents on a page. Directly across from navy blue is yellow. Thus, in your blue page, your accents might be a blue icon that reads NEW in gold lettering.

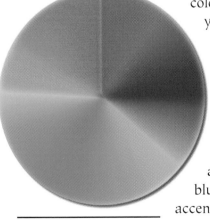

Figure 5.4 The color wheel.

USING COLOR TO SET A TONE

When you begin to design a Web page, you have to consider the overall color. Sometimes, this is the most difficult part of designing for me. Often, I'll look through books and magazines to find a color combination that suits the mood and feeling of the artwork I'm designing. I might find the right color combination in a landscape, a swatch of fabric, a photograph, or a painting. Think about it: If a color scheme works well for Monet or da Vinci, why wouldn't it work well as an inspiration for your own color selection?

Color can also have emotional connotations and expectations. When red, white, and blue are used together, it symbolizes to many American patriotism. Black and red used together can convey violence. Pastels can symbolize tranquility. Think of the color associations you form with the following words: *love, death, Halloween, Christmas, springtime, baby*. The point here is, if you get feedback that a graphic or page isn't working or is somehow disturbing, consider whether the colors you're using are contributing to the problem.

All that said, however, there's no reason you can't use any of this information on color to break the rules. Creating a page on chaos and dissonance? Maybe you want to use as many of the 16 million colors as possible.

CHANGING CONTRAST

In Photoshop

We created some wonderful seamless pattern tiles in the last chapter. Unfortunately, some of them are completely unusable as background tiles because they overwhelm the type that will go on top of them. By adjusting the contrast and overall lightness of the image, you can transform these into subtle backgrounds for Web pages.

1. Open the example in Figure 5.5, a seamless pattern tile from the Recipes section of Chapter 4. Select **Image/Adjust/Levels**. Drag the Output Levels black slider from the left side toward the center. You will see that the tile lightens as you do this. If you wanted to create a very dark tile, so that you could add white text over the top, you would drag the white slider toward the center.

2. Temporarily add some text to this tile, to see if it has been lightened enough. Select **Window/Show Layers**.

3. Use the Type tool to add text to the Type Layer as in Figure 5.6. We're using Layers for this example so that you can manipulate the type and background separately. If the tile still seems too dark, you can select the **Background Layer**, then return to **Image/Adjust/Levels**. When the contrast seems right, discard the Type Layer by dragging it to the trashcan icon. Save your tile (Figure 5.7).

Figure 5.5 The seamless pattern tile.

Figure 5.6 Type on top of the lightened tile.

Figure 5.7 The finished background tile.

In PhotoPaint

In Chapter 4, we created some great seamless pattern tiles to use as backgrounds on Web pages. Until we lower the contrast on the pattern tiles, however, type won't be legible when placed on top of the patterns. Using PhotoPaint, we will correct the legibility problem.

1. Open the image shown in Figure 5.8, which was created in the PhotoPaint recipes in Chapter 4. Apply **Effects/PhotoLab/CSI Levels**. Drag the Shadow slider to the right to lighten the tile. Raise the brightness and lower the contrast in this tile.

Figure 5.8 The original tile.

Figure 5.9 The tile darkened.

Figure 5.10 The lightened tile.

2. To make this a very dark tile, darken the image by dragging the High Light slider to the left as in Figure 5.9.

3. Add some type to the tile using the Type tool. If you think the tile isn't light enough, apply the **Effects/PhotoLab/CSI Levels** filter again. When the tile looks right, delete the type and save your tile (Figure 5.10).

HTML HELL

We've avoided it long enough. It's time to face the HTML monster. I used to think of writing HTML as a chore, so I tried a slew of HTML editors to create HTML for me but finally gave up in frustration and started learning the tags and writing it out in a text editor. Now I'm amazed at the flexibility and power of HTML. Remember, when you create a Web page, it's an elastic form that will reformat itself to the monitor of the person viewing the page. You never know whether the person viewing your page is using a black and white display for a handheld computer at 640 x 200 pixels, WebTV, or a huge 21-inch monitor. As long as you design with this diverse audience in mind, your page will be viewable by anyone in the world. I know you may yearn to specify a certain typeface at a precise point size, but I promise that what you give up in micro-control you'll gain in flexibility and audience for your Web site.

Even if you decide to use a software package that does the HTML for you, I do insist that you memorize four HTML tags: <HTML>, <HEAD>, <TITLE>, <BODY>. After helping thousands of America Online members put up their first Web sites, I've seen nearly every HTML problem possible, and I know there is no perfect HTML editor. Knowing these four simple tags will help you out in the long run. Whenever I check a problem page, these are the first elements I look for: Are they in the right order? Are any of them missing? Are they spelled correctly?

You can type these tags in any simple text editor to create the upcoming page example. In Windows, use Notepad or Wordpad. On the Mac, use Simple Text or Teach Text. If you use a word processor like Microsoft Word or WordPerfect, be sure to save your file as MS DOS Text or plain text. Don't use an HTML editor to create this example, as most automatically add these tags and you'll end up with duplicate tags.

These four HTML tags must be present on *every* Web page in the order shown, or the page will not display in some browsers. Further, each of these tags must appear only once on any Web page. Duplications of any of these tags can cause some browsers to fail to display a page.

Ready? Here we go. Type the following:

```
<HTML>
<HEAD>
<TITLE>
Memorizing HTML Tags
</TITLE>
</HEAD>
<BODY>
The body of your HTML Document will go here.
</BODY>
</HTML>
```

To save your file, add an .htm or .html file extension, for example, page.htm.

Generally, the main Web page on a site is named index.htm or index.html. Notice that each tag has an opening, <HTML>, and closing, </HTML>, format, although not all tags have a closing tag.

Now, here's what each tag means:

<HTML>   Tells the Web browser that this is an HTML page.

<HEAD>   The head portion of the document. The only tags you'll usually see in this portion of the Web page are META tags and JavaScript tags.

<TITLE>   The title appears at the top of the Web browser, not on the Web page itself.

<BODY>   The body portion of the document. Between <BODY> and </BODY> is where most of your Web page information will go, including text, images, animations, and links. The <BODY> tag itself can contain information about page color, link colors, and more.

That wasn't so bad, was it?

Hexing Colors

Once you decide on the colors you want to use for the background and text for your page, you need to know the hexcodes for the colors to specify them in the HTML for your page. The HTML code for specifying a black background color with white text looks like this:

```
<BODY BGCOLOR="#000000" Text="#FFFFFF">
```

which will appear in your HTML document like this:

```
<HTML>
<HEAD>
<TITLE>
Memorizing HTML Tags
</TITLE>
</HEAD>
<BODY BGCOLOR="#000000" TEXT="#FFFFFF">
The body of your HTML Document will go here.
</BODY>
</HTML>
```

Hexcodes and Browsers

Because the two most popular browsers, Internet Explorer and Netscape Navigator, display colors for 256-color monitors for Mac and Windows, there is a specific group of colors that generally will not dither. Therefore, there are some colors that you will probably want to use more than others for Web page text colors and backgrounds. When you select the Web palette in Photoshop or the Internet Explorer or Netscape palette in Corel PhotoPaint, you are indexing your images to this palette. On pages 98 to 100, you'll find examples of these colors along with their hexcodes.

Internet Explorer and Netscape Navigator have a fixed palette of 256 colors for Mac and for Windows. If you're using a 256-color monitor, all images will be dithered to this palette. Be aware that the palettes are slightly different between Mac and Windows, and they have only 216 colors in common.

Higher-color monitors, of course, won't dither any colors, as shown in Figures 5.11 and 5.12. Lower-color monitors, say, 16 colors or even black and white or grayscale monitors, would have completely different color palettes. If you're designing a Web page for a known audience—for instance, a human resources page that will be viewed only by a company's employees, all of whom have 16-color displays—it makes sense to find out the exact 16-color palette that is used. But let's face it, most Web pages are designed to be viewed by the general public, so there's no way of knowing the color depth of all the monitors in use, although most people assume that the majority of Web users have 256-color monitors.

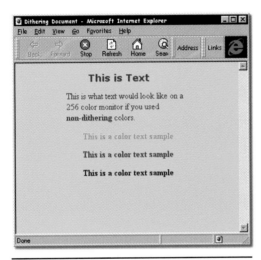

Figure 5.11 Our HTML page on a high-color display

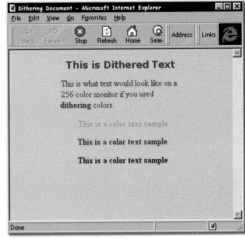

Figure 5.12 The HTML page on a 256-color display.

Figure 5.13 Dithering close up.

We tested this palette with version 3.0 of AOL and found that colors also did not dither for AOL users. AOL 3.0's built-in browser is Internet Explorer.

But there were occasions when even the nondithering 216-color palette dithered with both Internet Explorer and Netscape. We were able to track down the problem to Windows utilities that change screen resolutions on the fly. We found that, consistently, these utilities, whether supplied by the video card manufacturer or shareware utilities, would dither everything to a smaller palette, sometimes as small as 70 colors, when a standard 256-color display was selected. Obviously, a bug to watch for.

The point is, even if you use the 216-color palette, it won't guarantee that your lovely peach background won't turn puke green on someone else's monitor. It just means that the background won't dither. Monitors will interpret colors differently, and it's always a good idea to check out your Web site on more than one browser and more than one monitor. In general, though, images display darker on PCs than they do on Macs, so keep in mind that while you can't control color shifts, as long as your images and your text and background have enough contrast, your page should display at least legibly on most monitors.

The hexcodes that follow can be used to specify colors for the following HTML tags. Note that the *0* specified in the hexcodes are zeros, not the uppercase letter *O*.

```
<BODY BGCOLOR="#FFFFFF" TEXT="#000000" LINK="#000099" VLINK="#0000FF"
ALINK="#6600FF">
```

This code would produce a white background with black text. The unvisited link would be dark blue, a visited link a lighter blue, and an active link the lightest blue.

The default colors, or what you would see on a Web page if these hexcodes were not specified in a document are a blue link, a red active link, and a purple visited link. The specific hexcodes for the defaults in Internet Explorer and Netscape Navigator are:

```
LINK="#0000FF", VLINK="#400040", and ALINK="#FF0000"
```

But what if you would like to use one of the background tiles we created in the last chapter? That is specified in the BODY tag as well. You can have both a BGCOLOR and a BACKGROUND tag within the BODY tag. With most browsers, if you use both a hexcode and a background GIF or JPG, the hexcode background shows up while the GIF or JPG loads. So, your BODY tag looks like this:

```
<BODY BACKGROUND="stripe.gif" BGCOLOR="#FFFFFF" TEXT="#000000"
LINK="#000099" VLINK="#0000FF" ALINK="#6600FF">
```

if you have uploaded the file named **stripe.gif** to the same directory as your HTML file. If the file is on another Web site, the tag would look like this:

```
<BODY BACKGROUND="http://www.mccannas.com/backgrounds/stripe.gif"
BGCOLOR="#FFFFFF" TEXT="#000000" LINK="#000099" VLINK="#0000FF"
ALINK="#6600FF">
```

Does the order of the elements within the BODY tag matter? As long as the BODY tag is first, no.

```
<FONT COLOR="#FF0000"> This would render the text within your document a
different color from that specified in the BODY tag. </FONT>
```

The results from this and the body tag appear as shown in Figure 5.14. If you change the body tag for the same Web page to:

```
<BODY BGCOLOR="#000000" TEXT="#FFFFCC" LINK="#FF0000" VLINK="#CC00CC"
ALINK="#FFFF00">
```

the page would look as it does in Figure 5.15.

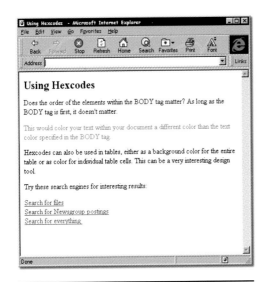

Figure 5.14 Hexcodes used for a Web page.

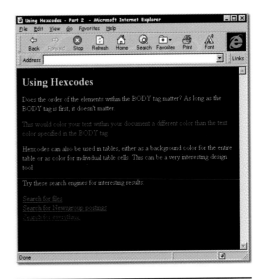

Figure 5.15 Different hexcodes used for the same Web page.

Hexcodes can also be used in tables, either as a background color for the entire table or for individual cells, which can be a very interesting design tool.

Hex Color Chart for Internet Explorer and Netscape Navigator
Nondithering Color Palettes

RGB	255-153-0	204-153-0	153-153-0	102-153-0	51-153-0	0-153-0
Hex	#FF9900	#CC9900	#999900	#669900	#339900	#009900
RGB	255-153-51	204-153-51	153-153-51	102-153-51	51-153-51	0-153-51
Hex	#FF9933	#CC9933	#999933	#669933	#339933	#009933
RGB	255-153-102	204-153-102	153-153-102	102-153-102	51-153-102	0-153-102
Hex	#FF9966	#CC9966	#999966	#669966	#339966	#009966
RGB	255-255-0	204-255-0	153-255-0	102-255-0	51-255-0	0-255-0
Hex	#FFFF00	#CCFF00	#99FF00	#66FF00	#33FF00	#00FF00
RGB	255-255-51	204-255-51	153-255-51	102-255-51	51-255-51	0-255-51
Hex	#FFFF33	#CCFF33	#99FF33	#66FF33	#33FF33	#00FF33
RGB	255-204-0	204-204-0	153-204-0	102-204-0	51-204-0	0-204-0
Hex	#FFCC00	#CCCC00	#99CC00	#66CC00	#33CC00	#00CC00
RGB	255-204-51	204-204-51	153-204-51	102-204-51	51-204-51	0-204-51
Hex	#FFCC33	#CCCC33	#99CC33	#66CC33	#33CC33	#00CC33
RGB	255-204-102	204-204-102	153-204-102	102-204-102	51-204-102	0-204-102
Hex	#FFCC66	#CCCC66	#99CC66	#66CC66	#33CC66	#00CC66
RGB	255-204-153	204-204-153	153-204-153	102-204-153	51-204-153	0-204-153
Hex	#FFCC99	#CCCC99	#99CC99	#66CC99	#33CC99	#00CC99
RGB	255-255-102	204-255-102	153-255-102	102-255-102	51-255-102	0-255-102
Hex	#FFFF66	#CCFF66	#99FF66	#66FF66	#33FF66	#00FF66
RGB	255-255-153	204-255-153	153-255-153	102-255-153	51-255-153	0-255-153
Hex	#FFFF99	#CCFF99	#99FF99	#66FF99	#33FF99	#00FF99
RGB	255-255-204	204-255-204	153-255-204	102-255-204	51-255-204	0-255-204
Hex	#FFFFCC	#CCFFCC	#99FFCC	#66FFCC	#33FFCC	#00FFCC
RGB	255-255-255	204-255-255	153-255-255	102-255-255	51-255-255	0-255-255
Hex	#FFFFFF	#CCFFFF	#99FFFF	#66FFFF	#33FFFF	#00FFFF

RGB	255-204-204	204-204-204	153-204-204	102-204-204	51-204-204	0-204-204
Hex	#FFCCCC	#CCCCCC	#99CCCC	#66CCCC	#33CCCC	#00CCCC
RGB	255-204-255	204-204-255	153-204-255	102-204-255	51-204-255	0-204-255
Hex	#FFCCFF	#CCCCFF	#99CCFF	#66CCFF	#33CCFF	#00CCFF
RGB	255-153-153	204-153-153	153-153-153	102-153-153	51-153-153	0-153-153
Hex	#FF9999	#CC9999	#999999	#669999	#339999	#009999
RGB	255-153-204	204-153-204	153-153-204	102-153-204	51-153-204	0-153-204
Hex	#FF99CC	#CC99CC	#9999CC	#6699CC	#3399CC	#0099CC
RGB	255-153-255	204-153-255	153-153-255	102-153-255	51-153-255	0-153-255
Hex	#FF99FF	#CC99FF	#9999FF	#6699FF	#3399FF	#0099FF
RGB	255-102-153	204-102-153	153-102-153	102-102-153	51-102-153	0-102-153
Hex	#FF6699	#CC6699	#996699	#666699	#336699	#006699
RGB	255-102-204	204-102-204	153-102-204	102-102-204	51-102-204	0-102-204
Hex	#FF66CC	#CC66CC	#9966CC	#6666CC	#3366CC	#0066CC
RGB	255-102-255	204-102-255	153-102-255	102-102-255	51-102-255	0-102-255
Hex	#FF66FF	#CC66FF	#9966FF	#6666FF	#3366FF	#0066FF
RGB	255-51-255	204-51-255	153-51-255	102-51-255	51-51-255	0-51-255
Hex	#FF33FF	#CC33FF	#9933FF	#6633FF	#3333FF	#0033FF
RGB	255-51-204	204-51-204	153-51-204	102-51-204	51-51-204	0-51-204
Hex	#FF33CC	#CC33CC	#9933CC	#6633CC	#3333CC	#0033CC
RGB	255-51-153	204-51-153	153-51-153	102-51-153	51-51-153	0-51-153
Hex	#FF3399	#CC3399	#993399	#663399	#333399	#003399
RGB	255-51-102	204-51-102	153-51-102	102-51-102	51-51-102	0-51-102
Hex	#FF3366	#CC3366	#993366	#663366	#333366	#003366
RGB	255-0-255	204-0-255	153-0-255	102-0-255	51-0-255	0-0-255
Hex	#FF00FF	#CC00FF	#9900FF	#6600FF	#3300FF	#0000FF
RGB	255-0-204	204-0-204	153-0-204	102-0-204	51-0-204	0-0-204
Hex	#FF00CC	#CC00CC	#9900CC	#6600CC	#3300CC	#0000CC

RGB	255-0-153	204-0-153	153-0-153	102-0-153	51-0-153	0-0-153
Hex	#FF0099	#CC0099	#990099	#660099	#330099	#000099
RGB	255-0-102	204-0-102	153-0-102	102-0-102	51-0-102	0-0-102
Hex	#FF0066	#CC0066	#990066	#660066	#330066	#000066
RGB	255-0-51	204-0-51	153-0-51	102-0-51	51-0-51	0-0-51
Hex	#FF0033	#CC0033	#990033	#660033	#330033	#000033
RGB	255-0-0	204-0-0	153-0-0	102-0-0	51-0-0	0-0-0
Hex	#FF0000	#CC0000	#990000	#660000	#330000	#000000
RGB	255-102-102	204-102-102	153-102-102	102-102-102	51-102-102	0-102-102
Hex	#FF6666	#CC6666	#996666	#666666	#336666	#006666
RGB	255-51-51	204-51-51	153-51-51	102-51-51	51-51-51	0-51-51
Hex	#FF3333	#CC3333	#993333	#663333	#333333	#003333
RGB	255-51-00	204-51-00	153-51-00	102-51-00	51-51-00	0-51-00
Hex	#FF3300	#CC3300	#993300	#663300	#333300	#003300
RGB	255-102-51	204-102-51	153-102-51	102-102-51	51-102-51	0-102-51
Hex	#FF6633	#CC6633	#996633	#666633	#336633	#006633
RGB	255-102-0	204-102-0	153-102-0	102-102-0	51-102-0	0-102-0
Hex	#FF6600	#CC6600	#996600	#666600	#336600	#006600

Named Colors and Grays

Note: The colors below already appear in the hexcodes listed above. Sometimes it's helpful to use grays, since they don't conflict with any color.

RGB	255-255-255	204-204-204	153-153-153	102-102-102	51-51-51	0-0-0
Hex	#FFFFFF	#CCCCCC	#999999	#666666	#333333	#000000
Name	White					Black

RGB	0-255-255	0-0-255	0-255-0	255-255-0	255-0-0	255-0-255
Hex	#00FFFF	#0000FF	#00FF00	#FFFF00	#FF0000	#FF00FF
Name	Aqua	Blue	Lime	Yellow	Red	Fuschia

You'll notice that eight of the colors above have names. Microsoft Internet Explorer 3.0 and above and Netscape 3.0 and above support the use of named colors in lieu of a hexcode. Note that other browsers would not recognize these names as colors.

To use a named color, the HTML would look like this:

```
<FONT COLOR="blue"> This is blue text </FONT>
```

Decoding Hexcodes

There are two tips to remember about hexcodes, so you don't have to look them up each time: The first is that the RGB of every nondithering color is divisible by 51; the second is a simple RGB-to-hexcode conversion chart that makes up the nondithering colors (Table 5.1).

Table 5.1 RGB-to-Hexcode Conversion Chart

RGB Color	Hexcode Value
0	0
51	33
102	66
153	99
204	CC
255	FF

So, if you know that the RGB value is 153-204-104, that translates to the hexcode #99CC66.

A second alternative for finding hexcodes is to use the Windows calculator. Another Great Secret of the PC revealed! To do so, first find out the RGB number for the colors you want the hexcodes for. In Photoshop, use the Eyedropper to select the color you want for text or background. Double-click on the foreground color in the Tool palette, which will open the Color Picker. You will find the RGB value for the color.

To find the RGB value in PhotoPaint, use the Eyedropper to select the color. Double-click on the **Current Fill** swatch at the bottom of the screen. You'll find the RGB value in the dialog box that opens.

Now open the Windows Calculator (Figure 5.16). Don't bother to close the paint program; this is multitasking! From the Start button, select **Programs/Accessories/Calculator**. On the Calculator menu, select **View/Scientific**.

There are three numbers, one each for Red, Green, and Blue. In this example, R=51, G=153, and B=204. Select the **DEC** radio button (stands for decimal), and using the keypad, enter **51**, the number for the Red value.

Now select the **HEX** radio button. *Voilá!* The first two digits of your color's hexcode—33. Select **CE** (Clear Entry) and **DEC**, and enter the Green value, **153**. You will find that the hex value is 99. If you come up with a single digit, add a zero so that you end up with six digits for the entire hexcode. Use **CE**, **DEC**, and enter the Blue value, **204**. The hexcode is CC. So, the final six-digit hexcode is #3399CC.

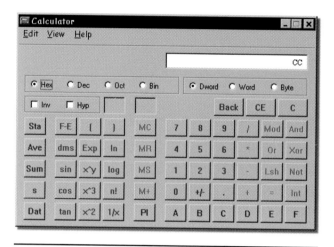

Figure 5.16 The Windows calculator.

A third alternative is to visit a Web site to select your hexcodes. Visit any of the following:

Thalia's Guide: Compose Page Color

http://www.sci.kun.nl/thalia/guide/color/

ColorMaker

http://www.missouri.edu/~wwwtools/colormaker/

Uses the nondithering Netscape/Internet Explorer palette.

HYPE Electrazine—The Color Specifier

http://www.users.interport.net/~giant/COLOR/hype_color.html

Uses the "named" colors.

Beach Rat

http://www.novalink.com/pei/hex/hex.html

Allows you to select a hexcode from any RGB color.

More Information on Color and Web Pages

http://www.microsoft.com/workshop/design/

Finally, there are a number of color selection utilities that you can use to create your hexcodes. Figure 5.17 shows a Windows hexcode utility named ColorMaster that allows you to select your colors from the nondithering palette. The URL for HTMLColorMaster is http://members.aol.com/WenRobbins/.

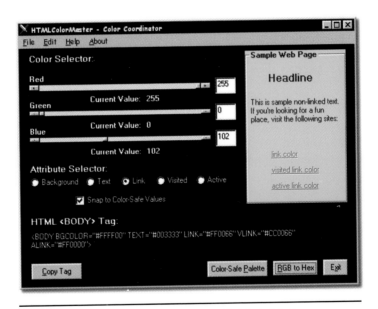

Figure 5.17 A Windows hexcode utility called ColorMaster.

Figure 5.18 shows ColorMeister, a hexcode utility for the Mac available at http://www.hotfiles.com.

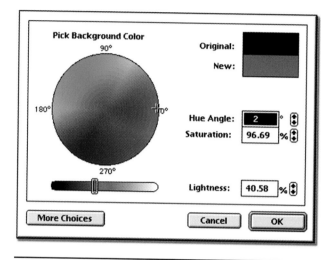

Figure 5.18 A Mac hexcode utility called ColorMeister.

AVOIDING WEB PAGE DESIGN CLICHÉS

Good organization and content are the secrets to good Web design. Unfortunately, many beginning Web builders focus on the minutiae of hexcodes and fonts to the exclusion of these basic elements. Remember to test your site for usability by sitting next to someone as he or she tries to navigate your Web site.

While you're deciding about design and organization for your site, ask yourself:

What information will people want to see?

How will they find it?

Why would they come back on a weekly or monthly basis?

Why would they recommend the site as a place to visit?

I firmly believe that everyone has the right to express themselves in whatever way they wish on their Web page, and if you think using as many colors as possible is the way to go, I'm not going to try to dissuade you. The wonderful thing about the Web is that your site can be anything and everything *you* want it to be. That said, however, experience is a great taskmaster, and mine has taught me to avoid the following clichés on Web pages. At least, consider these points:

1. Huge graphics. I've seen pages with individual graphics more than 1.5 MB in size. I never waited for any of them to download, however, which is exactly my point.

2. A big graphic on the front page, no text, and no information other than a logo that says "Click here to enter." Don't use your front page as a billboard, but as a way for people to select the most important 3 to 10 features at your Web site.

3. A long list of requirements for using the site. Give me a plain text site any day! I've seen sites that require no fewer than five browser plug-ins to navigate.

4. Big, bad Java apps that crash the Web browser. Some Web sites can be navigated only with a Java-enabled browser. Not only are there a lot of non-Java-enabled browsers out there, but many people with them turn Java off because of security concerns. If you're including Java, ActiveX, or JavaScript at your Web site, give folks another way to navigate.

5. Anything that makes displaying the coolest technology more important than the content. The Web is about communication, expression, and connection, not software. Think about how incredibly useful some text- and CGI-based tools, like guestbooks, message boards, and links, are. These tools sometimes get overlooked in favor of whizbang technology. The exception to this, of course, is a Web site where the topic is software or the latest technology.

6. Wonderful Web sites that never get the recognition they deserve because their owners haven't submitted their URL or invested enough time in publicizing their Web site. I still spend time every month publicizing my Web site, a little here, a little there. Doing a really good job of publicizing your Web site can take longer than building the site itself. See the Resources section in this book for places to publicize.

7. Web pages with no contact information. In my unofficial survey, about 20% of all commercial Web sites either don't have their contact information available or it's so hard to find it that it might as well be unavailable.

6

SCANNING FOR THE WEB, OR BRINGING CONTRAST UP AND LOOKING GOOD AT LOW RESOLUTION

Sooner or later, you will have to deal with a bad scan. Luckily, making a bad scan look better is not that difficult with Photoshop or PhotoPaint. Good tools are available to help you adjust, cover up, delete, or compensate for almost every bad scanning situation. The most common problem is that scans lose their original contrast. The darks may seem a little faded, and the whites are often dingy and gray looking. As the first project in this chapter, you'll learn how to bring back the contrast in a very poor scan and add an interesting background. The second project, colorizing a grayscale version of a scan, can enliven an otherwise mediocre photograph. It also answers one of the most frequently asked questions that I get at my Web site. However, you must promise never to use the colorizing techniques demonstrated in this chapter on lovely old black-and-white movies.

A few tips about scanning before we plunge into the tutorials. First, it's usually better to scan the photo or artwork for the Web at a higher-than-screen resolution, then resample down to the size you want to work at. Try scanning at 150 to 200 dpi. This means that you'll start with an image that has 150 or 200 pixels per inch and end up with an image at screen resolution, or 96 pixels per inch. Do some testing with your individual scanner to see if scanning at screen resolution or at a higher resolution, then resampling to a smaller size is the best method for working with your particular scanner. During the past two years, scanner prices have dropped and the quality of the software for scanners has improved. If you have an older scanner, you might be surprised at the increase in performance you will achieve if you update your scanner drivers. Contact the company that manufactured your scanner (most have Web sites).

Although you can compensate for certain defects in photos that you may scan, in general, the better the quality of the original image, the better the quality of your scan. I try to keep artwork to a width of 500 pixels or less. The three most common screen resolutions for PCs are 640 x 480, 800 x 600, and 1040 x 768. Using a width of 640 pixels, and taking into account the menu bars for the Web browser in use, 500 pixels means that most people won't have to scroll horizontally to see the entire graphic.

We will be saving all of the scans in JPG format, a 24-bit, lossy compression format that can handle a greater range of colors more smoothly than the GIF file format, which is limited to 256 colors or less. Lossy means that some information is lost during the compression process, so it's always a good idea to keep a 24-bit uncompressed copy for later revisions. In addition, for photographs and complex artwork with many colors, a JPG file is almost always much smaller than a GIF file would be. For example, the jukebox at my Web site is a 37K file saved in JPG format, whereas the GIF file of the same image is 200K, and much more dithered and less appealing. It's worth your time to experiment with the different JPG settings to see what you consider acceptable quality.

Since filters are used so often with scanned images, I've included a big visual reference of the most helpful filters in Photoshop and PhotoPaint for adding creative effects to images. Although both Photoshop and PhotoPaint include more filters than you may think you'll ever need, some users just never have enough. For these users there are pointers to Web sites with free, shareware, and demo filters in the Resources section. There are also lists of newsgroups (including one devoted solely to scanners) and mailing lists that cover PhotoPaint and Photoshop included in the Resources section.

If you don't have access to a scanner, you can still follow the tutorials in this chapter by using a photo from the Photoshop or PhotoPaint CD. On the Photoshop CD, the images are in a directory labeled Stockart/Photos. In PhotoPaint, there's a large selection of photos on CD number 2 in a directory named Photos.

FILTERS FOR SCANS

In Photoshop

The filters in Figures 6.2 to 6.4 are especially helpful for cleaning up scans. Figure 6.1 shows the original, unfiltered scan. Every scan will have its own individual problems that you'll need to compensate for.

Figure 6.1 The original image.

Figure 6.2 Filter/Sharpen/ Unsharp Mask applied.

Figure 6.3 Filter/Noise/ Despeckle applied.

Figure 6.4 Image/Adjust/Variations selected in Photoshop.

An indispensable filter for scans is Unsharp Mask, which actually sharpens details and edges, contrary to its name. In the second example (Figure 6.2), the Unsharp Mask filter was applied to the image. The third example, Figure 6.3, shows the use of the Despeckle filter, which evens out some of the graininess in an image. Figure 6.4 shows the Variations dialog box in Photoshop. Using **Image/Adjust/Variations**, you can select precisely the type of adjustment you'd like to make to your image.

Other Photoshop tools can be used to correct errors in scans. If you have a scan with a number of scratches in the sky, for example, you might want to use a cloning brush to cover the problem areas with a copy of the sky from a different portion of your photo. Cloning can look more natural than trying to paint over a problem using the paintbrush or airbrush.

Photoshop has added a variety of new filters in version 4, some of which are useful for transforming an otherwise hopeless scan into an acceptable, even "arty" image. The following filters were applied using the default settings unless otherwise noted.

Artistic Effects

These filters are found under **Filter/Artistic** in Photoshop 4.

Colored Pencil

Cutout

Dry Brush

Film Grain

Fresco

Neon Glow—
Flow Size: 10;
Brightness: 38;
Color: Red

Paint Daubs—
Brush Size: 4;
Sharpness: 15;
Brush Type: Simple

Palette Knife—
Stroke Size: 6;
Stroke Detail: 3;
Softness: 0

Plastic Wrap—
Highlight
Strength: 8;
Detail: 12

Poster Edges

Rough Pastels

Smudge Stick—
Stroke Length: 2;
Highlight Area: 6;
Intensity: 7

Sponge—
Brush Size: 1;
Definition: 25;
Smoothness: 2

Underpainting

Watercolor

Brush Stroke Effects

These filters are found under **Filter/Brush Strokes** in Photoshop 4.

Accented Edges

Angled Strokes

Crosshatch

Dark Strokes

Ink Outlines

Spatter

Sprayed Strokes

Sumi-E

Diffuse Glow

Glass

Ocean Ripple

Pinch

Polar Coordinates

Ripple

Shear

Spherize

Twirl

Wave—
Type: Square;
No. Generators: 1

Zigzag—
Amount: 33;
Ridges: 15

Pixelate Filters

These filters are found under **Filter/Pixelate** in Photoshop 4.

Crystallize

Facet

Fragment

Mezzotint

Mosaic

Pointillize

Render Filters

These filters are found under **Filter/Render** in Photoshop 4.

Lens Flare–
Brightness: 150;
Lens: 50–300mm

Lighting–
Style: 2AM Spot

Sketch Filters

These filters are found under **Filter/Sketch** in Photoshop 4. Most of these filters use the current foreground and background colors you have selected. For these examples, I had a dark red as the forground color and white as the background color.

Bas Relief

Chalk and Charcoal

Charcoal

Chrome

Conte Crayon

Graphic Pen

Halftone Pattern

Note Paper

Plaster

Reticulation

Stamp

Torn Edges

Water Paper

Stylize Filters

These filters are found under **Filter/Stylize** in Photoshop 4.

Diffuse

Emboss

Extrude

Find Edges

Glowing Edges

Solarize

Wind

Texture Filters

These filters are found under **Filter/Texture** in Photoshop 4.

Craquelure

Grain

Mosaic Tiles

Patchwork

Stained Glass

Texturizer

Fading Filters

To soften the effects of a filter, apply the filter then select **Filter/ Fade**. Figure 6.5 shows the **Filter/ Pixelate/Mezzotint** applied with the setting of **Fine Dots**. Figure 6.6 shows the effects of **Filter/Fade** applied with the settings **Opacity, 30; Mode, Color Dodge**.

Figures 6.5 and 6.6 The effects of a filter faded using the **Filter/Fade** command.

In PhotoPaint

The filters in Figures 6.7 to 6.10 are especially helpful for cleaning up scans in PhotoPaint, but every scan will have its own problems that you'll need to compensate for. Figure 6.7 shows the original, unfiltered scan.

An important filter for scans is Unsharp Mask, which sharpens details and edges, contrary to its name. In the second example (Figure 6.8), the Unsharp Mask filter was applied to the image. The third example, Figure 6.9, shows the use of the Noise/Remove filter, which evens out some of the graininess in an image. Figure 6.10 shows the image after the Intellihance filter has been applied. Intellihance is a good, quick color and tonal correction filter. If you're unsure where to start correcting an image, give this filter a try.

Figure 6.7 The original image.

Figure 6.8 Effects/ Sharpen/Unsharp Mask applied.

Figure 6.9 Effects/ Noise/Remove applied.

Figure 6.10 Effects/ Intellihance selected.

Other PhotoPaint tools can be used to correct errors in scans. If you have a scan of a landscape with a telephone wire crossing the sky, for example, you might want to use a cloning brush to cover the problem areas with a copy of the sky from a different portion of the photo. Cloning can look more natural than trying to paint over a problem using the paintbrush or airbrush.

PhotoPaint has added a nice selection of new filters in version 7, some of which are useful for changing a dull or unremarkable image into an acceptable, even "arty" image. The following filters were applied using the default settings unless otherwise noted.

Artistic Effects

These filters are found under **Effects/2D** in PhotoPaint 7.

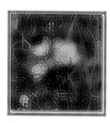

Band Pass–
Inner Band: 70;
Middle Band: 30;
Outer Band: 100

Displace–
Map: stars.pcx

Edge Detect

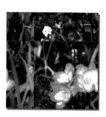

Offset–
Horizontal: 30;
Vertical: 30;
Wrap Around

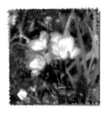

Pixelate–
Mode: Circular;
Opacity: 65

Puzzle

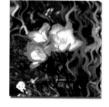

Ripple–
Period: 20;
Amplitude: 5

Shear

Swirl

Tile

Trace Contour

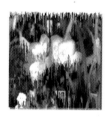

Wet Paint

Whirlpool

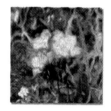

Wind

3D Filters

These filters are found under **Effects/3D** in PhotoPaint 7.

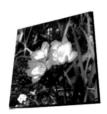

3D Rotate

Emboss

Map to Object

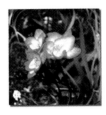

Mesh Warp

Page Curl

Pinch/Punch

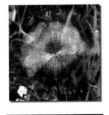

Zigzag

Canvas—
Map: Rocks2c.pcx

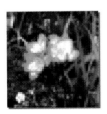

Glass Blocks—
Block Width: 6;
Block Height: 6

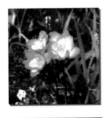

Impressionist—
Scatter Horizontal: 3;
Scatter Vertical: 3

Smoked Glass

Vignette

Color Transform

These filters are located on the **Effects/Color Transform** menu in PhotoPaint 7.

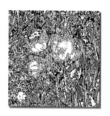

Bit Planes

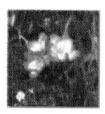

Halftone

Psychedelic

Solarize

Render Filters

These filters are located on the **Effects/Render** menu in PhotoPaint 7.

Lens Flare

Lighting Effects—
Style: Texturize

Fancy Filters

These filters are found under **Effects/Fancy** in PhotoPaint 7.

Alchemy—
Style: Planet Paint

Glass

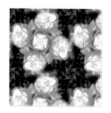

Terrazzo

The Boss

KPT 3.0 Filters

These filters are found under **Effects/KPT3.0** in PhotoPaint 7.

KPT Meta Toys—
Kaleida

KPT Meta Toys—
Twirl

KPT Video
Feedback

Gradient Designer—
Glue: Procedural+

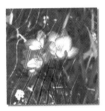

Texture Explorer—
Glue: Procedural-

PhotoLab Filters

These filters are found under **Effects/PhotoLab** in PhotoPaint 7. They are especially useful for tweaking photos and changing the colors in them.

CSI GradTone—
Electric Fire

CSI GradTone—
Sepia

CSI GradTone—
Green-Blue

CSI Hue Slider—
Strong Pink

CSI Hue Slider–
Green Glow

CSI Monochrome–
Turquoise

CSI Negative–
Color Negative

CSI Noise–
50% Cadmium

CSI PhotoFilter–
30% Mauve

CSI PhotoFilter–
Brushed Copper

CSI PhotoFilter–
Sienna

CSI PhotoFilter–
Ultramarine

CSI PhotoFilter–
Deep Blue

CSI PhotoFilter–
Green Filter

Transform Filters

These filters are found under **Image/Transform** in PhotoPaint 7.

Invert

Posterize

Fading Filters

To soften the effects of a filter in PhotoPaint, you can duplicate the image, paste the copy as a second object and apply the filter, then adjust the opacity and/or the merge mode for the object. Figure 6.11 shows **Effects/Fancy/Alchemy** applied with the **Bubbles Pastel** setting. The filter is strong enough to obliterate most of the original photo. For the second example (Figure 6.12), the entire original image was copied by selecting **Edit/Select All**, then **Edit/Copy (Ctrl+A, Ctrl+C)**. The copy was then pasted as a new object by selecting **Edit/Paste/As New Object (Ctrl+V)**. The Object roll-up was opened **(View/Roll-ups/Object)**. The filter was applied only to the second object, the merge mode was set to **If Lighter**, and the opacity was set to **90%**. These options are found at the bottom of the Object roll-up. By changing the merge mode, you control how the filtered copy will combine with the original image. The Opacity slider allows you to select how much of the original image shows through the filtered copy. You can, of course, create a second copy and apply another filter, and again adjust the merge and/or opacity settings. In this way, you can stretch the filter effects to create an infinite number of creative attributes.

Figures 6.11 and 6.12 The effects of a filter faded by creating a duplicate layer.

FIXING A BAD SCAN

In Photoshop

1. Scan your image using **File/Import**. You may need to experiment with your scanner to see if you achieve better results when you scan at a higher resolution (like 200 dpi), and then resize the image using **Image/Image Size**. Your image should be no larger than 400 pixels in any dimension. Using the Rectangular Marquee tool, select the area of the scan you wish to keep (see Figure 6.13). Select **Image/Crop**.

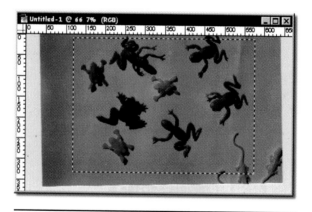

Figure 6.13 The original scan in Photoshop.

2. Next, compensate for dingy whites and dull darks. Apply **Image/Adjust/Auto Levels**. Sometimes this one-step adjustment is all you need to adjust a scan. However, in the case of the scan in Figure 6.14, the middle tones are still too dark. In order to adjust for this type of problem, select **Image/Adjust/Levels**. To darken the dark areas, drag the left Input slider toward the center. To lighten the light areas, drag the right Input slider toward the center. To adjust midtones, slide the middle slider to the left, to make them lighter as in this example, or right to darken the midtones. Every scan will be different, so watch the preview as you adjust the sliders. In this particular scan, the dark areas looked fine, but the light areas needed to be lightened (see Figure 6.14).

3. The next step is to select the background area and fill it with a pattern fill to make this scan more interesting. The background is very complex because of all the little fiddley parts on the toys. Using the Marquee tool and holding down the **Shift** key, make two or three selections from different parts of the photo. Next, apply **Select/Similar**. Everything in the photo that is similar to

Figure 6.14 Image/Adjust/Auto Levels used to lighten the scan.

the selected areas will be made part of the selection. If not enough of the background has been selected, undo (**Ctrl+Z**) and double-click on the **Magic Wand** to open the Magic Wand Options palette. Increase the tolerance number and apply **Select/Similar** again.

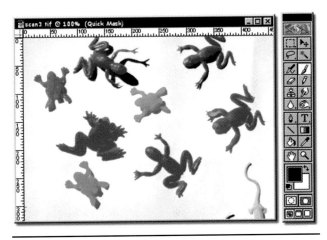

Figure 6.15 Using **Select/Similar** to create a complex selection.

In Figure 6.15, the bits of cropped toys I wanted to delete were added to the selection by holding down the **Shift** key and using the Selection tool. The little parts of the toys weren't well selected in this image, so I switched to Quick Mask mode, which transforms the selection into a red mask, as seen in Figure 6.15. You can select automasking by clicking on the icon directly below the color swatches on the tool palette, or by typing **Q**. This feature enables you to make small adjustments, by painting with black to subtract from the existing selection and painting with white to add to the current selection. You can use any of the paint tools, including the airbrush, paintbrush, pencil, and smudge tools, to create as accurate a selection as you like. When the selection is correct, click on the **Standard Mode** icon (or type **Q**).

4. Open one of the seamless pattern tile files you created in Chapter 4. Apply **Select All**, then **Edit/Define Pattern**. Returning to the scanned image, select **Edit/Fill/Pattern**. Alternatively, you can fill the selection with a color and then use a filter (Figure 6.16).

Figure 6.16 A pattern fill applied to the background.

In PhotoPaint

1. Scan your image by selecting **File/Acquire Image** (Figure 6.17). Experiment with your scanner to find out if it improves the quality of low-resolution images to scan first at a higher resolution (like 200 dpi) and then resample (**Image/Resample**) to the size you intend the image to be on your Web page.

2. Obviously, this image was a little out of kilter when it was scanned. Luckily, Corel has a nifty filter called Deskew that will automatically straighten out the image. Select **Image/Deskew** if your image needs to be adjusted. Next, compensate for those pesky dingy, dull whites and flat darks. Apply **Effects/PhotoLab/CSILevels**. For this scan, you'll want to raise the brightness and contrast quite a bit, but every scan will be different. Use the preview and experiment with the Shadows and Highlights settings (Figure 6.18).

Figure 6.17 The original scan in PhotoPaint.

Figure 6.18 The image adjusted using Deskew and CSI Levels filters.

3. The scan is still nothing to write home about. Sometimes, adding an interesting background helps. Select some of the background using a masking tool. Apply **Mask/Similar**. To adjust the range of color selected, double-click on the **Magic Wand** masking tool and raise or lower the tolerance.

4. Some areas of this image weren't selected well. To create a very accurate mask, select **Mask/Mask Overlay**. The mask on the image will appear as a red see-through area. You can then adjust the mask by selecting **Mask/Paint on Mask**. Then, by using a paint tool and white, you can delete areas of the mask. By using black, you can add to the mask. You'll be able to achieve a very accurate mask by using the paint tools (Figure 6.19).

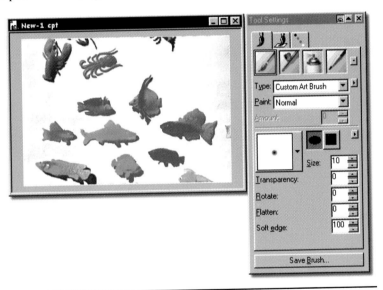

Figure 6.19 Adjusting the mask with paint tools.

5. To create an interesting background, I applied **Effects/Noise/Add Noise**, then **Effects/Blur/Radial Blur** to create the illusion of movement. Using the Cropping tool, select the area of the scan you wish to keep. Double-click inside the area you want to crop to; or use the right mouse button and select **Crop To Selection**.

To experiment with different JPG settings in Corel PhotoPaint, duplicate your original file several times by selecting **Image/Duplicate**. Save each image with a different JPG setting. Close the file and reopen it, because you can't view the effect the JPG compression has had on the image until you've reopened the image. Once you've saved your file, you can check the file size by selecting **Image/Info**. The size of the image is listed as Original File Size.

COLORIZING A GRAYSCALE PHOTO

In Photoshop

Let's start with a color photo and add some mood and warmth by hand-coloring it (see Figure 6.20). This is not a bad photo; it has good contrast, and it's in focus.

1. Select the area of the photo you want to keep, using the Rectangular selection tool, and apply **Image/Crop**. Next, apply **Image/Mode/Grayscale**. A dialog box will ask if you want to discard the color information. Select **OK**.

2. Apply **Image/Adjust/Levels**. Since you will be adding color over this grayscale photo, you will want to lighten it a little so that the photo doesn't become too dark. Drag the right Input Level slider toward the center, and apply. Next apply **Mode/RGB Color** (Figure 6.21). You have to return the image to RGB color in order to paint it.

3. Select the photo (**Ctrl+A** on Windows, **Command+A** on the Mac). Copy it (**Ctrl+C** on Windows, **Command+C** on the Mac), and paste it (**Ctrl+V** on Windows, **Command+V** on the Mac). The copy of the photo will be pasted as a new layer. Change the mode for this layer to **Multiply**. You'll need

Figure 6.20 The original scan in Photoshop.

the Layers palette open to do this, so if it isn't open, select **Window/Show Layer**. By changing the mode to **Multiply**, the grayscale photo will be visible through the color you apply.

4. Select the **Airbrush** tool, and set it to a large size. From the Options palette, set the pressure to 10% or less. In this photo, I painted in the background first. Don't worry about being sloppy or painting outside the lines. You can always delete the layer you're applying color to and start over. You also don't need to individually color each item in the photo (Figure 6.22). Be bold!

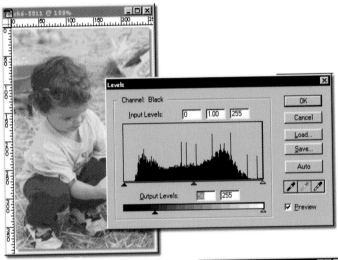

Figure 6.21 The image's mode changed to grayscale.

Figure 6.22 Finished colorized photo.

5. From the Layers flyout menu, select **Flatten** to combine the layers. Save the file as a medium-quality JPG. This particular image had a 16K file size when saved as a JPG.

In PhotoPaint

Let's start with a color photo for this project (see Figure 6.23). We could just as easily start with a line drawing (an old engraving, for example, or a black-and-white photo or black-and-white clip art).

1. Crop the image using the Crop tool and resample if necessary. Next select **Image/Convert To/Grayscale**. This removes the color information, as shown in Figure 6.24. Apply **Image/ConvertTo/RGB Color** so that you can begin colorizing. First, though, you'll want to lighten the image. Apply **Image/Adjust/Levels**, and raise the Gamma number to lighten the image.

2. Next you'll be adding a new layer to the image so that you can paint without affecting the image below it. Select **View/Roll-ups/Object**, if your Object roll-up isn't already visible on screen. Select the **Layer** icon. Next select the **New Object** icon at the bottom of the roll-up, as seen in Figure 6.25. The icon isn't labeled, but it has a picture of a curled page. Change the merge mode to **Multiply** for the new object.

Figure 6.23 The original scan in PhotoPaint.

Figure 6.24 Image changed to grayscale.

3. Double-click on the **Paintbrush** tool to open the Tool Settings palette. Select the **Airbrush; Type, Wide Cover; Transparency, 80**. Paint loosely and freely. Don't worry about staying within the lines.

4. Continue to paint, changing colors as necessary. When you're finished, save the file as a JPG. In this image I saved one area (the top of the waterfall) as white and did not add any color to it. It then becomes the focal point for the image.

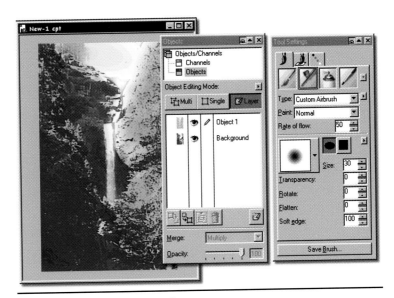

Figure 6.25 Painting on a new layer.

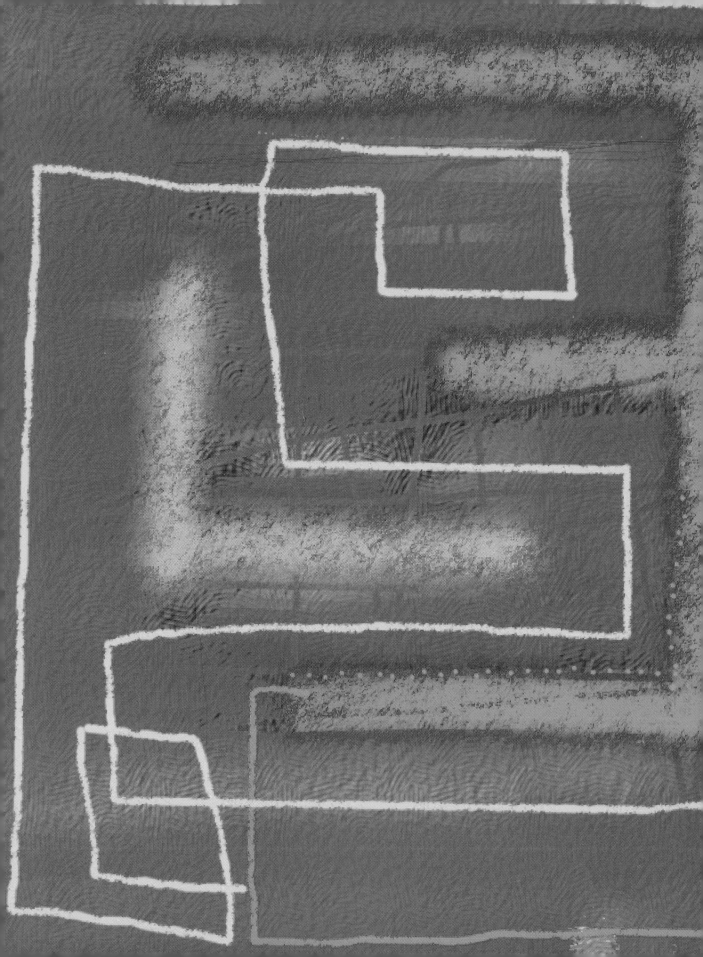

7 GIVING GRAPHICS INTERESTING EDGES, OR THERE'S MORE TO LIFE THAN RECTANGLES

Asquare is a rectangle, but a rectangle is not a square. Remember this from geometry class in the fourth grade? Well, sometimes even a rectangle shouldn't be a rectangle. The tendency when designing Web graphics is to design right up to the corners of the image area, which results in every graphic becoming a boring rectangle. If you do this, you're missing an opportunity to give your pages a more interesting look by changing the outside shape of your images.

In Chapter 5, I discussed how color can unify your Web pages and give them a unique personality. Similarly, giving your graphics more interesting edges can enliven your pages with a more dynamic yet unified look. In fact, sometimes it's the only area where you can be creative with an image. If, for example, you have a large number of product photos or portraits of company officers to add to a Web site, you could add interesting edges to elevate the collection of pictures to a uniquely stylized group of images that would really stand out.

If you use some of these techniques, be aware that you may need to make more careful decisions about cropping your graphics, because when you feather or texturize the edges, important information can be lost. And note that you can use the methods and recipes in this chapter not just for header graphics and photos, but also for icons.

In this chapter, I'll also show you how to take any group of images you'd like to use on your Web site and colorize them to match. This is a nifty trick to invoke if you have a hodgepodge of images that you need to use on your Web page, but you want them to look like they belong together.

One piece of advice before we begin: Because creating artwork is supposed to be fun and easy, I've found that people tend to blame themselves when they reach a plateau in the learning curve or run into a problem with software or hardware. Consider this: Learning about computer graphics often is more like math class than art class. So remember to take breaks, and learn the **Ctrl+Z** keystroke (**Command+Z** on the Mac). Now, on to the importance of not being rectangular all the time.

CREATIVE EDGES IN PHOTOSHOP

The color that you select for the area surrounding an image should be the same as that of the Web page for the image. If your Web page is light gray, then the area surrounding your image should be light gray instead of white, as I've used in these examples.

1. Start with an image 200 pixels wide x 150 pixels tall (Figure 7.1). You can use a portion of a scanned photo or a photo from the Adobe Photoshop CD (located in the Stockart directory). Don't forget to correct any errors in the image using the tools and techniques discussed in Chapter 6.

2. Set the background color to white. Apply **Image/Canvas Size**, using a width of 300 pixels and a height of 250 pixels. You may want to use **Image/Duplicate** at this point, if you want to try some of the other recipe variations on the same file.

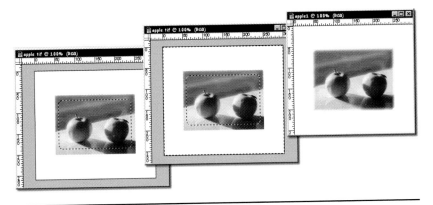

Figure 7.1 Creating an interesting edge in Photoshop.

3. Make a rectangular selection using the Marquee tool a little in from the edges of the image. The selection you're creating will protect the main area of the image from being affected by the filter. Apply **Select/Feather**, with the feather amount set to **5**. Apply **Select/Inverse**, as shown in Figure 7.1. The area now selected includes only a little of the outside of the image, along with the white border area.

4. Apply **Filter/Blur/Motion Blur**; **Angle, 45; Distance, 10,** as in the third example in Figure 7.1.

Creative Edges Using Filters

There's a filter specifically for creating interesting edges called AutoFX's Photo/Graphic Edges. This is a commercial add-on filter available from Auto F/X. Its Web site is located at http://www.autofx.com.

1. Make sure your image is in RGB mode; select **Image/Mode/RGB** to change it if necessary. Your image should be cropped to the edges of the image without the extra white space we added in the first tutorial in this chapter. You'll lose some of the photo at the outer edges, so be careful not to crop too closely.

2. Select **Filter/AutoFX/Photo-Graphic Edges**, and select the **Outset Effect** button. You'll then be able to browse through the effects for your image, then preview the effect on the image. By changing the Inset Scale, Inset Blur, Outset Scale, and Outset Blur sliders, you can create an infinite number of subtle effects. Figure 7.2 shows some of them.

Figure 7.2 Edge effects created with Auto F/X filter.

CREATING MATCHING ARTWORK IN PHOTOSHOP

You'll often be confronted with a situation where a certain amount of artwork has to go on a Web page, yet none of it matches or fits together very well, as in Figure 7.3. In this case, the artwork is in different styles, different colors, and different textures. Seemingly it's a hopeless task to make this motley group of artwork come together. Not so. Keep reading.

Figure 7.3 Artwork that doesn't work well together.

Creating a Duotone

We'll examine two methods of changing the artwork so that it goes together. The first is to change the artwork to a duotone. A duotone is usually used only in printing, but it has benefits for Web artwork as well. A duotone in printing remaps an image so that it is printed in two colors. In Web work, using fewer colors means that an image can be saved to a smaller color palette if it is saved as a GIF, thus creating a smaller file size.

1. Make sure the Info palette is open by selecting **Window/Show Info**. Select the **Eyedropper** tool, and select a color you'd like to use as the basis for the duotone images you'll create, as seen in Figure 7.4. I recommend a dark color so the duotones won't look too washed out. Jot down the RGB number you see on the Info palette.

2. Select the image you'd like to match. Select **Image/Mode/Grayscale**. In order to create a duotone, you have to reduce the image to grayscale first. Next, select **Image/Mode/Duotone**. Click the **Black** swatch, which will reveal the Color Picker. Enter your RGB values, as in Figure 7.5. We're only using one color for this example, but you could select a second color. Be sure to experiment, as it's the best way to learn and discover new things about your paint program. If the duotone ends up looking a little wimpy, you can adjust the contrast by selecting **Image/Adjust Levels**. Figure 7.6 shows the finished product.

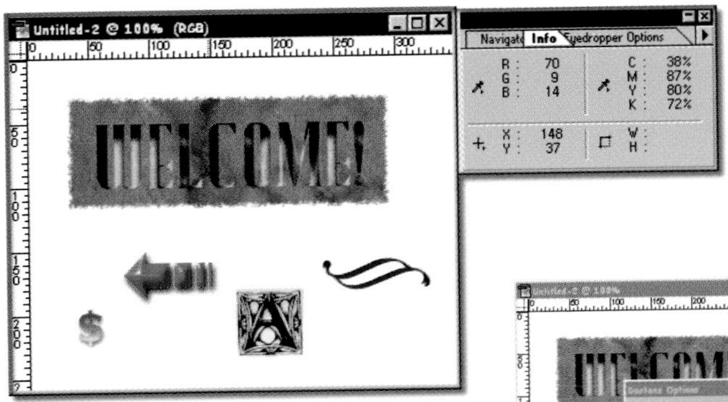

Figure 7.4 Selecting a color.

Figure 7.6 The matching artwork.

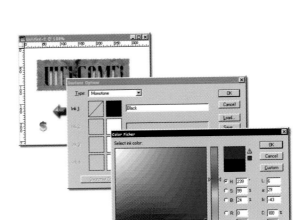

Figure 7.5 Creating a duotone.

Adjusting Color in Photoshop

In this exercise, we'll manipulate the existing colors in the artwork so that they match the header graphic.

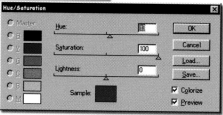

Figure 7.7 Altering the colors in the image in Photshop.

1. Open an image, and if it isn't in RGB mode, select **Image/Mode/RGB**. Next, select **Image/Adjust/Hue-Saturation-Brilliance**. Drag the Hue slider and watch your image as it previews the color change. Select **OK** when your image reaches a color that appears to match your main image.

2. In some cases, you can't manipulate the existing colors to match, which was the case with the initial letter and the swash image in this example. If that happens, open an image, and if it isn't in RGB mode, select **Image/**

Mode/RGB. Next select **Image/Adjust-Hue-Saturation-Brilliance**. Drag the Hue slider and watch your image as it previews the color change. If that doesn't work, select the **Colorize** checkbox, as in Figure 7.7. Then manipulate the Hue slider until you get a color that matches. The finished graphics are in Figure 7.8.

Figure 7.8 The finished, matching images.

CREATIVE EDGES IN PHOTOPAINT

The color that you select for the area surrounding an image should be the same as the Web page for the image. If your Web page is light gray, then the area surrounding your image should be light gray instead of white as I've used in these examples. You can use a scanned photo or a photo from the collection found on CorelDRAW 7 CD number 2.

1. Start with an image 200 pixels wide x 150 pixels tall. You can use a portion of a scan or a texture fill, as shown in Figure 7.9. Don't forget to fix any problems with your image using the tools and techniques demonstrated in Chapter 6.

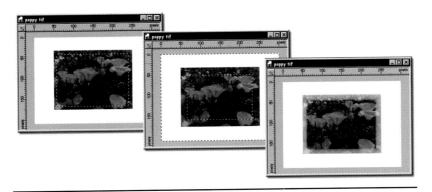

Figure 7.9 Creating an interesting edge in PhotoPaint.

2. Set the paper color to white. Apply **Image/Paper Size**, deselecting the **Maintain Aspect Ratio** checkbox and using a width of 300 pixels, a height of 250 pixels, placement centered, and paper color white. This will add the extra area around your image to which you'll be applying a filter. Using the Rectangle Mask tool, create a mask that is a little smaller than the image. Select **Mask/Feather**; **Width, 5; Direction, Middle; Edges, Curved**.

3. Select **Mask/Invert**. The mask will protect the image from the filter you will use in the next step. You may want to use **Image/Duplicate** at this point, if you want to try some of the recipe variations on this same file later. You can save the file as a TIF or CPT file, and the mask will remain intact.

4. Apply **Effects/Artistic/Vignette**; **Vignette Color, White; Offset, 100; Fade, 75; Shape, Rectangle.**

Creative Edges Using Filters

There's a set of filters specifically for creating interesting edges called AutoFX's Photo/Graphic Edges. This filter is included with Corel PhotoPaint 7 (Figure 7.10).

Figure 7.10 The Auto F/X Photo/Graphic filter.

1. Make sure your image is in RGB mode; select **Image/Convert To /RGB** to change it if necessary. Your image should be cropped to the edges of the image without the extra white space we added in the first tutorial for creating interesting edges in this chapter. You'll lose some of the photo at the outer edges, so be careful not to crop too closely on the focal point of the photo. You may want to use **Image/Paper Size** to increase the area available for the filter to work on.

2. Select **Filter/AutoFX/Photo-Graphic Edges**, and select the **Outset Effect** button, as shown in Figure 7.11. You'll then be able to browse through the effects for your image and preview the effect on the image. By changing the Inset Scale, Inset Blur, Outset Scale, and Outset Blur sliders, you can create an infinite number of subtle effects. Figure 7.11 shows some of the edge effects possible using this set of filters.

Figure 7.11 Edge effects created with the Photo/Graphic filter.

Creating a Duotone

We'll examine two methods of changing the artwork so that it goes together. The first is to change the artwork to a duotone. A duotone is usually used only in printing, but it has benefits for Web artwork as well. A duotone in printing remaps an image so that the color images are printed in two colors. In Web

work, using fewer colors means that an image can be saved to a smaller color palette if it is saved as a GIF, thus creating a smaller file size. Using a duotone is a good way to create a cohesive group of page elements from dissimilar images. Figure 7.12 shows a group of images that couldn't have less in common. By using a duotone, we'll match the images to the main banner colors.

Figure 7.12 A disparate collection of artwork.

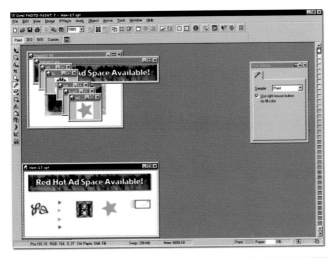

1. Select the **Eyedropper** tool, and select a color you'd like to use as the basis for the duotone images you'll create, as seen in Figure 7.13. Select a dark color so the duotones won't look too washed out. Jot down the RGB number you see in the status bar at the very bottom of the screen.

Figure 7.13 Finding the target RGB value.

2. Select the image you'd like to match. Select **Image/Convert To/ Grayscale**. In order to create a duotone, you have to reduce the image to grayscale first. Next select **Image/Convert To/Duotone**. Click the **Black** swatch, which will reveal the Color Picker. Enter your RGB values, as in Figure 7.14. We're using two colors for this example, a dark red and a yellow. Be sure to experiment, as it's the best way to learn and discover new things about your paint program. Figure 7.15 shows the finished product.

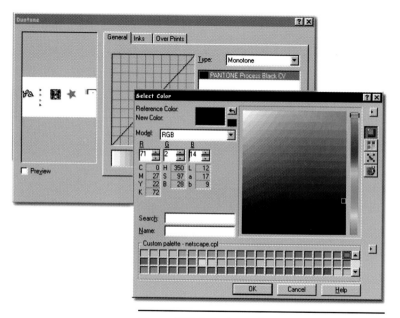

Figure 7.14 Selecting a duotone color.

Figure 7.15 The matching artwork.

Adjusting Color in PhotoPaint

In this exercise, we'll manipulate the existing colors in the artwork so that they match the banner graphic.

1. Open an image, and if it isn't in RGB mode, select **Image/Convert To/RGB**.

2. Select **Effects/PhotoLab/CSI HueSlider**.

3. Use the Eyedropper tool to select a target color from your main image, as shown in Figure 7.16.

4. Adjust the Flood Amount slider until the preview looks right.

The finished graphics are in Figure 7.17.

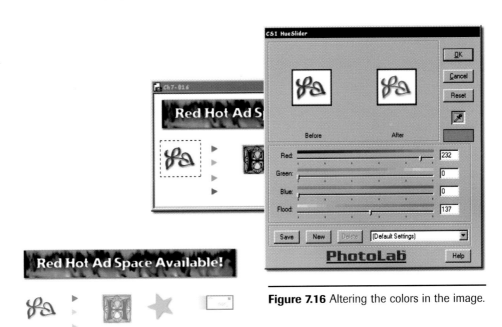

Figure 7.16 Altering the colors in the image.

Figure 7.17 The finished artwork.

PHOTOSHOP RECIPES

All of the recipes start with a photo that has a feathered selection as described for the example in this chapter. All of the filters are applied using the typical defaults unless otherwise specified.

 Apply **Filter/Distort/Wave**, **Number of Generators, 1; Type, Square; Wavelength Maximum, 10; Wavelength Minimum, 10.**

 Apply **Filter/Stylize/Diffuse**, with a setting of **Amplitude Minimum, 5; Amplitude Maximum, 5.** Apply the filter a second time by selecting **Filter/Apply Last Filter**, or by using **Ctrl+F** on Windows, **Command+F** on the Mac.

 Apply **Filter/Blur**, **Gaussian Blur at 2 pixels.** Apply **Filter/ Stylize/Find Edges.**

 Apply **Filter/Stylize/Tiles; Number of Tiles, 20; Maximum Offset, 20%; Fill Empty Areas with Unaltered Image.**

 Apply **Filter/Artistic/Cutout.**

 Apply **Filter/Blur/Radial Blur; Amount, 15; Blur Method, Spin; Quality, Good.**

 Apply **Filter/Noise/Dust and Scratches; Radius 10; Threshold, 0.**

 Apply **Filter/Artistic/Palette Knife; Stroke size, 35.**

Apply **Filter/Pixelate/Color Halftone**.

Apply **Filter/Pixelate/Crystallize**; **Cell Size**, **5**.

Apply **Filter/Sketch/Grain**; **Grain Type**, **Sprinkles**.

Apply **Filter/Brush Stroke/Sumi-e**.

Apply **Filter/Brush Strokes/Sprayed Strokes**; **Stroke Direction**, **Right Diagonal**. Repeat the filter by selecting **Filter/Apply Last Filter**, or by using **Ctrl+F** on Windows or **Command+F** on the Mac.

Apply **Filter/Brush Strokes/Dark Strokes**, with the black intensity set to **7**.

Apply **Filter/Artistic/Poster Edges**.

Extra Credit

Use some of the same edge effects, but start with an oval selection created with the Ellipse Marquee tool (click and hold the Rectangular Marquee tool to reveal) instead of a rectangular selection. Or try using the Lasso tool to draw a rough, freehand selection.

C h a p t e r

7

PHOTOPAINT RECIPES

All of the recipes start with a photo that has a feathered selection as described for the example in this chapter. All of the filters are applied using the typical defaults unless otherwise specified.

Apply **Effects/2D/Pixelate; Circular; Width, 10; Height, 10; Opacity, 100.**

Apply **Effects/2D/Ripple; Direction, Vertical; Period, 18; Amplitude, 5.**

Select **Image/Flip/Vertically**. Apply **Effects/2D/Wet Paint; Percentage, 80; Wetness, 45**. Select **Image/Flip/Vertically**. Apply **Effects/Last Filter (Ctrl+F).**

Apply **Effects/3D/Mesh Warp**. Pull in the center nodes (control points) to create the desired warping effect.

Apply **Effects/Fancy/Alchemy; Style, Vasili.**

Apply **Effects/2D/Whirlpool; Style, Smudger,** and select the checkbox for **Warp.**

Apply **Effects/3D/Zigzag; Type, Out from Center; Waves, 40; Strength, 40.** Next, apply **Effects/Blur/Smooth.**

Apply **Effects/Fancy/Alchemy; Style, Cubist.**

Apply **Effects/Fancy/Alchemy**; **Style, Ripple Detail.**

Apply **Effects/Artistic/Impressionist**; **Scatter Horizontal, 20; Scatter Vertical, 20.**

Apply **Effects/Noise/Diffuse**; **Level, 100.**

Apply **Effects/Fancy/Julia Set Explorer**. Select **Corel Presets; Rings of Saturn.** Select **Options/Lighten only.** Select **Image/Flip/Horizontally.** Repeat the filter (**Ctrl+F**). Select **Image/Flip/Horizontally.**

Apply **Effects/Render/Lighting**; **Style, Texturize.**

Apply **Effects/Color Transform/Color Halftone**; **Radius, 2.**

Apply **Effects/Artistic/Smoked Glass**; **Tint, 70; Percent, 90; Other Color, White.**

Extra Credit

Use some of the same edge effects, but start with an oval selection created with the Circular Mask tool (click and hold the rectangular Mask tool to reveal) instead of a rectangular selection. Or try using the Lasso tool to draw a rough, freehand selection.

8 INDEXING COLORS AND CREATING TRANSPARENT GIFs, OR 8 BITS IS ENOUGH

This chapter addresses the not-so-fun part of Web graphics: file formats and color indexing. But these topics also offer the opportunity to learn about transparency and how to make graphics smaller and therefore quicker to download. The latter is especially important since few visitors to the Web will wait for slow-moving graphics to appear; they'll just go elsewhere.

Let's review the two basic file formats for Web graphics, GIF and JPEG. GIF is a compressed file format that allows a maximum of 256 colors in any image. JPEG, also a compressed file format, allows the total spectrum, or 16 million colors, in any image. It is essential to understand how and when to use GIF and JPEG files, and transparency, so that you can produce better-looking, faster-loading Web graphics. To that end, this chapter explains how to decrease the file size of GIFs by indexing, or limiting the available colors to a specific palette.

After we get through these lessons, we'll move on to Chapter 9, where your graphics wizardry will ignite when you discover how to create drop shadows and other cool type effects. But for now, back to indexing and transparency.

GIF VERSUS JPEG

A GIF file is an 8-bit (or less) graphics standard file format. JPEG is a 24-bit compression standard. The more bits you have, the more precise information you have in your file. The JPEG file format is considered "lossy," as shown in the examples in Chapter 1, meaning that each time you save a JPEG you lose a little more data from the file. In contrast, the GIF file format is not considered lossy, but by the time you've indexed an image that started out as 24-bit, you've thrown away (and therefore lost) more than 15 million colors. Thus, it's a good idea to always keep a copy of the original, uncompressed, 24-bit file.

Only GIF files are indexed; that is, constrained to a set of colors. If a file being indexed contains more than 256 colors, the missing colors are created by dithering, which is approximating the missing colors by using pixels of colors that are close in value. The more colors there are in the original image and the fewer colors there are in the indexing palette creates a great deal of dithering.

The rules of thumb for deciding between GIF and JPEG formats are:

- Use JPEG if your image is a photo or an illustration with many colors or smooth gradations of color. For example, a photograph often has a significant amount of color variation that will be handled best by JPEG.

- Use GIF if your image has large areas of the same color (such as line art), or if you would like to create an image with a transparent background (which will be discussed later in this chapter). An image with few colors can often be saved as a very small GIF since this format can be saved as a 4- or 5-bit image or even fewer colors.

The first example, Figure 8.1, is an 18K JPEG file, saved with the low-quality setting. This is an image with many color subtleties and variations. It looks better on a monitor than what you see in Figure 8.2, which is a 53K GIF file, which was indexed to the Web palette. This image has a lot of colors, and its soft focus makes it an ideal candidate for JPEG compression. Harder edges maintain their quality better in GIF files than in JPEG files.

Figure 8.1 This image is an 18K JPEG file, 400 x 267 pixels.

Figure 8.2 This Image is a 53K GIF file, 400 x 267 pixels.

I encourage you to experiment by saving your images in several different formats in order to compare the file sizes and appearance. Sometimes it's difficult to judge whether an image will make a better GIF or JPEG and what the trade-off will be between file size and image quality.

Both Photoshop and PhotoPaint have built-in Web palettes; that is, you can index your GIF images to the same palette we discussed in Chapter 5, and be assured that they won't dither again for Mac or Windows users who have 256-color monitors. However, there may be some trade-offs in file size that you might want to consider. Remember, the palette contains 216 colors that don't dither on either Windows or Mac 256-color monitors. When you index a GIF to this palette, you ensure that the image won't dither again. However, this is rarely the best solution for an image that contains more than a few simple flat colors. Figures 8.3 through 8.5 show that by using an adaptive palette, you can create a smaller GIF file. Although an image generated this way will dither again for users viewing Web pages with Internet Explorer or Netscape with 256 colors, it is not very noticeable, as seen in Figure 8.5.

Figure 8.3 GIF indexed to the Web palette, file size 39K.

Figure 8.4 GIF indexed to an adaptive 4-bit palette, 25K.

Figure 8.5 An adaptive palette image displayed on a 256-color monitor.

C h a p t e r

8

A Checklist for Creating Smaller Files

The following guidelines are helpful for creating smaller files:

- Use GIF and JPEG appropriately.

- Use JPEG if your image is a photo or a complex illustration with smooth gradations of color.

- Save your JPEGs as medium- or low-quality images in Photoshop. Generally speaking, this is good enough for Web pages and will substantially reduce the file size over a high-quality JPEG. Corel PhotoPaint offers a much wider range of JPEG settings. Frankly, the lowest setting of JPEG on PhotoPaint is almost guaranteed to turn your gorgeous image into clothes dryer lint. Try saving JPEGs in PhotoPaint with a setting somewhere between 100 and 200.

- Use GIF if your image has large areas of the same color or if you would like to have a transparent background. JPEGs don't support transparency.

- Experiment with different color depths when saving GIFs. Most images can be saved in 5- or 6-bit or even smaller format without much loss of quality, as seen in Figures 8.6 through 8.8.

Figure 8.6 A 260 x 325 pixel GIF indexed to an adaptive palette of 256 colors (8-bit); 38K.

Figure 8.7 A 260 x 325 pixel GIF indexed to the 216 Web palette; 29K.

Figure 8.8 A 260 x 325 pixel GIF indexed to an adaptive palette of 16 colors (4-bit); 15K.

- If you need to resize a GIF, change the color back to RGB before you resample. Index the colors again after you've resampled. This won't generate a smaller file size, but it will result in a less jaggy image.

- It's rare that an image needs to be wider than 500 pixels. Truly. If you think you need to tell people to set their browsers to a certain size, you're not really designing for the Web.

- Consider using an image in more than one place on a page. This is electronic recycling: The browser will download the image only once, but it can place the image in numerous places on the page.

- If you have a Web page with many images, consider using thumbnails, or smaller versions of the images, that act as buttons linking to the larger images.

- To dither or not to dither the GIF? In general, the fewer colors in the image, the more likely it is to look better with no dithering. Dithering, in general, results in larger file sizes.

BROWSERS AND THEIR LIMITATIONS

Not all browsers are the same, nor are monitors and computers, and while it's good practice to check how your images display on as many monitors and browsers as you can, there is no way to accommodate all the browsers or monitors that will be used to display your images. How does this affect your design choice? Essentially, it presents you with an either/or decision: You can decide either to accommodate for as many browsers and monitors as possible, or choose to design your page as you want it to look under optimum conditions.

What makes this decision more difficult is that there is no accurate way of counting the users of the various browsers or monitor settings. We know, for instance, that there are around 8 million America Online users, some half or more who have upgraded to the version of AOL that uses Internet Explorer as the default browser. However, each AOL account may have up to five screen names, or users. Add to that the fact that any one person can use his or her account from both home and work, where they may have two completely different computer setups, and you can begin to understand the difficulties in determining who uses which monitor resolution, platform, or browser for viewing the Web.

For a while, it looked as if most of the market would favor two browsers: Microsoft's Internet Explorer and Netscape's Navigator. But a number of consumer products are now adding Web access via their proprietary Web browsers. You've no doubt heard of WebTV, which enables users to view the Web on a television set. Other products range from handheld computers, which may have tiny black-and-white screens, to laptops to cell phones and other consumer electronic devices.

The bottom line? There is no definitive answer to this dilemma. As long as there are many different browsers and monitors out there, how you design your graphics and Web site will depend on your particular audience. There are, thankfully, sites and tools to help you make this decision and then to produce your best work within the framework you've chosen. Check out the Resources at the back of this book.

INTERLACING HAS NOTHING TO DO WITH SHOES

Interlacing is a nifty trick that you can apply to GIFs and JPEGs. While the browser is loading the Web page, interlaced GIFs will show up immediately at a very low resolution. As the browser continues to receive the rest of the GIF or JPEG file information, it rewrites the image until it is completely rendered. This gives the illusion that the graphic is being transferred quickly. In reality, interlaced GIFs can be about 10% larger than noninterlaced GIFs, but progressive JPEG files tend to be a bit smaller than standard (or nonprogressive) JPEGs. The only problem with interlaced GIFs is that sometimes they fail to render completely, leaving a lower-resolution image than intended. This can usually be corrected by using the browser's **Reload** command.

If a GIF is intended as a background pattern for a page, it shouldn't be interlaced, because using an interlaced GIF in this way will prevent the page from loading until it is fully interlaced.

There are two flavors of GIFs: GIF87a and GIF89a. Catchy names, right? Use GIF89a to use transparency or interlacing, which can be saved as either interlaced or noninterlaced files; GIF87a cannot be saved as interlaced or transparent files.

TRANSPARENCY

As you may know, bitmap files are geometrically challenged; that is, a GIF or any other bitmap can only be a rectangle. Fortunately, transparency enables you to integrate your bitmaps seamlessly with the background of your Web page. Transparent images appear to "float" over a background. In other words, your image will not appear to be placed on a rectangular background, as shown in Figures 8.9 and 8.10

Figure 8.9 Nontransparent background.

Figure 8.10 Transparent background.

Transparent backgrounds can be produced in a number of ways. Photoshop has a plug-in export filter for setting the transparent background; PhotoPaint has a transparency option built into the Save as GIF function. But before we start discussing how to create transparent backgrounds, be aware that a few potential problems may arise when creating transparent GIFs. First, only one color can be defined as transparent in any GIF. So, if your background has been dithered to more than one color in the indexing process, you can end up with an ugly spotted mess since only the one color will be transparent. Another transparency problem can occur when the color that you have made transparent is used in places other than the background, causing the background to appear in unseemly (no pun intended) areas. The star in Figures 8.11 and 8.12 illustrates both of these GIF problems. The background was dithered to two colors, and only one color was made transparent. Then the background color was present in more than just the background; it also was present on the star. When the color was defined as transparent, it made a portion of the star transparent as well. Fortunately, both of these problems can be corrected.

Figure 8.11 The original image.

Figure 8.12 One color made transparent.

CREATING A TRANSPARENT GIF IN PHOTOSHOP: TWO METHODS

You'll find the GIF89a Export filter under **File/Export** in Photoshop. If it's not there, try reinstalling Photoshop. Both of the methods I demonstrate here will work fine for most images. If you have an image in which the background color is similar to other colors in the image, you'll want to use Method 1, which allows you to define transparency using Layers in Photoshop, and not by selecting a specific color. If you want very precise transparency for your image, use Method 2 to create your transparent GIF.

Method 1

In this example, we'll try the trickiest transparent GIF effect: creating an image that will be transparent against a patterned background. Figure 8.13 shows the background we'll use in this example. Why is this tricky? Remember, you can make only one color transparent when you create a transparent GIF. Obviously, in a patterned background, a number of colors are involved. What to do? In this first method, we'll define the area to be transparent by using Layers in Photoshop. First, we'll create the image, making sure that the artwork is *not* on the background layer of the file.

Figure 8.13
The patterned background.

1. Open the Layers palette if it isn't already by selecting **Window/Show Layer**, as in Figure 8.14.

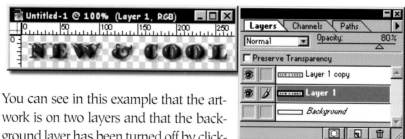

2. You can see in this example that the artwork is on two layers and that the background layer has been turned off by clicking on the eye icon on the Layers palette. Now find out which color should be defined as transparent. Open the Info

Figure 8.14 The Layers palette.

palette by selecting **Window/Show Info.** Then use the Eyedropper tool to select a color from the background pattern, as in Figure 8.15. See the R, G, and B values? Jot those down; well be using them in just a minute.

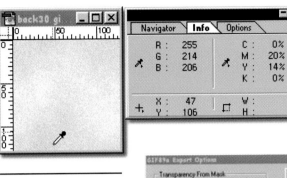

Figure 8.15 Choose a color that tends to be darker rather than lighter.

3. Now select your layered file to make it the active image; then select **File/Export/Gif89a**. You'll see a gray square in the upper-left corner of the dialog box that reads (Default) Transparency Index Color, as in Figure 8.16.

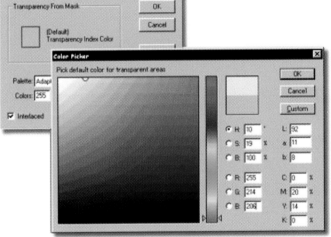

Figure 8.16 Changing the default transparency color.

4. Click on this gray square. A color picker will open. Type in the R, G, and B values that you jotted down a moment ago. This is where most transparent GIFs go wrong: Most people make the mistake of leaving the default transparency color set to gray, and this can cause a funny "aura," or ghosting effect, around the GIF.

5. Select **OK**, then **OK** again. You can see the image as it would appear in an application that did not support transparency in Figure 8.17.

Figure 8.17 The finished GIF.

Method 2

We'll create a second example using different steps to achieve a more accurate, if slightly more tedious, method.

1. Before creating the image for your Web page, fill the background of the image with the color selected from your seamless pattern file, as described in Method 1, using the Info palette. Create the image, and flatten and index the file. Select **Image/Mode/Indexed**.

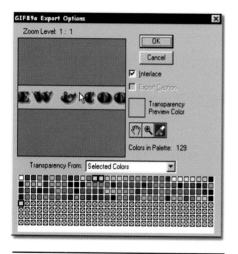

Figure 8.18 Selecting which colors will be transparent.

2. Select **File/Export/Gif89 Export**. Use the Eyedropper tool to select as much of the background as you'd like to have transparent, as in Figure 8.18.

3. Locate the gray square in the upper-left corner of the dialog box that reads (Default) Transparency Index Color, as in Figure 8.19. Click on it. A color picker will open. Type in the R, G, and B values that you jotted down when you used the Eyedropper to select a color from the background image.

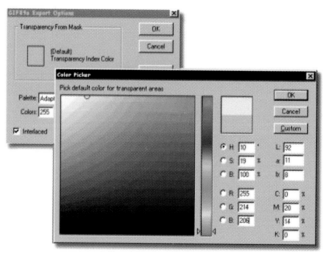

Figure 8.19 Changing the default transparency color.

4. If you're not using the Gif89a filter, you'll either need to bucket-fill the problem area or use a very small pencil or brush to retouch the dithered areas. This is single-pixel tweaking time, but it's worth the effort to avoid creating a GIF that is unattractive.

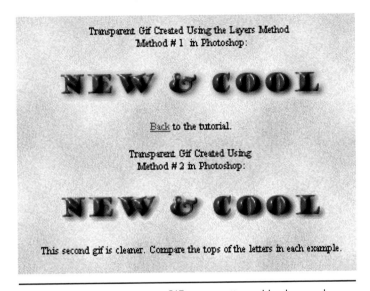

Figure 8.20 The transparent GIFs on a patterned background.

Figure 8.20 shows the results of using both these methods to create transparent GIFs.

CREATING A TRANSPARENT GIF IN PHOTOPAINT

For this example, we'll be using the background tile shown in Figure 8.21 as the background for our transparent GIF. Creating a transparent GIF that will appear against a patterned background is one of the more ticklish tasks you can undertake in creating great Web graphics, because you can make only one color transparent when you create a transparent GIF, and, obviously, in a patterned background, you have a number of colors involved.

Figure 8.21 The background for the transparent GIF.

1. Choose a color from the background to use for your transparent GIF background. Using the Eyedropper tool in conjunction with the **Shift** key, select a color from the background pattern; choose one that is darker rather than lighter. Using the **Shift** key, set this color as the Fill color. Jot down its RGB value that appears in the status bar on the bottom of the screen.

2. Fill an image with this color, and create the rest of the image. In this example, I've used type with a drop shadow. When you're finished creating the image, select **Combine/All Objects with Background**, then select **Image/Convert To/Paletted 8Bit**. Select **Adaptive** and **Error Diffusion**. This may cause the background color to dither to several colors, but that's okay because we'll compensate for it in the next step.

3. Create a mask of the area of the image you'd like to make transparent. Use the Magic Wand Masking tool and select any areas that should be transparent. When you're finished, select **File/Save as GIF**. You'll see another dialog box. Select **Transparent, Masked Area**, and **Invert Mask**.

4. This final step is important to achieve the best possible transparent GIF. Type in the RGB value of the background color that you jotted down in step 1 (Figure 8.23). This will guarantee that your image edges blend seamlessly into the background, as seen in Figure 8.24.

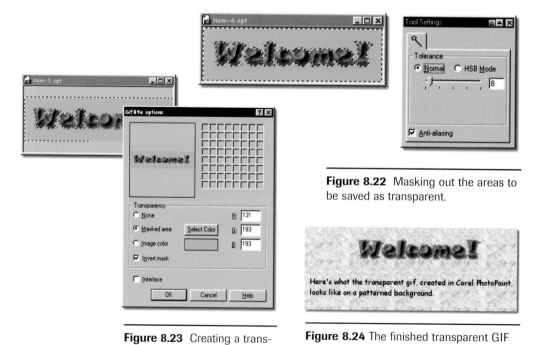

Figure 8.22 Masking out the areas to be saved as transparent.

Figure 8.23 Creating a transparent GIF.

Figure 8.24 The finished transparent GIF on the patterned background.

GIF SHOWDOWN: TESTING SOFTWARE FOR GIFs

There are a handful of tools that excel at compressing and saving files in GIF format. In this section, I'll show you the tests I performed on the more popular filters and programs with a difficult piece of artwork to demonstrate how each software application deals with creating GIFs.

Figure 8.25 shows the original uncompressed artwork. Note the subtleties in this artwork, especially in the figure and behind the type, which might be easily lost. Figures 8.26 through 8.30 show this image saved with HVS Color, DeBabelizer, Ulead, Photoshop, and Corel PhotoPaint, respectively. All were saved with 64-color (6-bit) adaptive palettes and diffusion dithered.

Figure 8.25 The original uncompressed image.

Figure 8.26 GIF saved with HVS Color, 38K.

Figure 8.27 GIF saved with DeBabelizer, 41K.

Figure 8.28 GIF saved with Ulead GIF SmartSaver, 39K.

Figure 8.29 GIF saved with Photoshop, 39K.

Figure 8.30 GIF saved with Corel PhotoPaint, 43K.

Chapter

8

DeBabelizer

DeBabelizer has been used for many years by game and multimedia artists. It excels at batch conversions and supports more file formats than perhaps any other graphics application (see Figure 8.31). You can find out more about this commercial software at http://www.equilibrium.com. This software is available for both Mac and Windows.

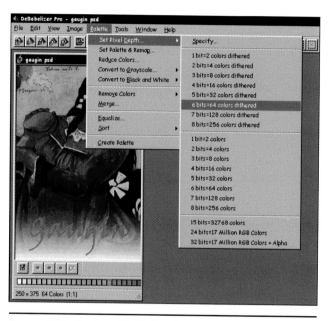

Figure 8.31 Saving with DeBabelizer.

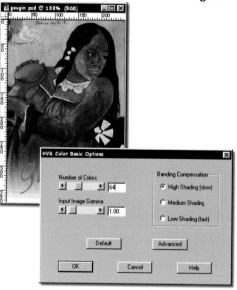

Figure 8.32 Using HVS Color, 39K.

HVS Color Saver

HVS is another plug-in for Windows and Mac, Photoshop or Corel PhotoPaint (see Figure 8.32). When installed with Photoshop, it's found under **File/ Export/HVS Color**. When used with PhotoPaint, it's found under **File/Export Image/HVS Color**. This software's strong point is compressing colors while maintaining the best possible visual appearance. You can find out more about this commercial software package at http://www.digfrontiers.com/.

Ulead GIF SmartSaver

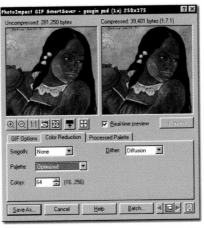

Ulead makes GIF SmartSaver for Windows that works either as a stand-alone software application or as a plug-in for Photoshop (Figure 8.33). When installed with Photoshop, it's found under **File/Export/GIF SmartSaver**. When used with PhotoPaint, it's found under **File/Export Image/GIF SmartSaver**. This software allows you to select color depth and type of dithering, and, as a unique feature, you can preview both the image and the file size before you save it. This can be a lifesaver if you have a job where you have to keep your images smaller than a certain file size. You can download a 30-day evalua-

Figure 8.33 Using the GIF SmartSaver.

tion copy of both GIF and JPEG SmartSavers at http://www.ulead.com.

GIF Transparency Tools

The following shareware tools can also create transparent GIFs.

GIF Construction Set

GIF Construction Set for Windows enables you to create transparent GIFs, and it supports interlacing. You can also load a palette from one GIF and apply it to others, and create GIF animations.

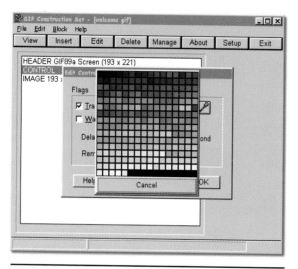

Figure 8.34 Using GIF Construction Set.

To create a transparent GIF with this tool, open your image and select the **Insert/Control** icons. Then, from the button bar, select **Edit.** From the Edit menu, check the **Transparent Color** checkbox. To the right of the checkbox is a color swatch. Click on the color swatch to view the GIF's palette and select the color that you wish to make transparent, as shown in Figure 8.34. Click on the **View** icon to preview the transparency.

Paint Shop Pro 4

Paint Shop Pro is a very nice Windows shareware paint package with many capabilities that you would expect only from higher-end commercial paint packages. The only drawback to using Paint Shop Pro to create transparent GIFs is that you can't preview which area of your GIF is being made transparent. You can download a shareware copy of Paint Shop Pro at http://www.jasc.com.

To make a transparent GIF in Paint Shop Pro, first you need to reduce the color depth. Go to **Colors/Decrease Color Depth/X Colors.** Select the number of colors that you would like to reduce your GIF to. For the method of color reduction, choose **Error Diffusion.** This will dither your image when reducing your colors.

Zoom in on your image to make sure that your background color hasn't dithered. If it has, use the Paint Bucket tool to fill the background with a single color; or use a paintbrush or pencil to eliminate colors from the background. Once your background is a single color, use the Eyedropper tool to select it, as shown in Figure 8.35. At the right edge of the window, Paint Shop Pro will display the RGB number and the index number, which is preceded by an *I.* This is the number in the image's palette that you'll make transparent.

Select **Save As**. The file type should be GIF89a. Select the **Options** button. Select **Set Transparency Value to Palette Entry,** and enter the index number. The number you use for the index color is the number displayed when you used the Eyedropper tool.

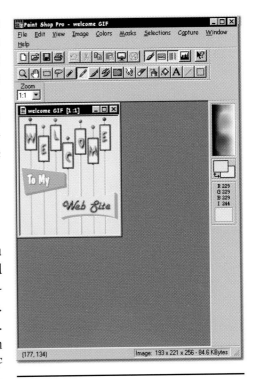

Figure 8.35 Using Paint Shop Pro.

Transparent GIFS on the Macintosh

For Macintosh users, there's a simple effective program called Transparency 1.0. You can download Transparency from Shareware.com at http://www.shareware.com. Transparency will work only with GIF files. To use it, open your GIF in Transparency. Select the color you wish to make transparent. Once you select a color, a small box appears that contains all the colors that are part of your image (Figure 8.36). One box contains an X; this is the color that is currently transparent. If there is no X, there is no transparent color set.

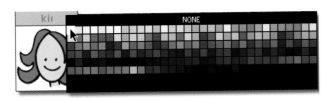

Figure 8.36 Creating a transparent GIF on the Mac with Transparency.

To select a color as transparent, move your cursor over to the color you want to make transparent while holding down the mouse button. Let go. You have just marked the color as transparent. From the File menu, choose **Save as GIF89**. Rename the image, and there you have it—a transparent GIF.

When you close the program, you will see a message box that asks you if you want to resave your original file. Since you've already saved a copy, this is not necessary.

PART 3
ADVANCED
WEB TOPICS

9 CREATING FLOATING TYPE, OR THE SHADOW KNOWS

Within a graphic, you have complete freedom to use any font in any style, color, or combination that you like. One of the great things about working with type is that once you learn a few basics, such as how to create a drop shadow, you can produce very professional-looking artwork fairly easily.

Here are the all-important basics of working with type. First, type has to be legible, so the more complex the typeface, the larger it should be. If you're working at a very small size, it is best to select a simple sans serif typeface, such as Arial, Futura, or Verdana. Serif typefaces tend to be a little more complex, and thus more difficult to make out at smaller sizes; script fonts especially can be difficult to read at low resolutions.

If you use a purposely degraded font (like a grunge font) at a small point size, as in Figure 9.1, instead of appearing intentionally rough, it will just look unclear and poorly anti-aliased. Using a large point size along with a drop shadow can help clarify your intentions and the legibility of the type, as shown in Figure 9.2.

Figure 9.1 Type in small size—12 points.

Figure 9.2 Type at a larger size—40 points.

Another tip for keeping type legible is to heighten the contrast between the type and its background; if you're using a dark color for the type, use a light color for the background, and vice versa. You can also tweak the contrast by using the **Adjust Levels** command, as I discussed in Chapter 5. In these examples, I'll be using bold or extra bold versions of typefaces to help them stand out. All of the projects and recipes included in this chapter can be used with logos, symbols, or line art. So be creative: Use some of the edge treatments from Chapter 7 on the finished graphic.

The main elements to look for when selecting typefaces for a Web page are legibility and how the design of the font contributes to the overall design. A good thing to do is to glance through a type catalog; you'll quickly see that each typeface has its own personality—informal or conservative, fun or conventional, loose or stiff, aggressive or subtle. Check out the list of type resources at the end of the book for further inspiration.

USING FONTS WITH HTML

Before we start working with fonts, I'll explain how they are specified in an HTML page. HTML doesn't give you a great deal of control over how type appears on a Web page. Although you can use different fonts on a Web page, there are some restrictions. With Netscape 3.0 or Internet Explorer

3.0, you can specify a number of options for fonts on a Web page, including the specific typeface, size, and color. But because we're discussing HTML, there are limits. I'll give you a brief overview of all the FONT tags and then display the entire HTML script for a specific example so that you can see how the whole page fits together.

Bold, Italic, and Underline Tags

You can display bold, italic, or underlining reliably on most browsers, using the following tags:

```
<U> This text would be underlined. </U>
<B> This text would be bold</B>
<I> This text would be italic</I>
```

And, of course, you could combine these:

```
<I><B>This text would be both bold and italic.</B></I>
```

The FONT SIZE Tag

You can specify the size of the font displayed on a Web page by using the FONT SIZE tag:

```
<FONT SIZE=4> Here's a Size 4 font.</FONT>
```

You can select a size from between 1 (the smallest) and 7 (the largest). This is the opposite of heading tags, <H1> through <H6> tags, where H1 is the largest. The default size displayed on a Web page is 3.

You can also set a BASEFONT size for your Web page, if you would like, for instance, to display the font a little larger than normal:

```
<BASEFONT SIZE=4> This would be a font size a little larger than normal,
but it can <FONT SIZE=-1>be smaller </FONT> or even <FONT SIZE=+3> larger
than that within a single HTML page.</FONT>
```

Note that the BASEFONT SIZE tag does not require a closing tag.

You can see the differences between font and heading sizes in Figure 9.3.

The FONT FACE Tag

Although you can specify a specific typeface for use within an HTML document, for it to display properly, it must be installed on the computer of the person viewing the Web page. And therein lies the rub: Very few people have the same fonts installed on their computers.

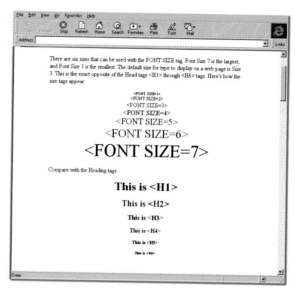

Figure 9.3 The FONT SIZE tag.

Microsoft is trying to change this, by providing a set of fonts for free. These fonts are available for both the Mac and PC, and you can download them at http://www.microsoft.com/truetype. They also come bundled with Internet Explorer. The fonts (shown in Figure 9.4) are:

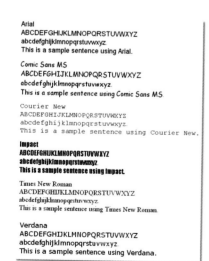

Arial

Comic Sans MS, Comic Sans MS Bold

Courier New, Courier New Bold, Courier New Italic, Courier New Bold Italic

Impact

Times New Roman, Times New Roman Bold, Times New Roman Italic, Times New Roman Bold Italic

Verdana, Verdana Bold, Verdana Italic, Verdana Bold Italic

Figure 9.4 The typefaces distributed by Microsoft.

To use the <FONT FACE> tag, you would specify one or more typefaces:

```
<FONT FACE="Comic Sans MS, Arial, Impact"> This would display as Comic Sans
MS if it was installed on your computer. </FONT>
```

To make this display as bold text, you would use both the FONT FACE and the bold tag:

```
<B><FONT FACE="Comic Sans MS, Arial, Impact"> This would display as Comic
Sans MS Bold if it was installed on your computer. </FONT></B>
```

If you don't have these typefaces on your computer, you can download them for free from http://www.microsoft.com/truetype.

The FONT COLOR Tag

You can specify the color of any section of text using the FONT COLOR tag. Using the hexcode color chart provided in Chapter 5 or any hexcode tool, you can easily change font colors within a page:

```
<FONT COLOR="#FF0000"> This text is red.</FONT>
```

Combining the FONT Tags

When you want to specify the font, color, *and* size, they can be combined in a single HTML tag:

```
<I><FONT COLOR="#FF0000" FACE="Verdana, Impact, Comic Sans MS" SIZE=6> This would
create a red text displayed in Verdana italic at a large size. </FONT></I>
```

Putting It All Together

Figure 9.5 shows an entire HTML document. Note the <P> tag, the paragraph tag, which is used to generate a new paragraph.

Chapter

9

```
<HTML>

<HEAD>

<TITLE>Font Tags Displayed</TITLE>

</HEAD>

<BODY BGCOLOR="#FFFFFF" TEXT="#000000" LINK="#000099" ALINK="#0000CC"
VLINK="#0000FF">

<H2>Font Tag Examples </H2>

<FONT FACE="Comic Sans MS, Arial, Impact"> This would display as Comic Sans
MS if it was installed on your computer. </FONT>

<P>

In order to make this display as bold text, you would use both the FONT
FACE and the bold tag:

<P>

<B><FONT FACE="Comic Sans MS, Arial, Impact"> This would display as Comic
Sans MS Bold if it was installed on your computer. </FONT></B>

<P>

<FONT COLOR="#FF0000"> This text is red.</FONT>

<P>

<I><FONT COLOR="#FF0000" FACE="Verdana, Impact, Comic Sans MS" SIZE=6> This
would create red text displayed in Verdana italic at a large size.
</FONT></I>

</BODY>

</HTML>
```

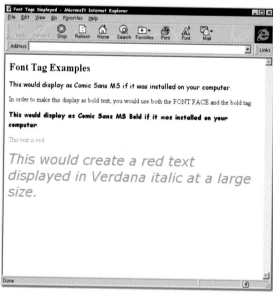

Figure 9.5 Using the FONT tags on a Web page.

CREATING TYPE WITH A DROP SHADOW

In Photoshop

Open a new file, 300 x 100 pixels. Open the Layers palette by selecting **Window/Show Layers**.

1. Fill the background layer with a pale yellow. Apply **Filter/Texture/Texturizer** with the **Sandstone** texture selected. Select **Red** as the foreground color, and click the Text tool on the image. Type **Welcome!** at about 40 points using a bold or extra bold typeface (Figure 9.6). By now I'm sure you know that this will be anti-aliased. The type will automatically be generated as a new layer called Layer 1.

Figure 9.6 Creating the type in Photoshop.

2. Duplicate the layer by selecting **Layer/Duplicate Layer**. This will create a new layer called Layer 1 copy. With **Layer 1** selected, apply **Image/Adjust Desaturate**; or use **Ctrl+Shift+U** on Windows or **Command+Shift+U** on the Mac. This will change the color of the type on Layer 1 to gray. If you have used a pale color for the type and you think the shadow color is too light, apply **Image/Invert**; or press **Ctrl+I** on Windows or **Command+I** on the Mac. Nudge the type down by using the **Control** key (**Command** key on the Mac) along with the arrow keys to offset the shadow from the type, as in Figure 9.7.

3. With **Layer 1** still selected, deselect the **Preserve Transparency** checkbox for Layer 1. Then apply **Filter/Blur/Gaussian Blur** at 2 pixels, as in Figure 9.8. You can adjust the strength of the shadow by changing the opacity setting.

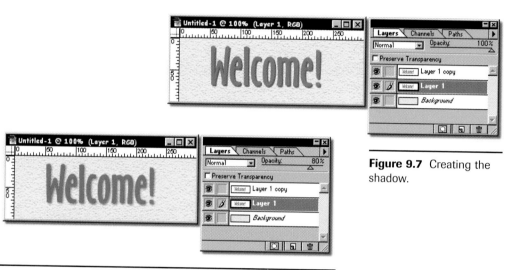

Figure 9.7 Creating the shadow.

Figure 9.8 Blurring the type layer.

4. At the top of the Layers palette, you'll see an opacity slider. Slide it until the shadow looks good, somewhere around 80%. Lessening the opacity of the shadow allows some of the background to show through, makes the shadow look more natural and less like it was painted on the background.

5. To save the file, select **Layers/Flatten**; or **Ctrl+Shift+E** on Windows, **Command+Shift+E** on the Mac. Select **Image/Mode/Indexed**, with an Adaptive palette set to 5 bits, and save your file as a GIF.

In PhotoPaint

For the Corel PhotoPaint examples, I've used the fonts available on the CorelDRAW CD. To install the fonts, go to CD number 1, Fonts/TTF, and copy the fonts you'd like to your Windows/Fonts directory. Symbol fonts, also called dingbat fonts, are located on CD number 1, in a Fonts/Symbols directory.

1. Open a new file 300 x 100 pixels, at 96 dpi in RGB color.

2. Apply **Effects/Fancy/Alchemy**, using the Vortex Thin preset. Select a violet as the paint color, and use the Text tool to type **Welcome** at about 40 points (Figure 9.9). You can select the **Bold** option to create a bolder type effect. This example uses a typeface called Informal011, also sometimes called Neuland.

3. Select **Object/Drop Shadow**, and create a drop shadow with the settings **Horizontal Offset**, **2**; **Vertical Offset**, **2**; **Feather**, **4**; **Opacity**, **60**; **Color**, **Black**. Drag your type into position using the Object Picker tool.

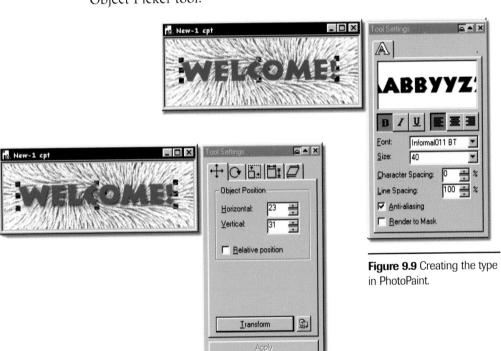

Figure 9.9 Creating the type in PhotoPaint.

Figure 9.10 Adding a drop shadow.

4. Select **Objects/Combine All Objects with Background**. Then apply **Image/Convert To/Paletted 8bit**, select **Adaptive**, **5 bit**, **Diffusion Dither** and save the image as a GIF. That's all there is to creating type with a drop shadow in Corel PhotoPaint (see Figure 9.10).

CREATING TYPE WITH A TRANSPARENT BACKGROUND

In Photoshop

This is a review of the transparent GIF skills we covered in Chapter 6. Type is often used on a transparent background to give it the illusion of floating over a patterned or textured Web page background.

First, find the RGB value for the color you will be using as a background on your Web page. Do this by using the Eyedropper tool to select the color, which will also become the color of the foreground. Double-click on the **Foreground Color** swatch to find the RGB value. Jot this number down, as you'll be using it to create a transparent GIF.

1. Fill the background layer with the color that most closely matches your Web page background. Apply **Filter/Texture/Texturizer**, with the **Sandstone** texture selected. Select **Red** as the foreground color, and click the **Type** tool on the image. Type **Celebrate!** at about 40 points using a bold font. The type will be created automatically as a new layer called Layer 1, as seen in Figure 9.11.

Figure 9.11 Creating the type in Photoshop.

2. Duplicate the layer by selecting **Layer/Duplicate Layer**. This will create a new layer called Layer 1 copy. With **Layer 1** selected, apply **Image/Adjust Desaturate**; or press **Ctrl+Shift+U** on Windows or **Command+Shift+U** on the Mac. If you used a pale color for the type and you think the shadow color is too light, apply **Image/Invert**; or use **Ctrl+I** on Windows or **Command+I** on the Mac. With **Layer 1** still selected,

deselect the **Preserve Transparency** checkbox for Layer 1. Next, apply **Filter/Blur/Gaussian Blur** at 2 pixels, as seen in Figure 9.8. You can adjust the strength of the shadow by changing the opacity setting.

3. To add a little extra pizzazz to this image, select a letter with the Marquee or Lasso tool, then apply **Image/Adjust/Hue-Saturation-Brilliance**, and move the Hue slider until you find a color you like. Repeat for each letter, applying a slightly different hue, as seen in Figure 9.12.

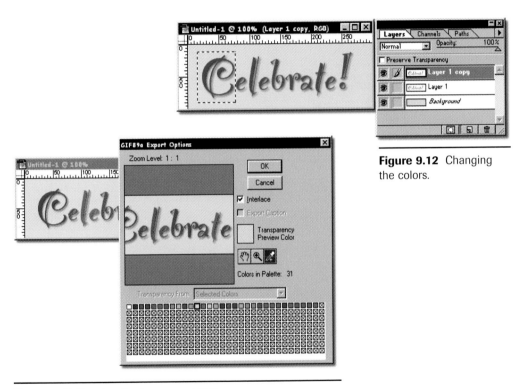

Figure 9.12 Changing the colors.

Figure 9.13 Creating the transparent GIF.

4. Select **Image/Mode/Indexed**. Select **5 bits, Adaptive Palette**, and **Diffusion, None**. We won't use diffusion dithering for this image because there are no subtle gradations or tiny details, and the image is made up of very few colors. Apply **File/Export/Gif89a**. Select the background as transparent, click on the **Transparency Index Color** swatch, and enter the RGB value for the transparent color (Figure 9.13).

In PhotoPaint

The steps for creating type on a transparent background in PhotoPaint are the same as those for creating a drop shadow, except that instead of using a pattern fill for step 1, you fill the background with the same color of the Web page, as shown in Figure 9.14. Jot down the RGB color of this background color.

1. Use the Text tool to type **It's a party!** at about 40 points. Select the **Bold** option to create a stronger effect. This example uses a typeface called Kaufmann Bold.

Figure 9.14 Creating type with a transparent background in PhotoPaint.

2. To add variety to this type, lock the background layer by selecting the **Lock** icon on the Objects roll-up. Then use the Lasso Mask tool to select an individual letter, and apply **Image/Adjust/Hue-Saturation-Lightness**. Drag the Hue slider to change the color. Repeat this for each letter (see Figure 9.15).

3. Select **Object/Drop Shadow** and create a drop shadow with the settings **Horizontal Offset, 2; Vertical Offset, 2; Feather, 4; Opacity, 60; Color, Black**. Drag your type into position using the Object Picker tool.

4. Select the background using the Magic Wand Masking tool. This will act as a mask for the transparency. Then select **Objects/Combine All Objects with Background**. Apply **Image/Convert To/Paletted 8bit**, and select **Adaptive, 5 bit, Dither, None**. This image won't need dithering because it has so few colors.

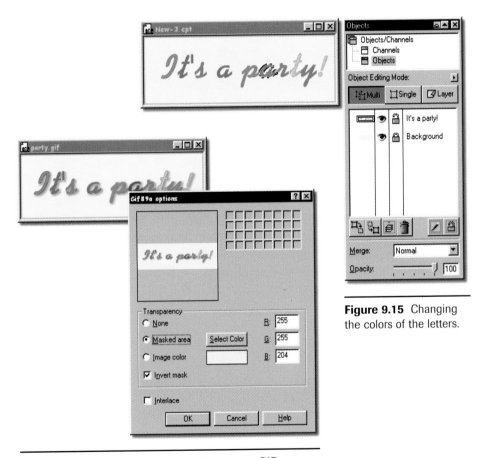

Figure 9.15 Changing the colors of the letters.

Figure 9.16 Saving the image as a transparent GIF.

5. Select **Save As GIF** (Figure 9.16), then select **Transparency from Mask**, and type in the RGB values of the background color you used.

TYPE RECIPES FOR PHOTOSHOP

All of these recipes begin with an image 300 x 100 pixels in RGB color.

Create purple type. Duplicate the layer by selecting **Layer/Duplicate**. Deselect the **Preserve Transparency** checkbox for Layer 1. Apply **Filter/Blur/Gaussian Blur** at a setting of 2 pixels. Select the **Layer 1 copy**, apply **Image/Adjust/Hue-Saturation-Brilliance**, and apply **Lightness** at a setting of +100. Flatten the image by using **Ctrl+Shift+E** on Windows, **Command+Shift+E** on the Mac and save.

Create yellow type. Deselect the **Preserve Transparency** checkbox. Select blue as the foreground color, and apply **Edit/Stroke** with a setting of **3 pixels, Outside**. Select red as the foreground color, and apply **Edit/Stroke** with a setting of **3 pixels, Outside**. Duplicate the layer, apply **Image/Adjust/Hue-Saturation-Brilliance**, and apply **Lightness** at a setting of -100. Apply **Filter/Blur/Gaussian Blur** with a setting of 2 pixels. Use the arrow keys on your keyboard while holding down the **Control** key (**Command** key on the Mac) to offset the shadow two or three pixels down and to the right. Adjust the opacity of the shadow layer (Layer 1) as needed. Flatten the image and save.

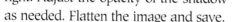

Fill the background with red, apply **Filter/Texture/Patchwork**. Create white type. Duplicate the layer, apply **Image/Adjust/Hue-Saturation-Brilliance**, and apply **Lightness** at a setting of -100. Deselect the **Preserve Transparency** checkbox. Apply **Filter/Blur/Gaussian Blur** with a setting of 2 pixels. Use the arrow keys on your keyboard while holding down the **Control** key (**Command** key on the Mac) to offset the shadow two or three pixels down and to the right. Adjust the opacity of the shadow layer (Layer 1) as needed. Select the **Layer 1 copy** of the white type, and apply **Filter/Texture/Patchwork**. Flatten the image and save.

Fill the background with light blue, and create medium blue type. Flatten the image. Apply **Filter/Render/Lighting**. Use the **Default Spotlight** setting and set the texture channel to **Blue** and the height to **60**.

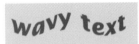

Fill the background with green. Apply **Filter/Noise/Apply Noise**. Create black type. Duplicate the layer and select **Layer 1**. Apply **Filter/Stylize/Emboss**,with the settings **Angle, 135; Height, 3; Amount, 200**. Change the mode for Layer 1 from Normal to **Hard Light**. Select the **Layer 1 copy** and invert it (**Ctrl+I** on Windows, **Command+I** on the Mac). Set the opacity for this layer to **20**. Flatten the image and save it. This technique can be used over any textured background, including wood grain, chrome, and so on to create a punched-out type effect.

Fill the background with pale blue, and create the text with medium blue. Deselect the **Preserve Transparency** checkbox. Apply **Filter/Distort/Wave** with the settings **Number of Generators, 2; Wavelength Minimum, 80; Wavelength Maximum, 120; Type, Sine**. Duplicate the layer twice. Apply **Image/Adjust/Hue-Saturation-Brilliance** with a **Lightness** setting of -100. Apply **Filter/Blur/Gaussian Blur** with a setting of 2 pixels. Use the arrow keys on your keyboard while holding down the **Control** key (**Command** key on the Mac) to offset the shadow seven or eight pixels down and to the right. Select the **Layer 1 copy** and apply **Image/Adjust/Hue-Saturation-Brilliance** with a **Lightness** setting of +100. Use the arrow keys on your keyboard while holding down the **Control** key (**Command** key on the Mac) to offset this highlight layer two or three pixels up and to the left. Flatten the image and save it.

Fill the background with black and create white type. Flatten the image. Select black as the foreground color and white as the background color, and apply **Filter/Sketch/Plaster**, with the settings **Image Balance, 15; Smoothness, 1**. Apply **Image/Adjust/Hue-Saturation-Brilliance** and select the **Colorize** checkbox.

Fill the background with light gray and create dark gray type. Duplicate the layer twice. Apply **Image/Adjust/Hue-Saturation-Brilliance** with a **Lightness** setting of -100. Deselect the **Preserve Transparency** checkbox. Apply **Filter/Blur/Gaussian Blur** with a setting of 2 pixels. Use the arrow keys on your keyboard while holding down the **Control** key (**Command** key on the Mac) to offset the shadow two or three pixels down and to the right. Select the **Layer 1 copy** and apply **Image/Adjust/Hue-Saturation-Brilliance** with a **Lightness** setting of +100. Use the arrow keys on your keyboard while holding down the **Control** key (**Command** key on the Mac) to offset this highlight layer two or three pixels up and to the left. Select the top layer and apply a linear gradient shading from pale gray to dark gray. Flatten the image and save it.

Fill the background with pale yellow. Create red type, and select blue as the background color and red as the foreground color. Apply **Filter/Distort/Twirl**, at an angle of **800**. Duplicate the type layer. **Apply Image/Adjust/Hue-Saturation-Brilliance** with a **Lightness** setting of -100. Deselect the **Preserve Transparency** checkbox. Apply **Filter/Blur/Gaussian Blur** with a setting of 2 pixels. Use the arrow keys on your keyboard while holding down the **Control** key (**Command** key on the Mac) to offset the shadow two or three pixels down and to the right. Flatten the image and save it.

Fill the background with light blue and create dark blue type. Duplicate the layer. Deselect the **Preserve Transparency** checkbox. Apply **Filter/Blur/Gaussian Blur** with a setting of 2 pixels. Select the **Layer 1 copy** and apply **Filter/Pixelate/Color Halftone**. Select red as the foreground color and apply **Edit/Stroke** with the settings **2 pixels, Inside**. Apply **Filter/Blur/Blur More**. Flatten the image and save it.

Fill the background with black and create light green type. Duplicate the layer. Deselect the **Preserve Transparency** checkbox for

Layer 1. Apply **Filter/Blur/Gaussian Blur** with a setting of 2 pixels. Flatten the image and save it.

Apply **Filter/Noise/Add Noise**. Create white type and duplicate it. Deselect the **Preserve Transparency** checkbox for Layer 1. Select the **Layer 1 copy** and apply **Image/Adjust/Hue-Saturation-Brilliance** with a **Lightness** setting of +100. Apply **Filter/Distort/Shear**, and drag the control point to the right. Apply **Filter/Blur/Gaussian Blur**, at 2 pixels. Flatten the image and save it.

Fill the background with black; create white type. Duplicate the type. With **Layer 1** selected, apply a linear white-to-black gradient. Constrain the gradient to a straight path by holding down the **Shift** key while you drag the Gradient tool. Select the **Layer 1 copy** and apply the same gradient in the opposite direction. Use the arrow keys on your keyboard while holding down the **Control** key (**Command** key on the Mac) to offset type down by two or three pixels. Flatten and save the image.

Open a photograph. Select pale green as the foreground color and create your type. Change the mode for the type layer from Normal to **Screen**. Flatten the image and save it.

Open a photograph, select it by using **Ctrl+A** on Windows or **Command+A** on the Mac; copy the photograph to the clipboard by using **Edit/Copy** or **Ctrl+C** on Windows, **Command+C** on the Mac. Create the type in black, and duplicate it. Select the **Layer 1 copy**, select the layer (**Ctrl+A** on Windows, **Command+A** on the Mac). Then, using the **Control key (Command** key on the Mac) and arrow keys, nudge the copy up and to the left. With the type selected, select **Edit/Paste Into**. The type shape should be filled with the photograph from the clipboard. Select **Layer 1**, and deselect the **Preserve Transparency** checkbox. Apply **Filter/Blur/ Gaussian Blur** with a setting of 2 pixels. Flatten the image and save it.

Extra Credit

Using symbols from dingbat typefaces, create matching icons using the techniques just demonstrated. Or, try adding an interesting edge to each of the text effects, using the directions given in Chapter 7 or by creating some of your own effects.

TYPE RECIPES FOR PHOTOPAINT

All of these recipes begin with an image 300 x 100 pixels in RGB color.

Fill the background with a Texture fill using the settings **Texture Library, Samples; Texture, Alabaster**. Create the type using the Text tool. This example uses Zurich Extra Condensed. Select **Mask/Create From Object**, then **Mask/Invert**. Apply **Mask/Feather** with the settings **Amount, 1; Direction, Middle**. Apply **Effects/Fancy/The Boss** with the settings **Width, 6; Smoothness, 20; Height, 12.** Apply **Object/Drop Shadow** with the settings **Horizontal Offset, 4; Vertical Offset, 4; Feather, 4; Opacity, 60; Color, Black**. Select **Object/Combine/All Objects with Background**, and save the image.

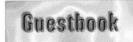

Fill the background with a Texture fill using the settings **Texture Library, Samples; Texture, Clouds, Morning**. Create the type using the Text tool. This example uses Ruach. Apply **Object/Drop Shadow** with the settings **Horizontal Offset, 0; Vertical Offset, 0; Direction, Outside; Feather, 4; Opacity, 100; Custom Color, Blue**. Select **Object/Combine/All Objects with Background**, and save the image.

Create the type using the Text tool. This example uses Aurora Bold Condensed. Select **Mask/Create Mask From Object**, then **Mask/Reduce**, with a setting of 1 pixel. Apply **Effects/Fancy/The Boss** with the settings **Width, 4; Smoothness, 30; Height, 15.** Apply **Mask/Select All**. Then apply **Mask/Feather** with the settings **Amount, 20; Direction, Inside**. Apply **Effects/Fancy/The Boss** with the settings **Width, 20; Smoothness, 30; Height, 24.** Select **Object/Combine/All Objects with Background**, and save the image.

Create the type using the Text tool. This example uses Serpentine Bold. Fill the type with a bitmap fill. Apply **Object/Drop Shadow** with the settings Horizontal Offset, 0; Vertical Offset, 0; Feather, 5; Direction, Outside; Opacity, 100; Custom Color, Pink. Select **Object/Combine/All Objects with Background**, and save the image.

Create the type using the Text tool. This example uses Skidoos. Select **Mask/Create Mask From Object**. Then apply **Mask/Feather** with the settings **Amount, 8; Direction, Inside**. Apply **Effects/Render/Lighting Effects** using the Texturize preset and changing the light color to violet. Apply this same filter twice more by using **Ctrl+F**. Apply **Object/Drop Shadow** with the settings **Horizontal Offset, 4; Vertical Offset, 4; Feather, 4; Opacity, 60; Color, Black**. Select **Object/Combine/All Objects with Background**, and save the image.

Fill the background with a Texture fill using the settings **Texture Library, Samples; Texture, Gouache Wash**. Create the type using the Text tool. This example uses Squire. Apply **Object/Drop Shadow** with the settings **Horizontal Offset, 0; Vertical Offset, 0; Direction, Outside; Feather, 4; Opacity, 100; Color, White**. Select **Object/Combine/All Objects with Background**, and save the image.

Create the type using the Text tool. This example uses Amelia. Select **Mask/Create Mask From Object**. Apply **Effects/Render/Lighting Effects** using the Texture preset. Apply **Object/Drop Shadow** with the settings **Horizontal Offset, 0; Vertical Offset, 0; Direction, Outside; Feather, 4; Opacity, 100; Custom Color, Green**. Select **Object/Combine/All Objects with Background**, and save the image. Apply **Effects/Render/Lighting Effects** using the Texture preset and changing the **Lighting Contrast** to +100.

Create the type using the Text tool. This example uses Dancin. Apply **Objects/Combine Objects with Background**. Apply **Effects/Blur/Gaussian** with a setting of 1 pixel. Apply **Effects/3D/Emboss** with the settings **Emboss Color, Gray; Depth, 2; Level, 220.** Apply **Effects/ PhotoLab/CSI GradTone** using the Electric Fire preset. Save the image.

Apply a gradient fill to the background using the preset named Cylinder Gold 03 and changing the angle of the gradient to 90. Create the type. This example uses Bedrock. Apply the same gradient to the type, with the angle changed to -90. Apply **Effects/Render/Lighting Effects**, using the Texture preset and changing the **Lighting Contrast** to +100. Apply **Object/Drop Shadow** with the settings **Horizontal Offset, 4; Vertical Offset, 4; Feather, 4; Opacity, 60; Color, Black.** Select **Object/Combine/All Objects with Background**, and save the image.

Create a two-color gradient fill using blue and yellow. Set the number of steps to 8. Create the type. This example uses Freehand 575. Apply **Object/Drop Shadow** with the settings **Horizontal Offset, 4; Vertical Offset, 4; Feather, 4; Opacity, 60; Color, Black.** Select **Object/Combine/ All Objects With Background.** Apply **Effects/ Render/Lens Flare**, using the 50–300mm Prime setting. Save the image.

Fill the background with a Texture fill using the settings **Texture Library, Samples 7; Texture, Cobwebs.** Create the type using the Text tool. This example uses Oz Handicraft. With the text selected, apply **Edit/Copy (Ctrl+C), Edit/Paste/As New Object (Ctrl+V).** Apply **Object/Flip Vertical.** Using the Object Transparency tool (found by clicking on the **Object Picker** tool), apply a transparency from the top to the bottom of the shadow. Select **Object/Combine/All Objects with Background**, and save the image.

Fill the background with a Texture fill using the settings **Texture Library, Samples 7; Texture, Psychedelic Cavern.** Create the type using the Text tool. This example uses Onyx. Apply **Effects/Artistic/Vignette** with the settings **Color, Black; Shape, Ellipse; Offset, 120; Fade, 50.** Apply **Object/Drop Shadow** with the settings **Horizontal Offset, 4; Vertical Offset, 4; Feather, 4; Opacity, 60; Color, Black.** Apply **Effects/AutoFX/ Photographic Edges.** Select **Object/Combine/All Objects with Background**, and save the image.

Fill the background with a Texture fill using the settings **Texture Library, Samples 7; Texture, Rock Face.** Create the type using the Text tool. This example uses Kabel Ultra Black. Apply **Mask/Create Mask From Object.** Apply **Effects/2D/Band Pass.** Repeat the filter by using **Ctrl+F.** Apply **Object/Drop Shadow** with the settings **Horizontal Offset, 0; Vertical Offset, 0; Direction, Outside; Feather, 4; Opacity, 60; Color, Black.** Select **Object/Combine/All Objects with Background**, and save the image.

Create the type using the Text tool. This example uses Eklektic. Apply **Mask/Create Mask From Object.** Apply **Effects/Render/Lens Flare**, using the 50–300mm Prime setting. Apply **Object/Drop Shadow** with the settings **Horizontal Offset, 0; Vertical Offset, 0; Direction, Outside; Feather, 4; Opacity, 100; Custom Color, Red.** Select **Object/ Combine/All Objects with Background**, and save the image.

Create the type using the Text tool. This example uses Slipstream. Select **Objects/Combine/All Objects with Background**. Apply **Effects/Blur/Motion Blur**, with the speed set to 10. Create the *Service* type using Futura Medium. Apply **Object/Drop Shadow** with the settings **Horizontal Offset, 4; Vertical Offset, 4; Feather, 4; Opacity, 60; Color, Black**. Select **Object/Combine/All Objects with Background**, and save the image.

Extra Credit

Using symbols from dingbat typefaces, create matching icons using the same techniques demonstrated here. Or, try adding an interesting edge to each of the text effects, using the directions given in Chapter 7, by using the **Effects/AutoFX** filter, or by creating some of your own effects.

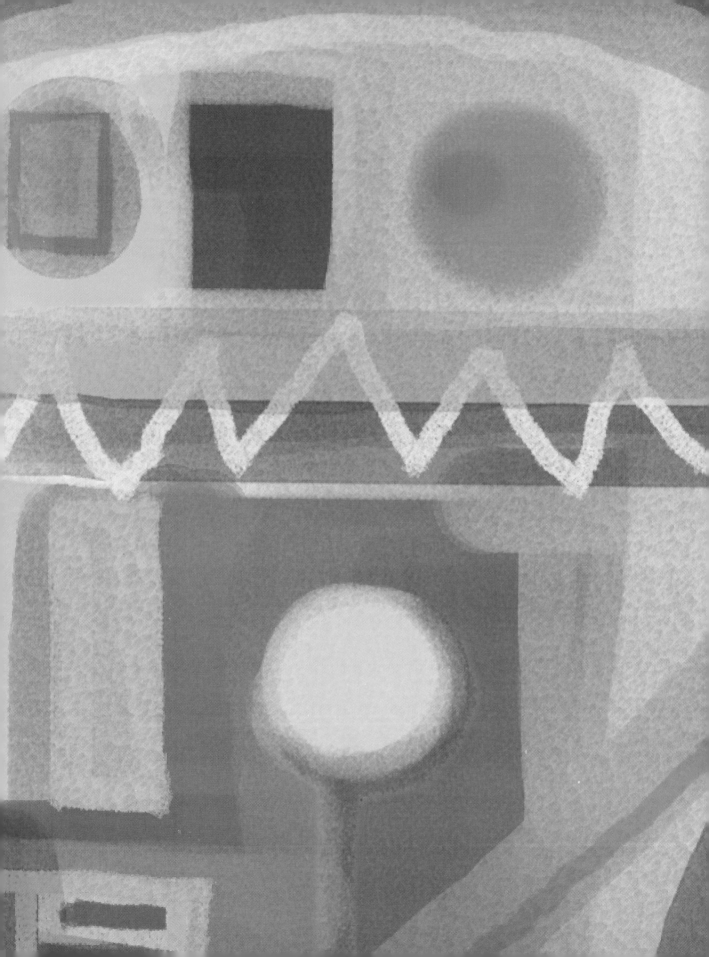

10 IMPORTING AND EXPORTING, OR SERRATED EDGES AND OTHER AMUSEMENTS

At some point, you'll need to convert files from different file formats to GIF or JPEG for the Web. Ideally, the files you'll be using won't be in some rare format that existed for only three months in 1982 within a proprietary graphics package that is now impossible to find. This chapter describes importing vector files from drawing packages like CorelDRAW, Adobe Illustrator, and Macromedia Freehand.

WELCOME TO PLANET VECTOR

Once upon a time, the differences between drawing software (like CorelDRAW, Adobe Illustrator, and Macromedia Freehand) and painting software (like Photoshop, PhotoPaint, xRes, and Paint Shop Pro) were very clear. Drawing packages were wonderful for creating designs that included type or that needed precise alignment. Painting packages were good for creating artistic, painterly effects. But with each new revision of software, paint programs become more objectlike, employing strategies such as layers (in Photoshop) or objects (in PhotoPaint) to enable you to manipulate portions of the image independently of other items within it. Similarly, drawing programs became much more bitmap-oriented, including tools such as bitmap fills, filters, or the Bitmap Lens Effects in CorelDRAW.

So what's the difference between vector graphics and bitmapped graphics? Vector graphics are stored in the program as mathematical formulas for the vectors, or directional lines, that make up the image. Thus, objects from drawing programs can be easily manipulated independently of one another. They can be resized, rotated, and rescaled without a loss of quality. In contrast, bitmapped objects are made up of individual pixels and have to be manipulated on the pixel level. They degrade in quality each time they are rotated, skewed, or resized.

Common vector-based applications include drawing programs such as CorelDRAW, Illustrator, Canvas, and Freehand. Type is also vector-based. Common vector file formats include CDR, EPS, and AI. Paint programs such as Photoshop, PhotoPaint, Painter, Paint Shop Pro, and xRes use bitmap file formats. Common bitmap file formats are BMP, TIF, GIF, JPEG, and PICT.

Photoshop 4 and PhotoPaint now both include guidelines for precise placement, as seen in Figure 10.1. To use guidelines in PhotoPaint or Photoshop, **click**+drag on the edge of the image to create and position. Use the rulers to help with placement by selecting **Ctrl+R** in Windows or **Command+R** on the Mac.

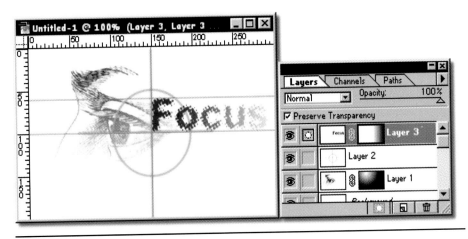

Figure 10.1 Using guidelines for placement in Photoshop.

As an example, examine Figures 10.2 and 10.3. The first image is a circle from a drawing program imported at three different sizes: 20 pixels x 20 pixels, 100 pixels x 100 pixels, and 300 pixels x 300 pixels. The second example is a TIF file that started out as 20 x 20 pixels and was resized to the same dimensions as the object from the drawing program.

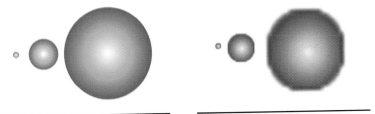

Figure 10.2 A drawing program file resized three times.

Figure 10.3 The same bitmap file resized three times.

With these definitions in mind, it is usually best to create your artwork in a drawing program instead of a paint program if you plan on using it for more than just a Web page. If, for instance, you are creating a logo or other artwork that will be used at many sizes—in a brochure, on letterhead, and on a Web site—create the logo either in a drawing program or as a high-resolution bitmap. As Figure 10.3 makes clear, bitmap artwork does not resize to higher resolutions very well.

Drawing programs like Macromedia's Freehand, Adobe's Illustrator, and Corel's Draw packages all have definite advantages and disadvantages when compared to paint programs like Photoshop or Corel PhotoPaint. The vector-based packages do an excellent job of manipulating type. If you need type curved, shaped, warped, or otherwise manipulated, the task will usually be accomplished more successfully in a drawing package.

These programs also enable you to export files as Web-ready. CorelDRAW publishes Web pages as Java applets, although you may want to think twice before using Corel's export to HTML feature known as Barista. In my tests, it worked fine with very, very simple graphics and text, but in the example in Figure 10.4, which contained a fairly complex graphic, after five minutes Corel failed to render the page completely. The type and graphics were not anti-aliased when exported as Corel Barista, a definite disadvantage. Figure 10.5 shows the original page layout in CorelDRAW. If you do use Corel's Barista to publish a Web page, remember that people using browsers that are not Java-enabled will see nothing at all when they look at the page. Consider offering an alternative to Java-only pages; publishing to a Web page from CorelDRAW is as simple as selecting **File/Save As/Corel Barista**. You'll need to upload the .htm page that is created, any other files created, and the Java Class files found in the Corel/Barista directory to your Web server. The Java Class files have to be uploaded to the same directory as the Barista HTML file.

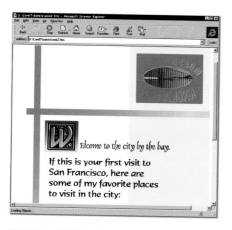

Figure 10.4 The incompletely rendered Barista file.

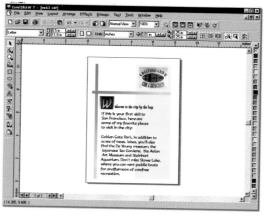

Figure 10.5 The original page layout in CorelDRAW.

From Vector to Photoshop

How do you make the leap from vector to bitmap? First, export your vector file as an AI or EPS file.

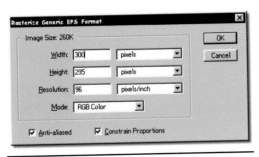

1. From within CorelDRAW, select your logo on the page; then select **File/Export**, **Adobe Illustrator AI/EPS** format, and **Selected Only**. From Adobe Illustrator, simply save your file in the default file format.

Figure 10.6 Opening an EPS file in Photoshop.

2. Select **Adobe Illustrator 3.0** as the format and select **Export Text as Curves**.

3. Open Photoshop and select **File/Open**. The Rasterize Adobe Illustrator Format dialog box (shown in Figure 10.6) will open. Make sure that the **Anti-aliased** checkbox is selected (of course!) and that the mode is set to **RGB Color**.

4. Set the width and height to any size you wish. The image will automatically have anti-aliased edges as long as the **Anti-aliased** checkbox is selected.

From Vector to PhotoPaint

Moving from CorelDRAW to Corel PhotoPaint is easier than it used to be, but you might stumble between file formats before finding the best way of getting images from CorelDRAW to a Web page. Once you've created your file in CorelDRAW, you can either export as a bitmapped file or open the CorelDRAW file from within PhotoPaint. You can export directly to GIF from CorelDRAW, but you can't select the type of dithering, color depth, or palette with this method. CorelDRAW's default dither looks a little like needlepoint, as you can see in Figure 10.7. In addition, CorelDRAW has failed to anti-alias the type.

Not to worry. You can successfully create GIFs by using PhotoPaint.

1. From within PhotoPaint, after you select **File/Open** and your CorelDRAW file, you'll see the Import Into Bitmap dialog box (Figure 10.8). It's always a good idea to import using the highest color value possible. There are a glut of choices under the Size dialog box. However, if you choose anything other than 1 to 1, your image will be squished horizontally or vertically to fit the dimensions you choose.

Figure 10.7 Exporting as GIF from CorelDRAW.

Figure 10.9 The imported image in PhotoPaint.

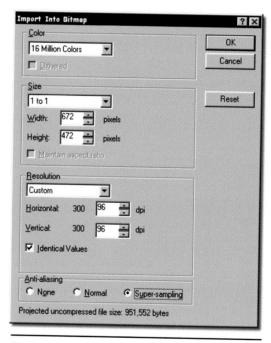

Figure 10.8 Import Into Bitmap dialog box in PhotoPaint.

2. To import at a size larger or smaller than the width and height specifies, change the size to **Custom**, and change the width and height amounts. Maintain the proportional values between the width and height.

3. Notice the **Anti-aliasing** checkbox. For this example, we've checked **Super-sampling.** The quality of this image, in Figure 10.9, is clearly superior to the image shown in Figure 10.8 that was exported as a GIF from CorelDRAW.

THE MAC-TO-PC AND PC-TO-MAC DANCE

"My computer can't read your disk." Not much can make me clench my teeth like that sentence. Honestly, usually it's not the files that are the problem; it's the darned disk.

Apple's latest operating system will read PC disks without a problem. Earlier versions, however, need a software conversion program to be able to recognize PC disks. On a PC, you will need a software conversion program to be able to read Mac disks. Here are a couple of resources for utilities that will help to read Mac diskettes on a PC:

MacAccess

http://www.syncronys.com/macaccess.html

MacAccess 2.0 is a software utility for Windows 95, Windows 3.1, and DOS that enables your PC to read, write, and format Macintosh floppy disks, removable hard disks, and other Macintosh media.

TransMac

http://www.asy.com

TransMac is a Windows utility that can read and write Macintosh high-density diskettes, CD-ROMs, and SCSI drives (SyQuest, Bernoulli, Zip, optical, hard drives, etc.). It can also format disks for the Mac.

You can avoid the disk problem entirely by attaching files to e-mail, by uploading the files to your Web site for the other person to download, or by uploading files directly to the other person's Web server.

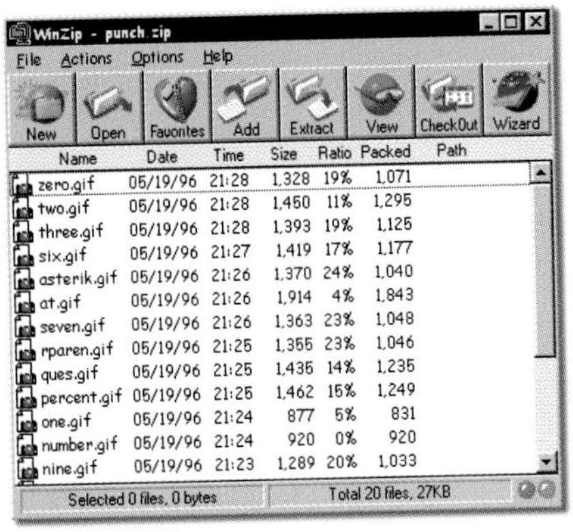

Figure 10.10 Creating a Zip archive using WinZip.

As for file formats, GIF and JPEG, TIF, and PICT bitmap files should be read easily on both platforms. I've also successfully traded PSD files, with layers intact, across platforms. Additionally, I've had no problem exporting CorelDRAW files as EPS files.

You can also transfer files back and forth between Mac and Windows users by archiving the files and offering them as either downloadable files from a Web site or as attachments to e-mail. When you archive a group of files, you not only group them into a single file, but also compress the file. The most common archive formats are ZIP and SIT, or StuffIt,

C
h
a
p
t
e
r

files (see Figure 10.10). Software applications to create and expand archives are listed next. If you offer a downloadable file in any archived format, it's a good idea to also offer a link to the software necessary to extract the file. The HTML for such a link to a file named **icons.zip** might read:

```
Download a collection of icons <A HREF="icons.zip"> here. </A>
<P>

Need help with Unzipping? Windows users can unzip using
<A HREF="http://www.winzip.com"> Winzip,</A> and Mac users can unzip using
<A HREF="http://www.awa.com/softlock/zipit/zipit.html">ZipIt.</A>
```

WinZip

http://www.winzip.com

A zip archiving program for Windows.

ZipIt for the Mac

http://www.awa.com/softlock/zipit/zipit.html

A program for the Macintosh that extracts and creates Zip archives.

StuffIt

http://www.aladdinsys.com

StuffIt is the most popular method of archiving on the Mac. You can find a version of StuffIt for the Mac and StuffIt Expander for Windows at the above Web site.

TRULY UNUSUAL FILE FORMATS, AND WHAT TO DO WITH THEM

If you're working on a corporate Web site, at some point you're sure to run across a file type you're not familiar with. You can refer to these Web sites for information on many file types:

Graphic File Formats FAQ

http://www.cis.ohio-state.edu/hypertext/faq/usenet/graphics/top.html

File Formats on the Internet

http://www.matisse.net/files/formats.html

Descriptions of different file formats, along with links to sites that feature applications that deal with each.

You may be surprised at the number of file formats that are supported by programs you already have.

Photoshop will open the following file formats:

AI–Adobe Illustrator	PCD–Kodak Photo CD	RAW–Raw Image
BMP–Windows Bitmap	PCX–PC Paintbrush	RLE–Run Length Encoded
FLM–Atari Filmstrip	PDF–Adobe Acrobat	SCT–Scitex Bitmap
ICB–Targa	PICT–Mac PICT	TGA–Targa
JPG–Joint Photographic Experts Group	PNG–Portable Network Graphics	VDA–Targa
	PSD–Adobe Photoshop	VST–Targa

CorelDRAW will open the following file formats:

AI–Adobe Illustrator	DRW–Micrografx Draw	PF–IBM PIF
CDR–CorelDRAW	DWG–AutoCAD Drawing	PIC–Lotus PIC file
CDT–CorelDRAW Template	DXF–AutoCAD	PICT–Mac PICT
CDX–CorelDRAW Compressed	EMF–Enhanced Metafile	PLT–HPGL Plotter
CGM–Computer Graphics Metafile	EPS–Encapsulated PostScript	PRN–PostScript Interpreted
	FMV–Frame Vector Metafile	PS–PostScript Interpreted
CMF–Corel Metafile	GEM–GEM file	WPG–WordPerfect Graphic
CMX–Corel Presentation Exchange	MET–Metafile	WMF–Windows Metafile
	PAT–Corel Pattern	

CorelDRAW will import these additional file formats:

BMP–Windows Bitmap	MAC–MacPaint Bitmap	SCT–Scitex Bitmap
CAL–CALS Bitmap	NAP–NAP Metafile	TGA–Targa
CPT–Corel PhotoPaint Image	PCD–Kodak Picture	TIF–Tagged Image Format
CUR–Windows Cursor	PCX–PC Paintbrush	WI–Wavelet Compressed Bitmap
DOC–MS Word Document	PNG–Portable Network Graphics	WPG–WordPerfect Files
GIF–Graphics Interchange Format	PP4–Picture Publisher 4	WSW–Word Star
JPG–Joint Photographic Experts Group	PP5–Picture Publisher 5	WSD–Word Star
	PSD–Photoshop	XY–XYWrite for Windows
ICO–Windows icon	RTF–Rich Text Format	

Corel PhotoPaint will open these file formats:

AI–Adobe Illustrator	DWG–AutoCAD Drawing	PICT–Mac PICT
AVI–Video for Windows	DXF–AutoCAD	PCD–Kodak Picture
BMP–Windows Bitmap	EMF–Enahanced Metafile	PCX–PC Paintbrush
CAL–CALS Bitmap	EPS–Encapsulated PostScript	PLT–HPGL Plotter file
CDR–CorelDRAW	GIF–Graphics Interchange Format	PNG–Portable Network Graphics
CDT–CorelDRAW Template	GIF Animation	PP4–Picture Publisher 4
CDX–CorelDRAW Compressed	JPG–Joint Photographic Experts Group	PP5–Picture Publisher 5
CGM–Computer Graphics Metafile	ICO–Windows icon	PSD–Photoshop
CMF–Corel Metafile	IMG–GEM Paint	RAW–Raster Image
CMX–Corel Presentation Exchange	MAC–MacPaint Bitmap	SCT–Scitex Bitmap
CPT–Corel PhotoPaint Image	MET–MET Metafile	TGA–Targa
CUR–Windows Cursor	MOV–QuickTime Movie	TIF–Tagged Image Format
DRW–Micrografx Draw	MPEG–MPEG Animation	WPG–WordPerfect Graphic
	NAP–NAP Metafile	WMF–Windows Metafile

Additionally, there are two software packages that excel at batch image processing, both of which support a wide variety of image file formats. These packages are DeBabelizer and Image Alchemy.

DeBabelizer is a commercial software package available for the Mac and Windows. Its Web site is found at http://www.equilibrium.com.

DeBabelizer will open these file formats:

AVI–Video for Windows	MSP–Microsoft Paintbrush	QDV–Random Dot Image
BMP–Windows Bitmap	NEO–Atari ST	RLE–Run Length Encoded
BOB–BOB Image	PBM–Portable Bitmap	SCN–Thunder Scan Image
CUT–Dr. Halo Image	PCD–Kodak	SGI–Silicon Graphics Image
GIF–Graphics Interchange Format	PCP–PC Paint	RAS–Sun Microsystem Raster
GIF Animation	PICT–Mac PICT image	TDIM–Digital FX
GL–Pictor Image	PIC–SoftImage	TGA–Targa
IFF–Amiga Image	PIX–Alias Image	TIM–Pstation Image
IMG–Ventura Publisher	PNG–Portable Network Graphics	WPG–WordPerfect Graphic
JPG–Joint Photographic Experts Group	PSD–Photoshop	XBM–X11 Bitmap
MAC–MacPaint	PXP–PixelPaint	XWD–XWindow Bitmap
	PXR–Pixar Image	YUV–Digital Video

If you're confronted by an unusual file format you need to convert for the Web, a very useful piece of shareware called Image Alchemy will convert between dozens of file formats, some of which I've never heard of. Image Alchemy is also available for the Mac. It's definitely worth investigating if you have to convert rare file formats. You can visit the Web site of Handmade Software, creators of Image Alchemy, at http://www.handmadesw.com/.

Image Alchemy converts the following file formats:

ADEX File	HSI Palette	PZL–Puzzle
Autologic	HSI RAW	PSD–Adobe Photoshop
AVHRR–Satellite Image Data	IBM Picture Maker	RAS–Sun Raster
BIF–Binary	ICO–Windows Icon	Q0–QLD Graphic
BMP–Alpha	IFF/ILBM–Interchange File Format	QDV–Mac Giffer File
BMP–Windows Bitmap	Imaging Technology	QRT RAW–Ray Trace Output
CALS–CALS Bitmap	Img Software Set	RIX–Color RIX
CEL–Lumena CEL	Intergraph	RLC
Collage	JEDMICS CCITT4	RLE–Run Length Encoded
Core IDC	Jovian VI	SGI–SGI Image
Cubicomp	JPEG–Joint Photographic Experts	Spaceward
CUT–Dr. Halo	Group	Spot Image
ER Mapper Raster	MAC–MacPaint	Stork
Erdas LAN/GIS/IMG	Mimaki MRL-1	Sun Icon
First Publisher	MTV–Ray Trace Output	TGA–Targa
FOP–Freedom of Press	Multi-Image Palette	TIFF–Tagged Image File Format
GPB–Sharp GPB	PC Paint/Pictor	US Patent Image
GEM VDI Image	PCX–PC Paint	Verity Image Format
GIF–Graphics Interchange Format	PDF–Adobe Acrobat	VITec
Histogram	PDS–Planetary Data System	WPG–WordPerfect Graphic
Hitachi Raster	PNG–Portable Network Graphics	XBM–XWindow Bitmap
HP PCL	PBM–Portable bitmap	XPM–XWindow Color Bitmap
HP-48sx	PICT–Macintosh PICT	XWD–XWindow Dump
HSI JPEG	PIX–Alias PIX	

Additional resources include Image Robot by JASC (http://www.jasc.com) for Windows and Graphic Converter for the Mac (http://www.goldinc.com/Lemke/gc.html).

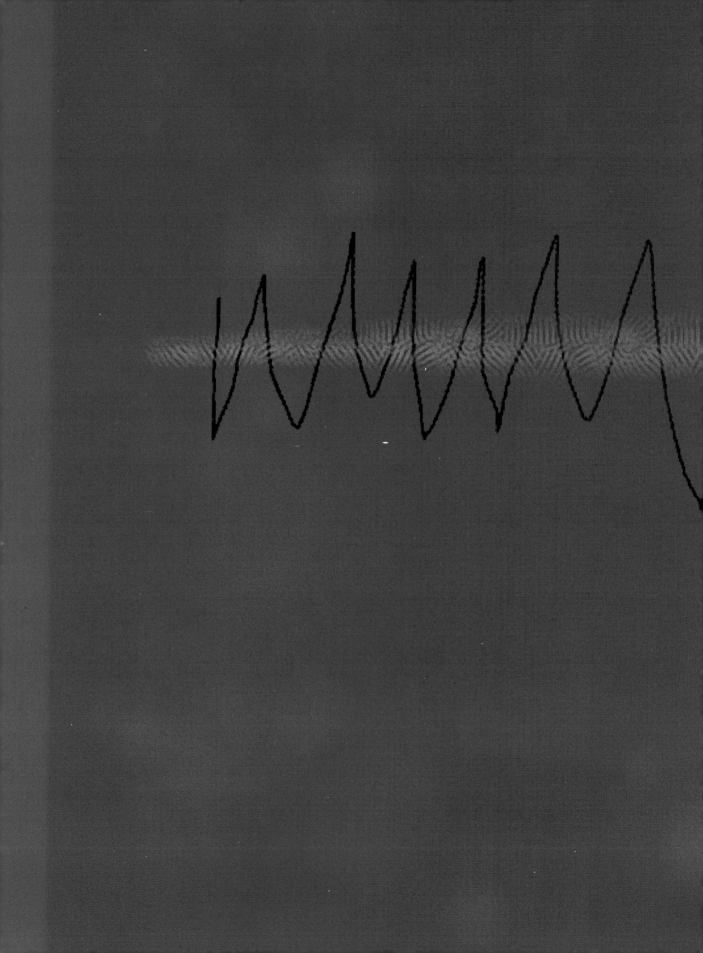

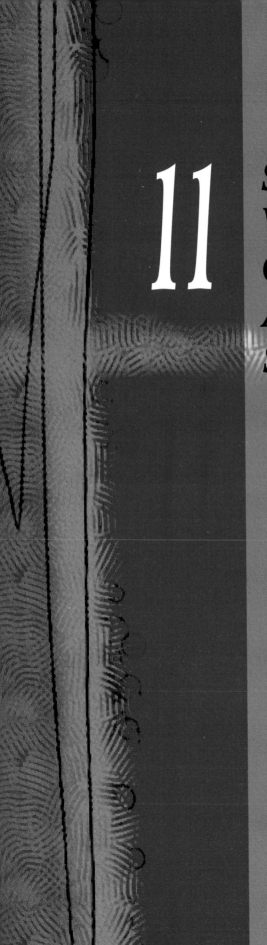

11 SPEEDING UP YOUR WORK WITHOUT CAFFEINE OR OTHER ARTIFICIAL STIMULANTS

Once you learn how to use the tools in a software program to achieve the effects you want, there are only two barriers that can stand in the way of enjoying your work. The first is a lack of organization, and the second is mind-numbing repetitive work. Any project that you work on in Photoshop or PhotoPaint will have some repetition, and certain projects (like creating a series of seamless pattern tiles) will have a lot. In the first part of this chapter, I lay out some strategies designed to cut down on some of the time-consuming aspects of repetitive work. In the second part, I offer suggestions to help you get and stay organized.

HOOKED ON SPEED IN PHOTOSHOP

In only two steps, you should be able to speed up your work in Photoshop considerably. The first is to learn some common keystrokes. This takes just a few minutes, and I promise you won't regret it. Here are the keystrokes I use most often:

Function	Windows	Mac
Select all	Ctrl+A	Command+A
Copy	Ctrl+C	Command+C
Deselect	Ctrl+D	Command+D
Apply Last Filter	Ctrl+F	Command+F
Hide a Selection	Ctrl+H	Command+H
Save	Ctrl+S	Command+S
Paste	Ctrl+V	Command+V
Cut	Ctrl+X	Command+X
Undo	Ctrl+Z	Command+Z
Merge Layers	Ctrl+Shift+E	Command+Shift+E
Invert a Selection	Ctrl+Shift+I	Command+Shift+I
Deselect Preserve Transparency	\	\
Toggle between Foreground/Background Colors	X	X

Once you have those committed to memory or pasted on the wall near your computer, add this shortcut: use the **Shift**, **Control (Command)**, and **Alt (Option)** keys in conjunction with Photoshop tools. For instance, using the **Shift** key along with any paint tool enables you to create a straight line by **Shift+clicking** the tool.

Creating Custom Actions in Photoshop

Wouldn't it be great to have an assistant who knew exactly how you liked to work in Photoshop and who did all the boring repetitive tasks for you, freeing you to spend more time experimenting with creative effects? Well, Photoshop provides such help in the form of a tool called Actions that makes it possible to automate your work in Photoshop. You can even process whole folders at once.

To demonstrate how Actions work, we'll create an Action for that ever-popular effect, the drop shadow. Creating a drop shadow involves first creating a layer with something on it (we'll use type), duplicating the layer, changing the darkness of the duplicate, then blurring it and moving the duplicate to offset it from the original.

1. Start with a new file, 300 x 200 pixels in RGB mode. Open the Actions palette by selecting **Window/Show Actions**. Select **New Action** from the flyout menu on the Actions palette. Name this Action **Type Effect # 1**, and select **Record** (Figure 11.1). (Note: Photoshop won't record some things, including using tools from the Tools palette; for instance, you can't record using a paint or selection tool. Photoshop will, however, record most menu items.)

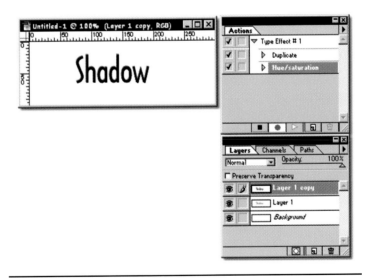

Figure 11.1 Creating a drop shadow.

2. Create your type using the Type tool. Deselect the **Preserve Transparency** checkbox for the layer. From the Photoshop menu bar, select **Layer/Duplicate Layer**.

3. Select **Image/Adjust/Hue-Saturation-Brilliance** and enter **-100** for the lightness setting. Select **Filter/Blur/Gaussian Blur** with a setting of 2 pixels.

4. You'll want to offset the shadow a little from the image, but Photoshop won't record actions from the Move or Selection tools. However, you can use filters, so apply **Filters/Other/Offset** with a setting of 2 pixels horizontal and 2 pixels vertical.

5. You're nearly done, but the shadow layer is on top of the type layer. Use a menu item to move this so that Photoshop will record it as part of the Action: Select **Layer/Arrange/Send Backward** as in Figure 11.2. Select the **Stop** button on the Actions palette.

Figure 11.2 Moving the shadow behind the type.

6. Test your Action by opening a new file, creating type, then selecting the **Type Effect # 1** Action and the **Play** icon from the bottom of the Actions palette. In the blink of an eye, Photoshop has created a perfect drop shadow for you!

If you discover you goofed and added steps that you don't want, you can always delete them from the Actions palette by selecting the item, then clicking on the trashcan icon. Likewise, you can add steps to any previously recorded Action by selecting where in the Action you would like to add a step, then selecting the **Record** icon from the bottom of the Actions palette.

Imagine the possibilities of using Actions palettes! You can record your most common Photoshop tasks and let Photoshop do the work while you savor another cup of coffee. You can also save your recorded Actions and swap them with others. Photoshop Actions can be used on either a Mac or in Windows, so you can even exchange your Actions with a Photoshop user on a different platform.

You can also add stops, or comments, to the Action. This is a helpful way to remind yourself what you need to do to complete an Action. To add a stop to the current Action, select **Insert Stop** from the Actions palette fly-out menu. You'll see the dialog box shown in Figure 11.3. If you want to continue after a stop, select the **Continue** checkbox. You can add a reminder or the date or project to which the Action belongs in this dialog box. For the drop shadow Action, this stop should be the first item, so drag it to the top of the list of commands for the Type Effect # 1 Action. Subsequently, when you use the action, you'll see the stop message after you select **Play**, as seen in Figure 11.4.

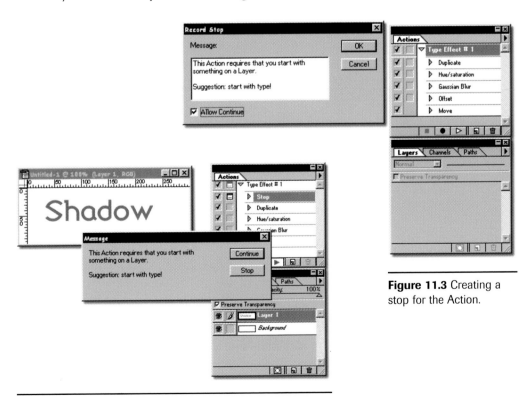

Figure 11.3 Creating a stop for the Action.

Figure 11.4 Viewing the stop message.

Batch Processing in Photoshop

At some point, you may be faced with what may seem like a Herculean task of converting a large number of files. This is another task for which Photoshop's Actions can save you time and prevent headaches.

For this example, we'll convert a group of BMP and TIF files to Web format, some of which are in 24-bit and 8-bit format, and all of which are larger than optimum for the Web. Additionally, to enable us to use these files as backgrounds, they need to be lightened. (Hint: Do a bit of experimenting with any Action you generate before you apply it to a lot of files.) The first step is to create the Action, using a single file. Then you'll apply the Action to a folder of files.

1. Open the Actions palette by selecting **Window/Show Actions**. Select **New Action** from the flyout menu on the Actions palette. Name this **Web Conversion** and select **Record,** as in Figure 11.5.

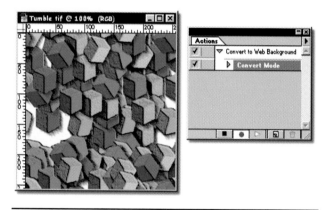

Figure 11.5 Starting to record an Action.

2. Open the sample file. Select **Image/Mode/RGB color.** Because some files are in indexed color and some aren't, we want to make sure they are all indexed to the same palette.

3. Select **Image/Adjust/Hue-Saturation-Brilliance** and enter **+80** for the lightness value. Select **Image/Mode/Indexed** with the settings **Palette, Web; Dither, Diffusion,** as in Figure 11.6.

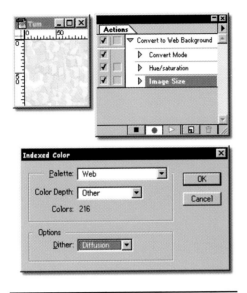

Figure 11.6 Indexing the image.

4. For this example, let's say we want the images to be no larger than 100 pixels wide. So select **Image/Image Size** and enter **100** in the Horizontal measurement box.

5. Select **File/Save As** and create a new folder if you need to, then save it as a GIF file.

6. Test the Action on another image to make sure it works well.

7. After you've tested the Action, from the Actions flyout menu, select **Batch**. Next, select **Source, Folder; Destination, Save and Close,** as in Figure 11.7. Select the folder you would like to open, and let Photoshop do the work for you.

Hooked on Actions? Photoshop includes a nice selection on the Photoshop 4 CD. And on the Web, you'll find more Actions to download, along with an Actions mailing list at the Action Exchange, http://jmc.mit.edu/photoshp/frames.htm.

Looking for still more? Go back to Chapter 9 or Chapter 7 and create Actions for your favorite effects. One thing more fun than creating Web graphics is creating Web graphics *really fast*.

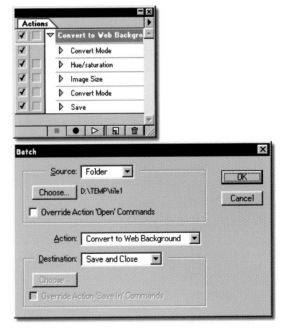

Figure 11.7 Getting ready to rock and roll with Actions.

HOOKED ON SPEED IN PHOTOPAINT

The first order of business to generate some speed in your work is to take a few minutes to learn the most common keystrokes in PhotoPaint. Memorizing is no fun, but I guarantee it will be worth every minute. And a bonus is that most of the keystrokes you use in PhotoPaint also work in CorelDRAW, so you're getting two for the price of one.

Function	Keystroke
Select All	Ctrl+A
Copy	Ctrl+C
Remove Mask	Ctrl+D
Repeat Effect	Ctrl+F
Hide Mask Marquee	Ctrl+H
Invert Mask	Ctrl+I
Create Mask	Ctrl+M
New File	Ctrl+N
Save	Ctrl+S
Paste as a new object	Ctrl+V
Cut (copies the cut portion to the clipboard)	Ctrl+X
Undo	Ctrl+Z
Zoom in	F2
Zoom out	F2

Customizing PhotoPaint

If you're one of those people who likes things a certain way—your way—you'll be happy to know you can customize the menus, toolbars, and keystrokes in PhotoPaint. Don't like where the menu items are stored? It's easy to change them using **Tools/Customize/Menu**, as shown in Figure 11.8. You can create a new menu item or topic, too. If you're always looking for something under the wrong menu topic, or if you'd like to create, say, your own list of favorite filters, select **Add Menu**, type in the name for the menu, then drag and drop items from the Effects menu or any other to this new menu.

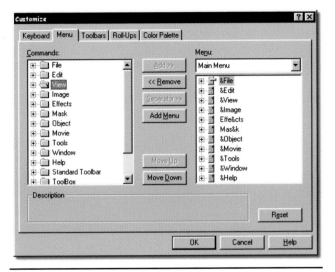

By selecting the **Toolbar** tab in the **Tools/Customize** command, you can create custom toolbars that contain your favorite tools, including some of PhotoPaint's built-in filters. To do so, select **Tools/Customize/ Toolbar** and **click+drag** as many icons as you want to the desktop, as in Figure 11.9. When you're done, you can even reshape the toolbar to a vertical or horizontal orientation by dragging the edges.

Figure 11.8 Customizing PhotoPaint's menus.

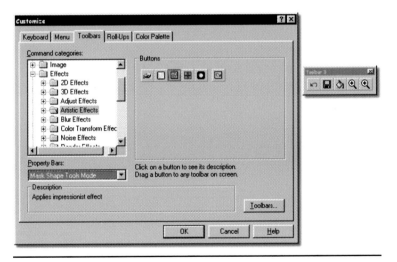

Figure 11.9 Creating a custom toolbar.

And last but not least, you can change or customize keystrokes within PhotoPaint by applying **Tools/Customize/Keyboard**. This is especially helpful if you have a keystroke memorized from another program; instead of memorizing a new keystroke within PhotoPaint, just remap the keystrokes. To print a complete list of keystrokes available within PhotoPaint, select **Tools/Customize/Keyboard**, then **Print**.

Using PhotoPaint's Command Recorder

PhotoPaint has a built-in Command Recorder that can record a series of commands that you perform within PhotoPaint. It will repeat actions you perform using PhotoPaint tools. So, for instance, if you selected the **Text** tool and typed **Welcome**, then recorded it, the Recorder would repeat that action. It will also repeat strokes created with a paintbrush, making it more useful as an artistic effect tool than as a production tool, as illustrated in Figure 11.10. The Recorder can also be used to script brushstrokes with Image Lists.

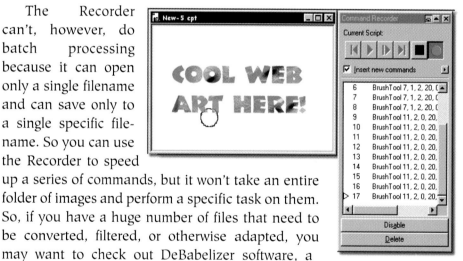

The Recorder can't, however, do batch processing because it can open only a single filename and can save only to a single specific filename. So you can use the Recorder to speed up a series of commands, but it won't take an entire folder of images and perform a specific task on them. So, if you have a huge number of files that need to be converted, filtered, or otherwise adapted, you may want to check out DeBabelizer software, a batch-processing package that supports a multitude of file types. Look for it on the Web at http://www.equilibrium.com.

Figure 11.10 Recording brushstrokes in PhotoPaint.

This next tutorial takes some of the grunt work out of converting files for the Web. In this example, we'll use a file that needs to be lightened, downsized, and indexed to the Web palette.

1. Open an image you'd like to use for this example, or create a quick sample. Open the Command Recorder by selecting **View/Roll-ups/Recorder.** Click on the flyout menu on the Recorder roll-up and select **New.** To begin recording, select the icon with the red circle (see Figure 11.11).

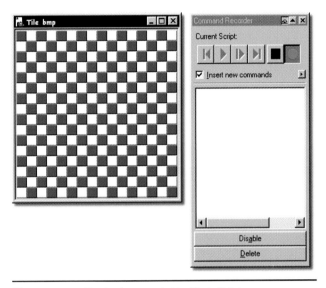

Figure 11.11 Beginning a script in PhotoPaint.

2. Select **Image/Adjust/Brightness-Contrast-Intensity** with the settings **Brightness, 80; Contrast, 25.** Select **Image/Resample** and enter **100 pixels** in the Horizontal Size box.

3. Select **Image/Convert To/Paletted 8Bit.** Select **Palette Type, Custom; Dither Type, Error Diffusion.** Select the black square icon on the Command Recorder roll-up to stop recording. From the flyout menu, select **Save** to save your script.

4. Test the script on a new image. You can remove commands by selecting the **Delete** icon. To add more commands, use the arrow icons to select where the new commands should appear in the script, then select the icon with the red circle to begin recording the additional commands.

For more on using PhotoPaint's Recorder, visit CorelNet's Scripting forum at http://www.corelnet.com.

GETTING ORGANIZED AND LIVING HAPPILY EVER AFTER

Getting organized is the secret to a happy life. Or at least it seems that way if you, like me, have ever spent more than half an hour trying to find a file that you need to deliver to a client. I wish I were a naturally gifted organizer, but, alas, I've had to learn it all the hard way.

A Web site, generally, is made up of a lot of small files that are linked together and need to be updated frequently, and being organized for this process from the beginning can save you hours of time in the long run. The following are some tips that work for me, but if staying up all night and organizing your files by day of the week works for you, who am I to stop you?

- Keep all the files for the same project in one directory (folder), broken down into subdirectories if necessary. I keep all my files for a client in a single directory: correspondence, HTML files, graphic files, typefaces, and so on.

- Create a file-naming convention that works for you, and be consistent. Use a file management utility like ThumbsPlus for Windows (Figure 11.12) or Corel's Image Manager to conduct visual checks on your files (Image Manager comes with Corel 7, but you may not have installed it). With either of these utilities, you can rename, move, or delete files. ThumbsPlus is shareware, available on the Web from Cerious Software at http://www.cerious.com.

- Can't find a file? Afraid it's lost and gone forever? Try the **Find** function off of the Start button from Windows.

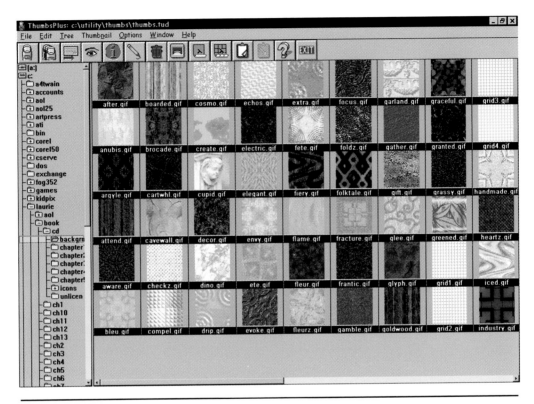

Figure 11.12 ThumbsPlus image management software.

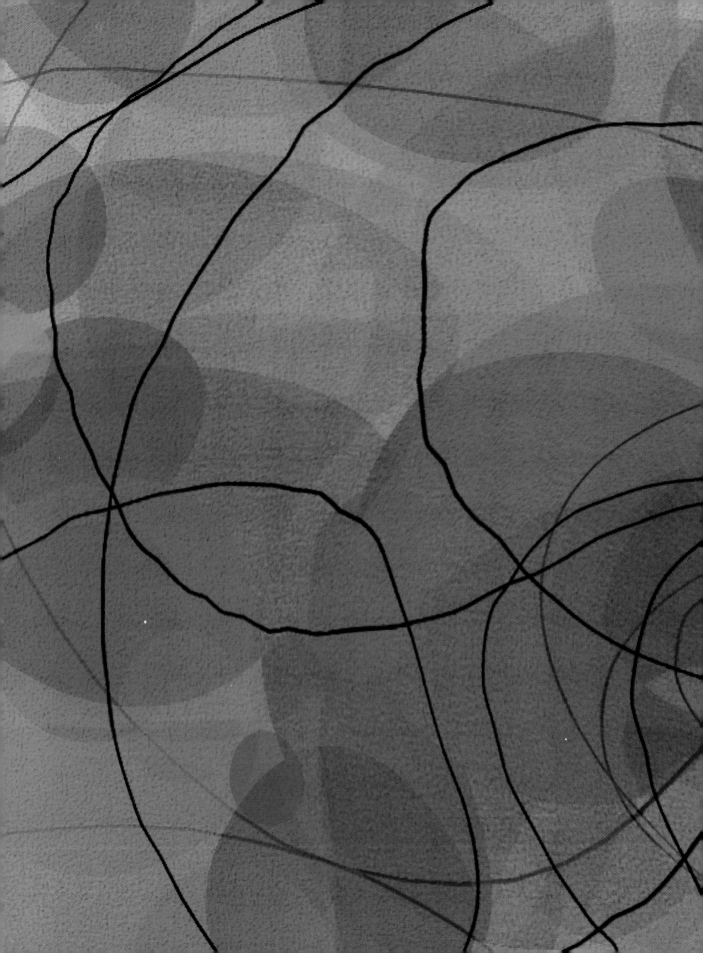

12 YOUR FAVORITE CARTOON CHARACTER HAS A VERY GOOD LAWYER

Not too long ago in an online forum, a Web designer asked for feedback on her new Web site. I looked it over; ironically, it was for a public relations firm that specializes in helping other companies recover from public relations disasters. Very prominently displayed on the main Web page was a very familiar—and very copyrighted—cartoon character. I immediately sent e-mail to the designer, alerting her to the problematic use of art on her Web page. The next day, the cartoon was gone.

WHAT'S MINE IS NOT YOURS

Easy access to artwork online, coupled with a misunderstanding of copyright law can get you into trouble. There are two areas of copyright to learn about: The first is using artwork created by someone else and the second area is how to copyright and then protect your artwork. In brief, what you create belongs to you, unless you specifically agree to sell your right to the work. This is an especially sticky problem area on the Web, where it is easy to download art. It is very easy for anyone to steal your artwork from the Web by clicking the right mouse button from within many browsers. And even if a browser doesn't support this function, capturing artwork is hardly brain surgery. In Figures 12.1 and 12.2, you can see the right mouse button in action on both Internet Explorer and Netscape Navigator.

When I wrote the first edition of *Creating Great Web Graphics* in 1996, I was aware that some people might download my artwork and use it without permission, but that it would be limited to a few clueless college students. Was I ever naïve! Within the last year, I have discovered artwork from my Web site in a number of commercial products and as a logo for a software program. Plus, a major Internet service provider included two dozen pieces of my artwork in its personal Web page service. All of this was done without my knowledge or permission. If it can happen to me, it can happen to you.

Copyrighting your work, unfortunately, does not mean it is protected from people who might misappropriate your artwork. It's up to you to identify people who have used your artwork without permission, and it's up to you to decide how to deal with it.

Although there is nothing you can do to prevent miscreants from downloading artwork from your Web site, I do have a few suggestions for tracking them down. Your first and perhaps best defense is to give your graphics unique names. (In my experience, people who take graphics without permission rarely rename an image.) Then, once a month, go to the search engine at http://www.altavista.digital.com, and type in your filename. Any Web site containing a file matching that name (which AltaVista has indexed) will be listed.

Figure 12.1 Using the right mouse button on Netscape.

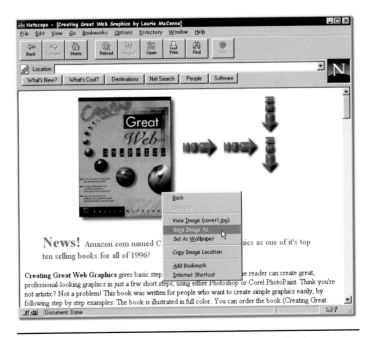

Figure 12.2 Using the right mouse button on Internet Explorer.

Using software, you can also add copyright information to your images. Photoshop 4 and Corel PhotoPaint 7 both include the Digimarc watermarking filter, which embeds information that can be read by anyone who has the filter installed. This filter does require that you pay an annual fee to Digimarc. You can also use one of the GIF tools like GIF Construction Set to embed a text comment block that is readable by other GIF tools.

Once you've tracked down the person or company using your images without your permission, what do you do? If you're like me, it'll take a few minutes, or a few days, to calm down. The next step is to write to the person misusing your image and ask (politely) that he or she remove it as soon as possible. Be sure to include your contact information and Web address. If you get no response, write to the Web master at the Internet service provider for the Web site containing your image. Let's say you find your image being used at the URL http://www.fictional.edu/~user/joehacker/index.htm. Go to the main Web site at http://www.fictional.edu and track down the contact e-mail address for the Web master. Again, write a polite letter. It's always best to assume initially that the person who has misappropriated your graphic did so out of ignorance, not maliciousness.

If polite requests fail, you have to decide how far you're willing to pursue the issue. You can continue to write to the owner of the Web site, you can hire legal representation, or you can give up. In any case, you should definitely become more familiar with copyright law. There are two FAQs (Frequently Asked Questions) of interest to consult. One is the general copyright FAQ at http://www.aimnet.com/~carroll/copyright/faq-home.html, and the other is the Copyright Myths FAQ, available at http://www.clari.net/brad/copymyths.html.

CLIP THAT ART FROM YOUR WEB PAGE!

If you've read the licensing agreement for the clip art you use on your Web site (and I know you have), you may recall a little paragraph prohibiting its electronic distribution, but this is still an area open to interpretation. Some companies will fax or e-mail you a copy of their usage requirements for their product upon request. Others have not yet formed a policy on it. At least one company I contacted wanted a guarantee that the artwork couldn't be downloaded or used in a screenshot. The bottom line: Check with the creator of the clip art you are using before you add it to your Web site.

13 ADDING PICTURES TO A WEB PAGE: ADVANCED HTML

The HTML tags I defined earlier demonstrated how to create a page, but they didn't include those for adding images to a Web site. This chapter fills that gap in your HTML arsenal by introducing the IMG SRC, or Image Source, tag and its attributes. More in-depth coverage can be had by contacting the HTML Resources at the back of the book, which include a guide to Web sites, mailing lists, and newsgroups that cover graphics and HTML topics.

Even if you're using a whizbang HTML editor that does everything but upload itself, you should familiarize yourself with this HTML information, because there is no perfect HTML editor and because paths and filenames are where most Web page designers run into trouble. If I had a dollar for every time I've heard "I uploaded my images but they don't show up on my Web page," I'd be vacationing in Tahiti now, instead of explaining it all to you.

RELATIVE AND ABSOLUTE PATHS: STAYING ON THE STRAIGHT AND NARROW

A path is the direction you give the browser to find an image. Remember, unlike desktop publishing files, HTML files do not have graphics embedded. You have to upload HTML files and graphics separately to your server. Then, in order for a Web browser to find the images you want to use in your Web page, you have to specify a path to the image on the server.

You can do this in two ways: using a relative path—a path relative to your HTML document—or using an absolute path that includes the full URL for the image. Generally, specifying a relative path is preferred, because if you move to a different domain, it will be easier to update your links. Think of a relative path as if someone were giving you directions from your house (the HTML page) to his or her house (the image). That person would give you directions relative to where you began. In contrast, an absolute path is like providing the longitude and latitude; you'd be able to follow directions from anywhere to find the destination.

As an example, let's say there's an HTML page named index.htm at:

```
http://www.mccannas.com
```

The URL for the page is:

```
http://www.mccannas.com/index.htm
```

So far, so good. Now let's say there's an image called **jukebox.jpg** uploaded to the same directory as the index.htm page. In order to display the **jukebox.jpg** image on the page named index.htm, you could use either of the following tags:

Absolute path: `<IMG SRC="http://www.mccannas.com/jukebox.jpg">`
Relative path: `<IMG SRC="jukebox.jpg">`

Both tags will successfully add the image to the page index.htm at http://www.mccannas.com/index.htm.

Now, for a little trickier example. Let's say there's a second image named **banner.gif** in a directory named images. Here are the respective pathnames:

```
Absolute path: <IMG SRC="http://www.mccannas.com/images/banner.gif">
Relative path: <IMG SRC="images/banner.gif">
```

The relative path tells the browser to look in a directory named images for the file named **banner.gif.** But let's now assume there's another HTML page at this location:

```
http://www.mccannas.com/corel/corel1.htm
```

How would you specify the path to **jukebox.jpg** and **banner.gif?**

```
Absolute path: <IMG SRC="http://www.mccannas.com/images/banner.gif">
Relative path: <IMG SRC="../images/banner.gif">
```

The ../ in the relative path tells the browser to go up one level in the directory structure. Using the ../ twice tells the browser to go back two levels to the images directory, and so on.

And the paths to the file **jukebox.jpg** are:

```
Absolute path: <IMG SRC="http://www.mccannas.com/jukebox.jpg">
Relative path: <IMG SRC="../jukebox.jpg">
```

That's it. Honest, HMTL never gets any worse than this.

THE **IMG SRC** TAG

Before we begin, one important note: HTML is case-sensitive to filenames, so if you want **wild.gif**, don't type **WILD.gif**. Let's go with that example. To add a GIF named **wild.gif** to a Web page, the code would read:

```
<IMG SRC="wild.gif">
```

Pretty simple, right? And notice that this points to the GIF uploaded to the same directory as the HTML page that points to it.

But let's say you want to add an image to your page, but the image is at another domain name. The code then would read:

```
<IMG SRC="http://www.mccannas.com/pshop/image1.gif">
```

This would load an image named **image1.gif** from a directory named pshop at the domain name www.mccannas.com.

More Fun with the IMG SRC Tag

There's more you can do with the IMG SRC tag than just point to an image. You can align your images and help a browser to render the Web page text more quickly.

Look at Figure 13.1, which displays three images, named **1.jpg**, **2.jpg**, and **3.jpg** with default alignment. Here's the HTML for it:

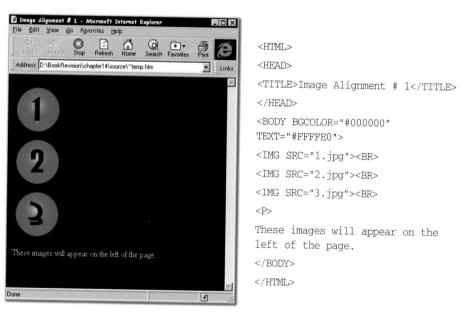

```
<HTML>
<HEAD>
<TITLE>Image Alignment # 1</TITLE>
</HEAD>
<BODY BGCOLOR="#000000"
TEXT="#FFFFE0">
<IMG SRC="1.jpg"><BR>
<IMG SRC="2.jpg"><BR>
<IMG SRC="3.jpg"><BR>
<P>
These images will appear on the
left of the page.
</BODY>
</HTML>
```

Figure 13.1 Three images using the <BR> tag.

The <BR> indicates a line break. Without it, the images line up as in Figure 13.2. Here's the HTML for Figure 13.2:

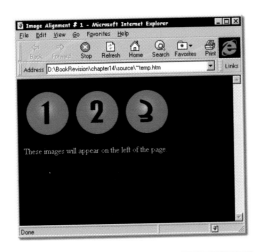

```
<HTML>
<HEAD>
<TITLE>Image Alignment # 2</TITLE>
</HEAD>
<BODY BGCOLOR="#000000" TEXT="#FFFFE0">
<IMG SRC="1.jpg">
<IMG SRC="2.jpg">
<IMG SRC="3.jpg">
<P>
These images will appear across the page.
</BODY>
</HTML>
```

Figure 13.2 Three images with default alignment.

And if you wanted to center the images, the code would read:

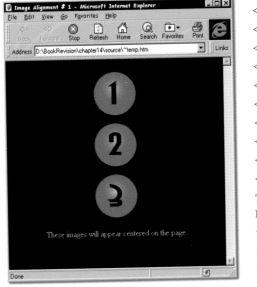

```
<HTML>
<HEAD>
<TITLE>Image Alignment # 3</TITLE>
</HEAD>
<BODY BGCOLOR="#000000" TEXT="#FFFFE0">
<CENTER><IMG SRC="1.jpg"></CENTER>
<CENTER><IMG SRC="2.jpg"></CENTER>
<CENTER><IMG SRC="3.jpg"></CENTER>
<P>
<CENTER>
These images will appear centered on the
page.
</CENTER>
</BODY>
</HTML>
```

Figure 13.3 Centering the images and text.

Chapter

13

The page would appear as it does in Figure 13.3. Note that the CENTER tag requires both an opening and a closing tag. You can also align images by using an ALIGN=RIGHT, ALIGN=LEFT, or ALIGN=CENTER tag within the IMG SRC tag, as in the following HTML example:

```
<HTML>
<HEAD>
<TITLE>Image Alignment # 4</TITLE>
</HEAD>
<BODY BGCOLOR="#000000" TEXT="#FFFFE0">
<IMG SRC="1.jpg" ALIGN=LEFT>
<IMG SRC="1.jpg" ALIGN=LEFT>
<IMG SRC="2.jpg" ALIGN=RIGHT>
<IMG SRC="3.jpg" ALIGN=RIGHT>
<IMG SRC="3.jpg" ALIGN=RIGHT>
<P>
</BODY>
</HTML>
```

This seems fairly straightforward until you look at Figures 13.4 through 13.6. This is the same page, viewed with the same Web browser, but with the browser set to different widths. You can see how important it is to test your Web page.

The ALIGN tag used in conjunction with the IMG SRC tag is used most often to align an image (like a bullet) to text, and it can be used in these configurations:

```
ALIGN=LEFT
ALIGN=RIGHT
ALIGN=TOP    aligns the image to the top of the text.
ALIGN=MIDDLE    aligns the middle of the image to the baseline of the text.
ALIGN=BASELINE    aligns the bottom of the image with the baseline of the text.
ALIGN=BOTTOM    aligns the bottom of the image with the baseline of the text.
```

Figures 13.4, 13.5, and 13.6 The same Web page viewed in different browser widths.

The following is the HTML for Figure 13.7, which demonstrates the different alignments possible with the ALIGN tag:

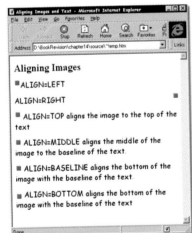

Figure 13.7 Using the ALIGN tag.

```
<HTML>
<HEAD>
<TITLE>Aligning Images and Text</TITLE>
</HEAD>
<BODY BGCOLOR="#FFFFFF" TEXT="#000000">
<H2> Aligning Images </H2>
<FONT FACE="comic sans ms" SIZE=+1>
<IMG SRC="icon1.gif" ALIGN=LEFT>ALIGN=LEFT
<P>
<IMG SRC="icon3.gif" ALIGN=RIGHT>ALIGN=RIGHT
<P>
<IMG SRC="icon1.gif" ALIGN=TOP>ALIGN=TOP aligns the image
to the top of the text.
<P>
<IMG SRC="icon3.gif" ALIGN=MIDDLE>ALIGN=MIDDLE aligns the
middle of the image to the baseline of the text.
<P>
<IMG SRC="icon1.gif" ALIGN=BASELINE> ALIGN=BASELINE aligns
the bottom of the image with the baseline of the text.
<P>
<IMG SRC="icon3.gif" ALIGN=BOTTOM> ALIGN=BOTTOM aligns the
bottom of the image with the baseline of the text.
</FONT>
</BODY>
</HTML>
```

USING **HSPACE** AND **VSPACE**

Two other tags, HSPACE and VSPACE, are essential for adding that all-important extra space around your images. You can use these tags with the IMG SRC tag in this form:

```
<IMG SRC="1.jpg" HSPACE=20 VSPACE=20>
```

This would add 20 pixels of space to the top, bottom, right, and left of an image. The following HTML code is for Figure 13.8, which demonstrates a few different settings for the HSPACE tag:

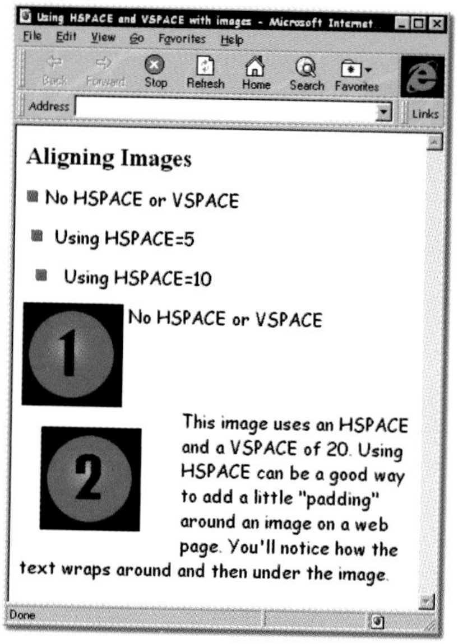

```
<HTML>
<HEAD>
<TITLE>Using HSPACE and VSPACE with
Images</TITLE>
</HEAD>
<BODY BGCOLOR="#FFFFFF" TEXT="#000000">
<H2> Aligning Images </H2>
<FONT FACE="comic sans ms" SIZE=+1>
<IMG SRC="icon1.gif" ALIGN=MIDDLE> No HSPACE or VSPACE
<P>
<IMG SRC="icon1.gif" ALIGN=MIDDLE HSPACE=5>Using HSPACE=5
<P>
<IMG SRC="icon1.gif" ALIGN=MIDDLE HSPACE=10>Using HSPACE=10
<P>
<IMG SRC="1.jpg" ALIGN=TOP>No HSPACE or VSPACE<BR>
<IMG SRC="2.jpg" ALIGN=LEFT HSPACE=20 VSPACE=20> This image uses an HSPACE
and a VSPACE of 20. Using HSPACE can be a good way to add a little
"padding" around an image on a Web page. You'll notice how the text wraps
around and then under the image.
</FONT>
</BODY>
</HTML>
```

Figure 13.8 Using HSPACE and VSPACE to add white space.

THE **ALT** TAG

The ALT tag is intended as an accommodation for users whose browsers don't support the display of images, or who may be browsing the Web with the image option turned off in order to load pages more quickly. You use ALT in the following way:

```
<IMG SRC="globe.gif" ALT="A picture of the earth">
```

IMAGE **WIDTH** AND **HEIGHT**

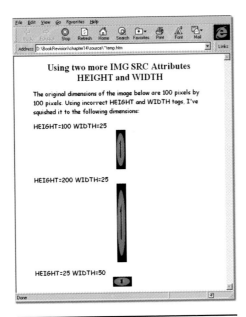

It's a good idea to specify the HEIGHT and WIDTH of your image in the IMG SRC code so that while your page is loading, the text of your page will appear. If you don't use the WIDTH and HEIGHT tags, the browser will wait for the images to download completely before adding the text, thereby increasing the potential that viewers will exit your page without ever seeing it completely.

Be careful to use the exact measurements of your image in the WIDTH and HEIGHT tags; otherwise it may end up squished or otherwise degraded. You can see the dire consequences of using incorrect HEIGHT and WIDTH tags in Figure 13.9.

Figure 13.9 Using incorrect HEIGHT and WIDTH tags.

THE **LOWSRC** TAG

One way to hold the attention of your viewers while an image is loading is to show them a lower-resolution version of the file. Oh, yech, you're saying. But I'm going to show you how to create a Really Big GIF that will load very quickly. In fact, this trick produces such nice images that you may want to use them as-is on your Web page, and not just as a preview. One note: This technique works best with a photograph or line art.

1. In Photoshop, open your image. Select **Image/Mode/Grayscale**. If you can't select **Grayscale**, select **RGB Mode**, then **Image/Mode/Grayscale**. Next select **Image/Mode/Bitmap** as shown in Figure 13.10. Select **Diffusion Dither**.

2. Select **Image/Mode/Grayscale**, then **Image/Mode/RGB**. Next select **Image/Mode/Indexed**, then **Palette**, **Exact**, which should be 2 colors.

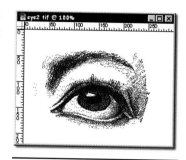

Figure 13.10 Creating a 1-bit GIF.

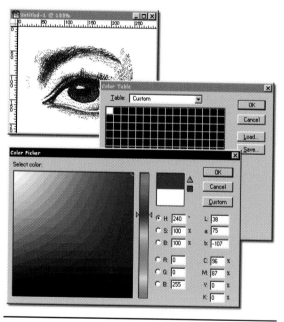

Figure 13.11 Editing the color table.

3. Select **Image/Mode/Color Table**. Click on the white color swatch, as shown in Figure 13.11. Next, from the Color Picker, enter one of the RGB values for a non-dithering color from Chapter 5. In this example, I've used blue.

4. Save the image. This example, 300 pixels x 220 pixels, was only 4K when saved (Figure 13.12).

Figure 13.12 The finished 1-bit GIF.

Creating a 1-bit GIF in PhotoPaint is a similar process:

1. Open an image in Corel PhotoPaint. Select **Image/Convert to Black and White**.

2. Select **Image/Convert To/Paletted 8Bit**. Choose **Palette Type**, **Custom**; **Dither**, **None**. From the next screen, select **Custom**. Double-click on the first swatch in the palette, which will reveal the color picker, shown in Figure 13.13. Select an RGB value from the list of nondithering colors in Chapter 5.

3. Save the file as a GIF. The artwork in Figure 13.14, at 225 pixels x 225 pixels, was only 4K when saved as a GIF.

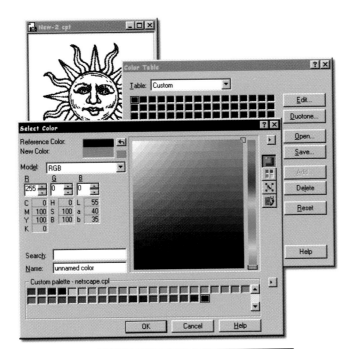

Figure 13.14 The finished PhotoPaint image.

Figure 13.13 Editing the PhotoPaint Color palette.

Creating these small GIFs is a great trick for animated GIFs, backgrounds, and other Web page artwork.

The HTML code for this technique looks like this:

```
<IMG SRC="color.gif" LOWSRC="eye.gif">
```

In this example, the image **eye.gif** would load first as a preview; then, after everything else on the page had loaded, the browser would render **color.gif.** You can use LOWSRC with GIFs or JPEGs. Browsers that don't support the LOWSRC tag will simply ignore it and load **color.gif.** By the way, both images will be rendered to fit the HEIGHT and WIDTH tags. But if you don't specify a HEIGHT and WIDTH for the images, both will be scaled to the dimensions of the image specified with the LOWSRC tag.

THE **A HREF** TAG

One last tag before we leave HTML again, and it's an important one, used to create a link on a Web page to another Web page. A sample text link would look like this:

```
<A HREF="page2.htm"> See my second Web page </A>
```

The *A* in this code stands for the Anchor tag; note that it must have a closing tag. Failure to add the closing tag would result in the remainder of the text on the page becoming a link.

The second element, HREF, stands for Hypertext Reference. An A HREF can point to a Web page or a page on another Web site using this form:

```
<A HREF="http://www.altavista.digital.com"> Altavista </A> is my favorite
search engine.
```

You can also point to a downloadable file, a sound file, or any other file type supported by the Web browser as shown here:

```
Like music? Listen to <A HREF="music.wav"> my favorite song. </A>
```

This would produce a clickable link leading to an audio file in WAV format, which wouldn't play until the Web site visitor clicked on the link.

```
Download <A HREF="icons.zip"> a collection of icons </A> in a zipped archive.
```

This would produce a link to a downloadable ZIP file, provided of course, that the file **icons.zip** was uploaded to the same directory as the HTML file that linked it. Refer to the beginning of the chapter for information on how to link to files with relative and absolute paths if you're getting lost.

To create a clickable icon, you need to nestle the IMG SRC tag between the opening A HREF and closing /A tags:

```
<A HREF="http://www.mccannas.com"> <IMG SRC="icon.gif"> </A>
```

This would produce a clickable link to the Web site at http://www.mccannas.com and would be displayed on the Web page surrounded by a border. To display a linked image without a border, include the BORDER=0 attribute in the IMG SRC tag:

```
<A HREF="http://www.mccannas.com"> <IMG SRC="icon.gif" BORDER=0> </A>
```

You can see these links displayed on a Web page in Figure 13.15.

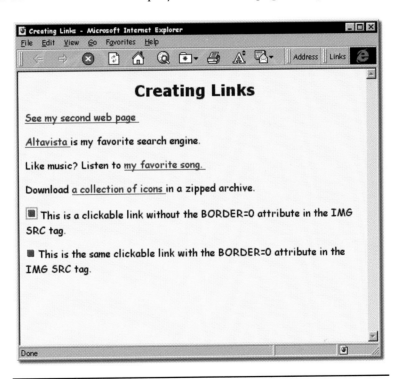

Figure 13.15 Creating links.

I hope this chapter has given you a better understanding of how to align images on a Web page and how to avoid some of the most common problems that occur with images and HTML.

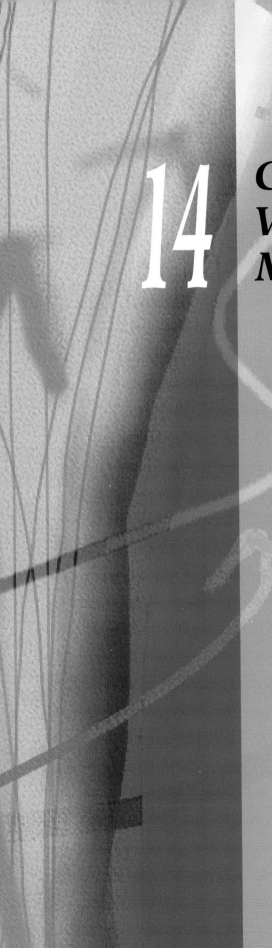

14 GETTING YOUR WEB PAGE MOVING

One of the easiest ways to add an eye-catching graphic to a Web page is to create a GIF animation. You can take any image you've created while following the tutorials in this book and animate it. The animation process for effects such as fade, wipes, and others is automated in one of the tools I'll describe—GIF Construction Set for Windows.

One of the benefits of GIF animations is that unlike many multimedia applications for the Web, they don't require browser plug-ins to view. Netscape versions 2.0 and higher and Internet Explorer versions 3.0 and higher support GIF animation, as does the current version of the America Online browser. With browsers that don't support GIF animations, either the first or last frame of the animation will be displayed in its place. GIF animations are more stable than many other types of applications, such as Java, and rarely crash a Web browser.

This chapter describes how to build an animation using GIF Construction Set on Windows and GIFBuilder on the Mac. GIF animations are fun to create, and you'll learn a lot by experimenting with different effects. You can design something as bold and brassy as a Saturday morning cartoon or as subtle as a leaf falling. In short, animations don't even necessarily need to move: A simple icon that changes color can be a nice addition to an otherwise dull Web page. An animation should complement your Web site design, reflecting its color scheme and tone.

In general, I recommend no more than one or two animation effects per Web page, as they can distract your visitors from reading the text on your page.

Unfortunately, there is no adequate way to demonstrate the full effects of an animation within the static boundaries of a book. Therefore, I suggest you fire up your Web browser and point it to http://www.mccannas.com/ book/gifan/, where you can view samples from this chapter in action. And don't miss the extensive list of Web sites in the Resources section. You'll find pointers to traditional animation resources, which will be helpful in understanding how to create unique effects for your own Web graphics. You'll also find pointers to archives of animations, which you can then open with your GIF animation program to view each frame individually and see how the effect was created.

To get motivated, you may want to take a short jaunt to Royal Frasier's GIF animation Web site at http://members.aol.com/royalef. There you'll find an extensive gallery of GIF animations along with links to GIF animation tools for every platform.

ANIMATION TOOLS

You can create the images that will be compiled as an animation in any paint program. Within the animation program, you establish the order in which the images will appear, set the timing for the animation, and select how many times (from one to an infinite number) the animation will repeat or loop.

Whether you are using Photoshop or Corel PhotoPaint, download a copy of a GIF animation program. PhotoPaint does include a GIF animation feature, but the animations it creates are substantially larger (about 50%) than the identical GIF animations compiled in the GIF Construction Set.

If you use Windows, download a copy of the GIF Construction Set from any of these sites:

Alchemy Mindworks Web Site

http://www.mindworkshop.com

Shareware.Com

http://www.shareware.com

Tucows

http://www.tucows.com

On America Online, use keyword: WEB DINER, then select **Software Libraries, PC Web Software.**

On the Mac, get a copy of GIFBuilder, available at:

Shareware.Com

http://www.shareware.com

On America Online, use keyword: WEB DINER, then select **Software Libraries, Mac Web Software.**

CREATING AN ANIMATION WITH PHOTOSHOP AND GIF CONSTRUCTION SET FOR WINDOWS

This tutorial demonstrates how to create a simple logo animation that loops (or repeats) itself. You can begin with either an imported EPS or AI file, or you can start by using a symbol from a typeface to create the image.

1. If you're using an EPS (Encapsulated PostScript) or AI (Adobe Illustrator) file, select **File/Open**, then select the pixel size of the image (here I've used 80 x 76 pixels), and set the mode to **RGB.** Make sure to check the **Anti-aliasing** checkbox. Duplicate the layer, then fill the background with white, as in the example (Figure 14.1). If you're using type, open a new file at an 80 x 80 pixel size, and use the Type tool to create a symbol. In this example, the point size was set to 70, but the size will depend on the typeface you're using.

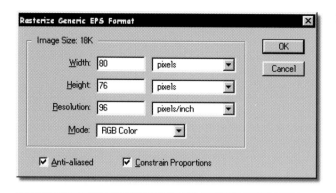

Figure 14.1 The EPS Import dialog box in Photoshop.

2. Once you have your logo on a separate layer from the background, select **Image/Duplicate** to create an exact copy. Select **Image/Mode/Indexed**, then **Palette**, **Adaptive**; **Color Depth**, **4 bits**; **Dither**, **None**. Now you have the first frame of your animation. Save it as **logo1.gif** (Figure 14.2).

3. Return to the original image, select the **Type Layer**, then **Filters/Render/Lighting** and use the **Default** setting. Select **Texture Channel**, **Red** and change the focus of the lighting to match the example in Figure 14.3. Select **Image/Duplicate** to create the second frame. Select **Image/Mode/Indexed**, and select **Palette**, **Adaptive**; **Color Depth**, **4 bits**; **Diffusion**, **None**. Save this file as **logo2.gif**.

4. Return to the original image, and with the **Type Layer** still selected, apply the same lighting filter again by using **Control+F**. Select **Image/Mode/Indexed**, then **Palette**, **Adaptive**; **Color Depth**, **4 bits**; **Diffusion**, **None**. Save this file as **logo3.gif**.

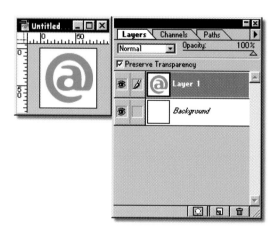

Figure 14.2 Beginning the logo animation in Photoshop.

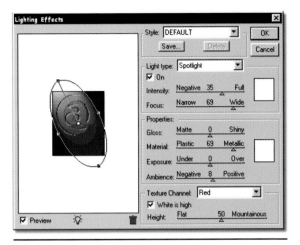

Figure 14.3 Using the Lighting Effects filter in Photoshop.

5. Return again to the original image, and with the **Type Layer** still selected, select **Filters/Render/Lens Flare** with the brightness set to **100** and the lens set to **105mm Prime**. Focus the lens flare on the upper-right edge of your logo. Select **Image/ Mode/Indexed**, then **Palette, Adaptive; Color Depth, 4 bits; Diffusion, None**. Save this file as **logo4.gif**.

You've created all the frames for your animation at this point, and they should look something like the example in Figure 14.4.

Figure 14.4 The four images that will make up the animation.

Compiling the Animation in GIF Construction Set

1. Open GIF Construction Set and select **File/Animation Wizard**. This will guide you through the process of creating a GIF animation. When prompted for the type of animation you would like to create, select **Web Page/Loop Indefinitely/PhotoRealistic**. Select **100/100** of a second delay (we'll customize this setting later). Next select the images that make up the animation: **logo1.gif, logo2.gif, logo3.gif**, and **logo4.gif**. Then, since we want this animation to loop, we'll work backwards. Add **logo4.gif, logo3.gif, logo2.gif**, and **logo1.gif**. Select **Next/Done**. GIF Construction Set will compile the animation but will not save the file until you select **File/Save**. You can preview the animation via the **View** icon.

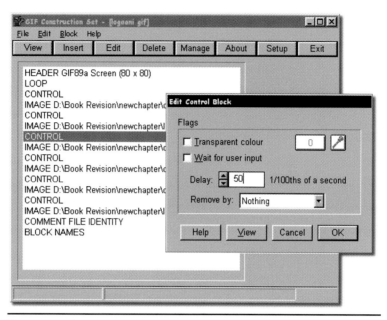

Figure 14.5 Customizing the delay time between frames in GIF Construction Set.

2. Next, we'll adjust the timing of the animation to make it a little more interesting. If we speed up the animation as it progresses, it will appear to come to life on the Web page. Select the second Control Block, where the transparency and delay information is stored for images in the GIF animation. Select the **Edit** icon. Change delay from 100 to **50** (Figure 14.5). Select the next Control Block, and the **Edit** icon again, and change delay to **15**. Select the fourth Control Block, and change delay to **30**. Change the last Control Block to **200**, which will give the illusion of a pause in the animation until it resumes its loop.

3. As a final step, you may want to use the **Supercompress** option from the File menu in GIF Construction Set. In this example, it was able to reduce the file size of this animation from 9K to 8K.

A nice feature of the GIF Construction Set is that the registered version automatically adds your name to the animation in a text field, as shown in Figure 14.6. You can edit that information, as illustrated in Figure 14.7, to add contact information, copyright information, or any usage restrictions.

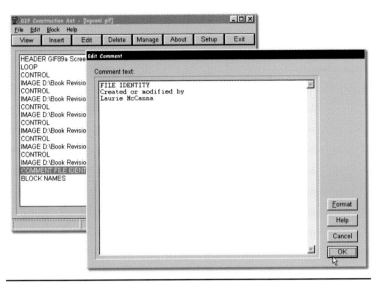

Figure 14.6 GIF Construction Set's text block.

One last word about the GIF Construction Set: It generates mysterious .THN files for all animations you create, thumbnails that are readable by another software program made by Alchemy Mindworks. You can either delete these files or turn off the option that generates them. To do the latter, select **Setup**, then uncheck the **Write THN Thumbnails** checkbox.

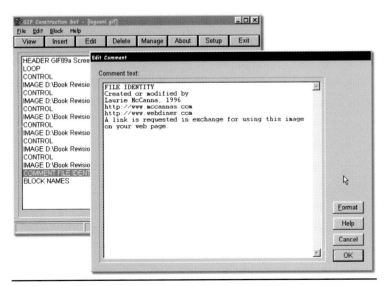

Figure 14.7 Adding copyright information in GIF Construction Set.

More Effects with GIF Construction Set

The GIF Construction Set has a number of functions that generate great-looking animation effects automatically. You can use them to create text effects or add animation transition effects to an existing GIF.

1. To create a text effect, select **Edit/Banner**. You will see the dialog box in Figure 14.8.

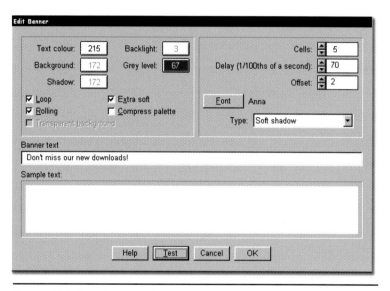

Figure 14.8 Creating a text banner.

2. Select **Text Color, White; Gray Level, 50; Font Type, Soft Shadow; Cells, 7; Delay, 20; Offset, 2.** Check the boxes for **Loop, Rolling,** and **Extra Soft** to create a scrolling text effect with a soft shadow, as in Figure 14.9. You can preview the animation by selecting **Test**. Use the **Escape** key to exit Test.

To create the neon text banner in Figure 14.10, use the same settings used in the GIF Construction Set, but change the font type to **Neon** and the backlight color to **Red.**

Figure 14.9 The animation frames.

Figure 14.10 A neon text banner.

You can also generate an animation from any existing GIF file in the GIF Construction Set. Simply select **File/Open**, then **Edit/Transition**, and you'll be able to choose from a variety of transitions for your animation. Figures 14.11 through 14.19 show nine different transitions.

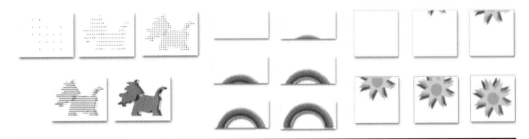

Figures 14.11, 14.12, and 14.13 Adam Interlace, Wipe in from Bottom, and Wipe in from Top, respectively.

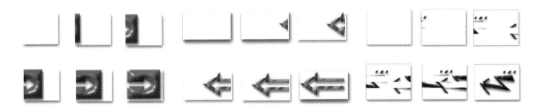

Figures 14.14, 14.15, and 14.16 Wipe in from Left, Wipe in from Right, and Raster transitions, respectively.

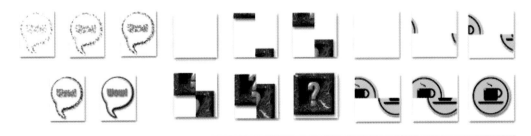

Figures 14.17, 14.18, and 14.19 Sandstorm, Vertical Split, and Horizontal Split transitions, respectively.

Chapter

14

CREATING A GIF ANIMATION USING GIFBUILDER ON THE MAC

This tutorial demonstrates how to create a simple yet eye-catching banner animation on the Mac. Before you begin, make sure you have the following items:

GIFBuilder, available at most shareware archives.

A single image, no more than 72 x 72 pixels (clip art, scanned image, photograph, etc.)

1. Open Photoshop and select **File/New** or **Command+N** to open a new file. Set the image size to 540 x 180 pixels, the resolution to 96 pixels per inch, RGB color, and the background to white.

2. In the new file, we'll be creating a black border around the outside of the image, so make sure that your foreground color is set to **Black**. Go to the Select menu and choose **All** (**Command+A**). From the Edit menu, select **Stroke** with the following settings: **Width, 5 pixels; Location, Inside; Blending, Default** (Figure 14.20). You should now have a blank file with a black border around it.

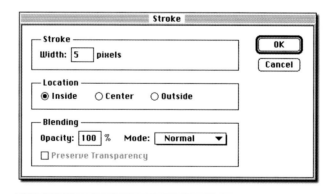

Figure 14.20 Creating a black border using **Edit/Stroke**.

3. Save this file as **template.psd.**

4. Make a duplicate of this file by selecting **Image/Duplicate**. Create a new layer, open your clip art image or photo, and copy the contents into this new layer. The easiest way to do this is by selecting the entire image (**Command+A**), copying it (**Command+C**), and pasting it into the duplicate template (**Command+V**). Position the image at the left side of the banner template. You can nudge the image into place in single-pixel increments by holding down the **Command** key and using the arrow keys to position the image precisely where you want it. If your image covers up any of the border, you might want to reduce the clip art and recopy it. Flatten the file (**Command+Shift+E**), index it (**Image/Mode/Indexed**), and save this file as **ANI001.gif**

5. Make a duplicate of **ANI001.gif** by selecting **Image/Duplicate**. Use the Type tool and click anywhere inside the right side of the file to open the Text window. Type the text you want to use in your banner.

6. Align your text with the image accordingly by using the arrow keys while holding down the **Command** key. Flatten the file (**Command+Shift+E**), index it (**Image/Mode/Indexed**), and save this file as **ANI002.gif.**

7. Make a duplicate of **ANI002.gif**. Using the Marquee tool, draw a selection directly around the outside of the text. Choose a new color and select **Edit/Stroke**. This time, set width to **3** and location to **Center.** Flatten the file (**Command+Shift+E**), index it (**Image/Mode/Indexed**), and save this file as **ANI003.gif**

8. Make a duplicate of **ANI003.gif.** Create another selection using the Marquee tool, select another color, and repeat the Stroke process again. Index this image (**Image/Mode/Indexed**) and save it as **ANI004.gif**

9. Make a duplicate of **ANI004.gif**. Create another selection, choose another color, and repeat the Stroke process one last time. Index this image (**Image/Mode/Indexed**) and save this file as **ANI005.gif.** Figure 14.21 shows all five images.

C h a p t e r

14

Animating the Image in GIFBuilder

Now it's time to add motion to the image.

1. Open GIFBuilder by double-clicking on the icon. You will see two windows: one titled Frames, the other untitled.gif. GIFBuilder considers each GIF file a frame.

2. With the Banner directory open in the background on your desktop, select **ANI001.gif** and drag it to the Frames window. Do this with each GIF file (Figure 14.22). As you drag the files, you will notice that the untitled window changes to reflect the graphics inside each frame.

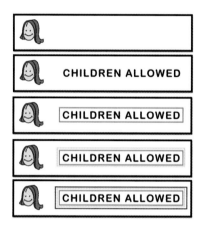

Figure 14. 21 The five frames of animation.

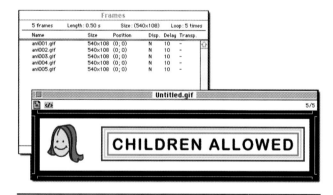

Figure 14.22 Opening the GIF files in GIFBuilder.

Setting GIFBuilder Options

1. To create the animation, select all frames (**Shift+click** each filename until all are highlighted). Select **Colors/System Palette/Remove Unused Colors**, then **Depth, 8 bits/pixel**. Select **Loop,** as shown in Figure 14.24. In this example, the number of loops was set to **5**.

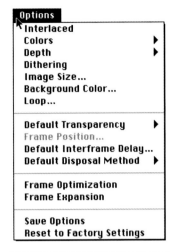

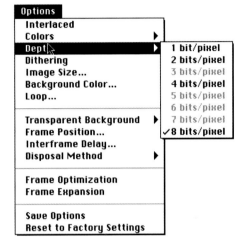

Figure 14.23 GIFBuilder animation options.

Figure 14.24 Selecting the depth options in GIFBuilder.

2. Click on **Interframe Delay.** When a new window opens, set your delay options, in this case **10/100** second. You may want to experiment with different delay settings to find the best ones for your particular animation. Check the **Frame Optimization** option.

Once your options are set, you can view the animation in the untitled.gif window. Click on **Command+R** to start the animation and **Command+T** to stop the animation. If it doesn't work properly, check your settings, adjust them accordingly, and review the animation. When your animation is to your satisfaction, save the entire image as **banner.gif**.

MORE FUN WITH GIF ANIMATIONS

The effects you can create with GIF animations are endless. For practice, go back through some of the instructions in this book for icons and text effects and use them to create more GIF animations. For instance, try starting with text, then add a drop shadow and a second or third effect from Chapter 9. Check out some of the animation Web sites listed in the Resources section for more inspiration.

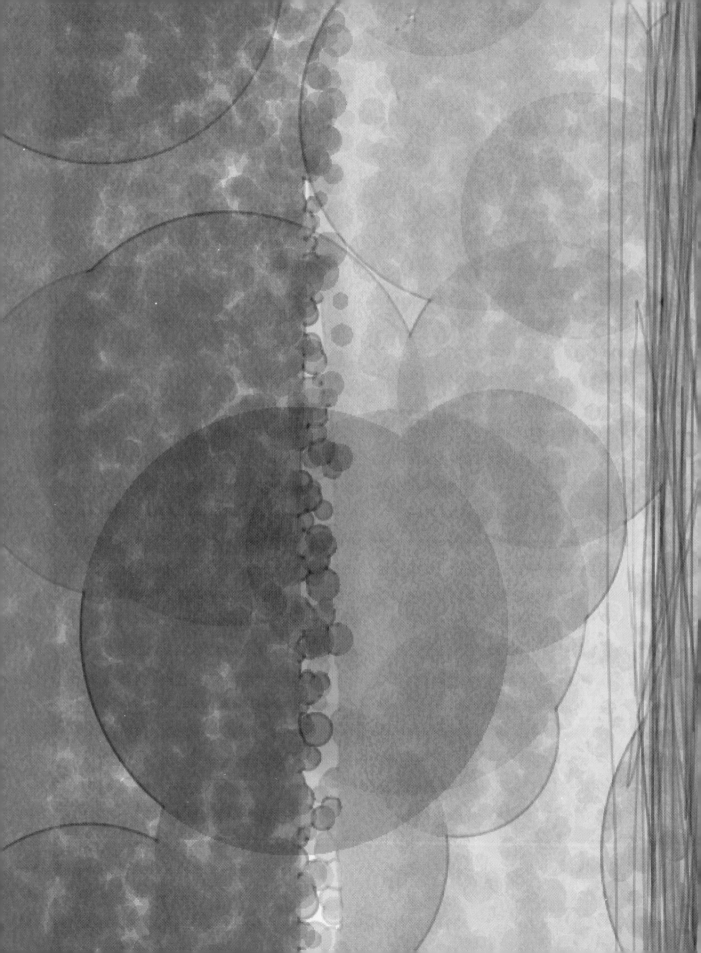

APPENDIX A: RESOURCES

What, no CD in this book? That's right, and for good reason. Web software would be as stale as last week's eclair by the time this book is on the shelf. Better that I give you pointers to Web resources and free and shareware software Web sites so that you'll be able to access the hottest, most up-to-date software available. Enjoy!

ANIMATION RESOURCES

Included here are examples of traditional animation, along with software, tutorials, and downloadable examples of animation for the Web.

Alchemy Mindworks: GIF Construction Set

Alchemy Mindworks offers a very nice demonstration page that includes a tutorial and explanation of the features of GIF Construction Set, a GIF animation shareware program for Windows.

`http://www.mindworkshop.com/alchemy/alchemy.htm`

If you can't get through to this site, you should be able to download the latest version from http://www.tucows.com or http://www.shareware.com.

Animator's Mailing List Web Site

This mailing list is for folks serious about traditional animation. It doesn't cover computer animation specifically.

`http://www.xmission.com/~grue/animate`

Animation Tour

This site, created by a student, discusses all aspects of animation. It's a very good overview of traditional and computer animation techniques, and you'll find examples from current films.

`http://www.art.uiuc.edu/local/anle/ANIMATION/ANIMATIONTGAL.ht`

Animation World Magazine

Lots of resources here for anyone interested in animation. You'll need to register (it's free) to read the back issues of the magazine. There are message boards and a newsletter you can sign up to receive via e-mail.

`http://www.awn.com/`

CleverMedia

CleverMedia carries a Shockwave tip of the week. If you've invested in Macromedia's Director software, this site can help you get the most out of it.

`http://clevermedia.com/`

Cartoon-O-Matic

Roll the dice, create a new cartoony face on the fly from this Web site. You can also download an off-line version of this tool for Windows, and save your cartoony creations as avatars for Virtual Places.

http://www.nfx.com/cgi-bin/livingart

GIF Animation Thrift Shop

An exotic mixture of GIF animations, including Celtic Knots, a lava lamp, and twirly things.

http://www.tiac.net/users/stacey/gifshop.html

GIFWorld: Download GIF Animations

GIFWorld offers a searchable site with more than 700 GIF animations that you can download and use on your Web site. They range from cartoons to business subjects, alphabets, animals, and much more. Most of the animations are of the cartoony type, but there are some nicely rendered examples here as well. If you're wondering how a particular animation was achieved, it might be worthwhile to download it, open the animation in GIF Construction Set (for Windows) or GIFBuilder (for the Mac) to see just how the effect was created.

http://www.gifworld.com

Learn to Write Chinese Characters

Learn to write Chinese characters by watching animated GIFs that draw characters stroke by stroke. This is a really wonderful use of GIF animation as a teaching tool.

http://www.ocrat.com/ocrat/chargif/

The MicroMovie MiniMultiPlex

A truly interesting site to browse. You can download these mini-movies in a mini-browser running in the background while you surf to animation-related links. Unfortunately, you don't get micro-popcorn, but you will see some clever and unique animations.

http://www.teleport.com/~cooler/MMMM/mmmm.html

Shock-Baubles

Don't have the bucks for Director? Don't worry, you can still experience the thrill of Shockwave on your own Web site, by downloading tiny Shockwave movies for your Web site. Each file is under 12K, and you'll find everything from the useful (a clock, a counter) to the absurd (bubbles, a hummingbird flitting across your page).

http://www.adveract.com/abtboble.htm

Royal Frazier's GIF Animation Site

You'll find many, many examples of GIF animation and specific instructions for creating GIF animations on Mac, Windows, and UNIX systems at this Web site.

http://members.aol.com/royalef

Smart Dubbing

Smart Dubbing is a GIF animation for the Mac that incorporates audio.

http://www.xs4all.nl/~polder

VideoCraft GIF Animator

VideoCraft GIF Animator is now available for a free 30-day trial from Andover Technologies. This Windows program supports GIF Animation and AVI and creates morphing and artistic filter effects across an animation. Worth a look.

http://www.andatech.com

Warner Brothers Animation 101

A fun overview of traditional animation techniques. This was written for kids, but it's a wonderful tour of everything that goes into creating an animated cartoon.

http://www.wbanimation.com/cmp/ani_01if.htm

Women in Animation

This is an organization for women animators, and includes job postings, a gallery of member work, a calendar of events, and more.

http://women.in.animation.org/

FONTS

As you've seen in the examples and recipes in this book, type can really expand your design horizons, and symbol (dingbat) fonts can be used as instant clip art. Browse through these Web sites for inspiration and type resources.

Astigmatic One Eye

A foundry with quirky type designs with names like Schrill, Schizm, and Scrawn. You can download freeware and shareware fonts at this site, including an unusual font with referee dingbats (Zeichens) and a typeface featuring bolts for that ultra-industrial look (Screwed). Who said fonts can't be fun?

http://www.comptechdev.com/cavop/aoe/fw.html

Comp.Fonts

Lots o' links here to lots of type resources, foundries, FAQs, and other information about type. Don't miss the Internet Font Archives.

http://www.ora.com/homepages/comp.fonts/

Fontaholics Anonymous

Feeling a little strung out? Or are you one of those who can give up fonts any time you want? Check out Fontaholics Anonymous for a fix!

http://home1.gte.net/tiaralyn/Fontaholics_Anonymous.htm

Fonts Unlimited

A new shareware font is featured every day at this site, and you can search the archives, too.

http://fonts.eyecandy.com/

Scriptorium Magazine

Scriptorium creates lovely shareware fonts inspired by historical art and documents. Its online magazine has covered such interesting topics as the Naming of Fonts, Arthur Rackham's Art, Type & Ornament, and Scriptorium Design Process.

http://members.aol.com/ragnarok/scriptorium

FREE, DEMO, AND SHAREWARE GRAPHIC SOFTWARE AND TUTORIALS

This is the good stuff: filters, add-ons, applications, and tutorials for your favorite Web software.

A Plug-In: Filters for Photoshop

You can download demo versions of Photoshop filters called Warper and Drop Shadow for Mac and Windows at this Web site. This company makes a set of filters that includes Lightening, Shape Cutter, Warper, Halo, Beveler, Puddles, and Drop Shadow.

http://www.almathera.co.uk/ppeople.html

Adobe Magazine

A little-known fact: If you own an Adobe product and would like to receive its magazine, you can go to its Web site and request it.

http://www.adobe.com/publications/magsubform.html

Adobe Software

Where do you go when your Photoshop install goes wonky? You'll find the latest patches and information on Adobe products at this Web site.

http://www.adobe.com

AFH Beveler

AFH Beveler Filter, a shareware filter for Windows, creates beveled edges on a rectangular image. Great for quick icons for Web pages.

http://www.afh.com/web/pshop/free.html

AlienSkin

AlienSkin makes Eye Candy, a set of filters that create beveling, drop shadows, glows, flames, and much more. You can download a demo of Eye Candy at the Web site.

http://www.alienskin.com

Andromeda Software

Andromeda makes filters for the Mac and PC, including Techtures, and offers demos of its three filter sets for Mac users.

http://www.andromeda.com

ArcSoft: PhotoStudio

ArcSoft makes a paint program for Windows that supports Photoshop style plug-ins. At this Web site you can download a 30-day trial version of its software. It has a low processor speed (386) and RAM requirement (4MB), making it a good program for older computers.

http://www.arcsoft.com

The Art Deadlines List

A listing of contests, grants, scholarships, internships, and more for art and art-related areas.

http://www.xensei.com/adl/

AutoF/X

Download demos of the AutoF/X filters for creating page and type effects.

http://www.autofx.com

Banner Design Tips

A large compilation of tips to creating effective advertising banners for Web sites.

http://www.photolabels.com/betterbanners.shtml

Banner Generator

The Banner Generator Form is a cool form-driven banner-creating utility. You can choose from a plethora of fonts and colors and select additional attributes such as transparency and rotation.

http://www.coder.com/creations/banner/
banner-form.pl.cgi

Boxtop Software

Boxtop Software offers a token handful of Windows filters and a plethora of Mac filters for download.

http://www.aris.com/boxtop/plugpage/welcome.html

Chromagraphics

Chromagraphics makes Photoshop plug-in filters for Mac and Windows. The Chroma filter takes a palette from one image and applies it to another, which may not sound that interesting until you see this filter in action. You can download a working demo at this Web site.

http://www.chromagraphics.com

Cool Type

Downloadable actions, plus browse tutorials and tips for creating cool type effects using Photoshop.

http://www.binary.net/cooltype/

Colleen's Filters

Photoshop filters for the Mac, available for download, called Colleen's Filters include Kwick Mask, Adjust Saturation, Rotate Color, and more.

http://www-leland.stanford.edu/~kawahara/
photoshop.html

Cool Tool

Every day, this Web site gives a humorous, honest review of a Web application. The reviews are worth reading for their irreverent humor and zaniness even if you never, ever (really) plan to use another piece of software. This site reviews both Mac and Windows applications.

http://www.cooltool.com/

Corel's Photo Studio

Is there anything as frustrating as being on deadline and knowing exactly which photo you need, but you can't find it? Corel has a huge library of stock photos that you can download for a small fee. At the time of this writing, prices started at $1 for a low-resolution copy of a photo. Da Vinci for a buck at 2 A.M.—what a concept!

http://commerce.corel.ca

Desktop Publishing Com

An excellent list of links to tutorials on the Web, and goodies galore for graphic artists and Web designers. There are also message boards for Photoshop users, product reviews, and much more.

http://www.desktoppublishing.com

Digital Effects

Download a demo version of a filter called OldPhoto, sample images, movies, and great free stuff!

http://www.digieffects.com

Digital Showbiz

Download the Flux collection sampler of fully working copies of ElectroSphere and Radial Noise, 2 of the 20 plug-ins in the flux collection. For Windows only.

http://www.dsb.com/freebies/

EDesign.com

EDesign has free downloads of two useful filters for the Mac: Grid Creator and Eliminate White.

http://www.edesign.com/filters/

FastEddie

A Mac and Windows shareware utility that claims to produce better dithering for GIFs than any other application.

http://www.lizardtech.com

Filters and Plug-ins

A cool collection of Photoshop filters, displacement maps, custom brush sets, and much more for both Mac and Windows users.

http://www.fns.net/~almateus/filplug.htm

Filter Factory Discussion Site

Die-hard users of Photoshop may already be familiar with the Filter Factory, a way to create homemade filters to sate the ever-growing need for more, more, MORE filters! Thankfully, there's now a support group for Filter Factory users. They'll tell you how to roll your own filters, and even share some of their discoveries with you. There are enough filters here to keep you busy for a month.

http://plug-in.eyecandy.com

Fractal Design Software

Download demos of Expressions, Painter, and more at the Fractal Design Web site. Expressions is a vector-based natural media program; Painter is a natural media paint program. These aren't filters, but they're just as much fun! Fractal also has a nifty background-a-day on its Web site.

http://www.fractal.com

GIF Transparency FAQ

A list of frequently asked questions about GIF transparency.

http://dragon.jpl.nasa.gov/~adam/transparent.html

GIF Transparency On-the-Fly

Select a GIF, and make it transparent at this Web site.

http://www.inf.fu-berlin.de/~leitner/trans

How to Make Icons for the Mac

This is a nifty tutorial on getting really small with your drawings. The instructions are specifically for Mac users, but the tips on drawing 3D objects on a very tiny scale are helpful to anyone working with Web graphics.

http://members.aol.com/gedeonm/create.html

Appendix

A

HumanSoftware

HumanSoftware makes Photoshop plug-ins for Mac and Windows, including Squizz, a distortion filter, and Textissimo, a text effects filter.

http://www.humansoftware.com

Image Alchemy

Image Alchemy is a graphics conversion utility, available for the Mac and Windows. At this site, you can give it a test drive and convert a graphic to a different format.

http://www.handmadesw.com

JPEG FAQ

A list of frequently asked questions about JPEG compression.

http://www.cis.ohio-state.edu/hypertext/faq/usenet/jpeg-faq/top.html

MediaSpark

This Web site offers a gaggle of filters for Windows, including Vignette White, Pixelate Edges Transparent, and many more.

http://mediaspark.com

MetaTools

MetaTools is the home of Kai's Power Tools, a set of nifty filters, Bryce, an other-worldly 3D rendering application, and KPT Actions, which work with Kai's Power Tools to create push-button effects. Browse tutorials, download demos, and much more.

http://www.metatools.com

Microsoft: Software for Web Developers

Sign up with Microsoft as a Web site developer, and snag valuable goodies including (at the time of this writing) Ray Dream Designer (a 3D rendering package); ImageComposer; and Fractal Design's new natural media, vector-based drawing package, Expressions; as well as Macromedia's Backstage Designer.

http://www.microsoft.com/sitebuilder

Morph Images on the Fly!

This Web site features a Java applet that allows you to apply morphing effects to an image.

http://web.cs.bgsu.edu/morph/morph.html

PC Resources for Photoshop

An alphabetical list of all of the filters available for Windows Photoshop users, along with a brief description of each. There's also a large archive of Filter Factory plug-ins for Photoshop at this Web site.

http://www.netins.net/showcase/wolf359/plugcomm.htm

Pixel Spy

Pixel Spy is a Mac shareware utility that allows you to match a color on the screen. For instance, this would be useful if you are in Photoshop and want to sample the color from a Web browser window. Just open Pixel Spy, examine the color of one of the pixels, and enter the values into Photoshop's color picker. It is also particularly helpful for determining the color hex codes needed in HTML documents.

http://shakti.trincoll.edu/~bhorling/pixelspy/

The Photoshop 4.0 Action Xchange

Can't get enough of those Photoshop Actions? You can download and exchange Actions at this Web site, where you'll find everything from Actions created especially for Web graphics to Actions for type effects.

http://jmc.mit.edu/photoshop

Stockphoto: Photo Discussion Group

This site is well worth visiting. It has a newsgroup and mailing list, links to stock photo Web sites, and information for and about professional photographers.

http://www.s2f.com/STOCKPHOTO/

TextureMill

TextureMill is a Photoshop plug-in for the Mac that creates seamless textures for Web pages, multimedia, and so on. You can download sample textures created with TextureMill and a demo version of TextureMill at this site.

http://members.aol.com/deepdevice

Ulead Software

Ulead makes two Windows Photoshop plug-ins that are especially helpful for Web work. With the GIF and JPEG SmartSavers you can preview an image's file size before you save it. Very cool. You can download a 30-day demo of the software, too. Ulead also now offers a demo download of its filter sets for Photoshop that create beveling effects.

http://www.ulead.com

The Ultimate Compendium of Photoshop Sites

Links to filters and plug-ins, tips and tutorials, Photoshop Actions, and much more.

http://www.sas.upenn.edu/~pitharat/photoshop/

Universe Space Paint Program

Yearning for that StarTrek look? If you are looking for a simple program that will generate starfields, nebula, and planets with the click of a mouse button, this is a great tool. The program will only save as .bmp, though, so you'll need to use another utility to convert these files to .jpg or .gif files for use on a Web page. This program is a lot of fun to use, too. This is Windows shareware.

http://home.earthlink.net/~jessd/

VRL's Imaging Machine

This site will do manipulations to graphic files on the fly. Here's how it works: You select the type of action you'd like to apply to your image (make transparent, combine with another image, use a filter, rotate an image, etc.); then you type in the URL of the image, submit your info, and voilà! Your transformed image is created on-the-fly!

http://www.vrl.com/Imaging/

WildRiver Filters

WildRiverSSK is a set of Mac demo filters available for download, including MagicCurtain, MagicFrame, MagicMask, and TileMaker.

http://www.datastrem.com

Xaos Software

Xaos makes some very cool filters for the Mac. You can download demos of TypeCaster, PaintAlchemy 2, TubeTime, and Fresco, Terrazzo. PaintAlchemy and Terrazzo are included with Corel PhotoPaint.

http://www.xaostools.com

GRAPHICS FOR WEB SITES

Of course, once you finish reading Creating Great Web Graphics , you won't ever need to visit a clip art archive again, right? Well, sometimes it's fun and inspiring to see what other designers are doing on the Web. Enjoy!

Bryce's Buttons and Widgets

Completely awesome Web artwork available for download, created by Bryce Glass. The truly nifty feature is that you can download the files in native Photoshop (PSD) or Painter format, with layers intact, so you can see how he created the work. Wonderful stuff that makes me positively puce with envy.

http://www.lcc.gatech.edu/gallery/widgets

Clip Art Connection

A nice variety of clip art at this archive, including decorative drop caps, and links to lots of other clip art resources.

http://www.acy.digex.net/~infomart/clipart/index.html

DocOzone

Although there's clip art here, you'll probably forget all about it, because DocOzone has some super Photoshop tips, mind-boggling animations, and much more to engage and entrance you.

Electronic Zoo

This site is a list of links to animal images on the Web. Few are clip art or copyright-free, but this is a useful resource nonetheless. Wonder what a scorpion or an Abyssinian cat looks like? A great reference of a variety of animals.

http://netvet.wustl.edu/pix.htm

Fine Arts Museums of San Francisco

Wouldn't it be wonderful if you could pop into your favorite museum whenever you wanted to? My favorite museum in San Francisco is the Palace of the Legion of Honor, which has joined forces with other San Francisco museums to form a huge searchable database of over 65,000 images. The Web site is well organized, and the pages load quickly. But the images at this site are for reference only, and not meant to be downloaded.

http://www.thinker.org

Julianne's Background Textures

A tasteful selection of seamless background tiles, suitable for the most conservative Web site builder.

http://www.sfsu.edu/~jtolson/textures/textures.htm

The Library of Congress

Uncle Sam... wired? You bet! Visit exhibits online from the Library of Congress. When I visited, there were exhibits on Frank Lloyd Wright, women journalists, Houdini, and the Gettysburg Address. There's also a searchable image database. You can download images, but only for personal use. There are some wonderful historical images to view at this site.

http://www.loc.gov

The Rocket Shop

Fun, funky clip art for your Web pages. Most of the images are very colorfully rendered, off-beat types of artwork, including a lava lamp and a wild armchair. You'll also find more typical headers, page dividers, and icons.

http://www.rocketshop.holowww.com/

Search for Clipart

A nifty page that lets you use several search engines at once to look for that perfect piece of clip art.

http://www.webplaces.com/search/

Texture Station

Nearly 400 backgrounds, organized by color.

http://www.aimnet.com/~bosman/TextureStation_Lobby.htm

Traditional Japanese Backgrounds

A really lovely, unique selection of geometric backgrounds based on traditional Japanese patterns.

http://web.mit.edu/asuwa/www/art.html

Wallpaper Boutique

A genteel collection of backgrounds that won't make your type unreadable; soothing and reminiscent of the 1930s.

http://www.wanderers.com/stormi/paper/paper.html

Web Ground: Free Background Textures

You'll find over 600 original background textures available at this Web site for downloading. But note: This site asks for a return link in exchange for using its backgrounds.

http://www.ip.pt/webground/front.htm

Windy's Fashionable Page Designs

This site offers a choice of graphics, designed around a common theme or color scheme. Choices include Ebony and Ivory, Dream Clouds, Orchid Swirls, Flaxen Honey, and more. Each group includes several icons and backgrounds designed to work with each other.

http://www.windyweb.com/design/

GENERAL REFERENCE RESOURCES

Just getting started on the Web? If you'd like to expand your basic understanding of the Web and how it works, browse these links to become Net savvy!

Classes on the Web—For Free

Spectrum Virtual University offers free online classes on a variety of topics, including IRC (Internet Relay Chat), Exploring the Internet, Building a Web Page, Fun Things to Do on the Net, PC Basics, Eight Weeks to Creative Writing, Writers' Roundtable, and more.

http://www.vu.org/campus.html

Cobb Tips

Get daily software tips either from this Web site or via e-mail for a number of popular programs, including Internet Explorer, Microsoft Access, and Pagemaker.

http://www.cobbtips.com

The Internet University

This site lists more than 700 courses you can take on the Web.

http://www.caso.com/iu.html

My Virtual Reference Desk

No need to run to the library; you can access the Virtual Encyclopedia from your desktop! It's a good thing, too, because it would be closing time at the library before you finished browsing through this extensive list of links.

http://www.vref.com

Surf School from Yahoo

This site covers everything for the beginning Web user (what do I click on?) to more advanced Web topics. Hop in for quick tips and pointers.

http://www.zdnet.com/yil/filters/surfjump.html

TidBITS

TidBITS is a weekly, electronic publication that covers news and views relating to the Macintosh and the Internet. You can also sign up to receive TidBITS via e-mail at this Web site.

http://www.tidbits.com

WhatIs.com

Sometimes, ignorance can be downright embarrassing. If you've been wondering what ASCII stands for, or if broadband is a good thing, or if you need an avatar or an AVI file, check out WhatIs—an alphabetically organized dictionary of computer and Internet terms.

http://whatis.com

WWW FAQ

The most frequently asked questions about the Web are answered here.

http://www.boutell.com

WWW Viewer Test Page

Test-drive your browser setup to see which file types you can view. There are links to plug-ins and helpful advice for getting your browser set up correctly. There's a wide range of file formats included for testing at this site, including AVI, MOV, VRML, and many others.

http://www-dsed.llnl.gov/documents/WWWtest.html

HTML AND WEB RESOURCES

Here are helpful guides, software and utilities for creating HTML. If you have a word processor or desktop publishing program that you use a lot, check with the company that makes your software to find out whether it has an HTML export or add-on utility for it.

AOLpress

AOLpress is a freeware Mac and Windows WYSIWIG HTML editor. AOL members and PrimeHost customers can use this tool to save files directly to the server. Others can use AOLpress as an HTML editor. On America Online, use keyword AOLPRESS.

http://www.aolpress.com

Bare Bones Software: HTML Editors for the Mac

BBEdit is the editor of choice for Mac users who are comfortable looking at the HTML tags in a document. This HTML editor has a lot of powerful features that make it a favorite with many Web developers.

http://www.barebones.com/

Calendars for the Web

A nifty gizmo for Windows that creates HTML pages in a calendar format.

http://www.hrworks.com/

Carl Davis' HTML Editor Reviews

Seems like there's a new HTML editor out every, oh, five minutes or so, and few of them have all of the features you want and need. Carl Davis has compiled helpful reviews of Windows HTML tools.

http://homepage.interaccess.com/~cdavis/editrev/index.html

Font Colorizer

This Windows Web gizmo takes a headline or bit of text and creates a color fade across it using the HTML FONT COLOR tag. This is a nifty little utility.

http://home1.inet.tele.dk/theill/hfc.htm

Frame Tutorial

Joe Barta has written a helpful, downloadable frames tutorial, available at his web site in both Mac and Windows format. This tutorial is one of the most popular downloads at our forum on AOL.

http://junior.apk.net/~jbarta/

Gomer

Gomer is a great HTML editor if you like to be able to view and work in raw HTML. It's the HTML editor I use, and it supports the FONT tags, tables, frames, and a lot more.

http://www.stoopidsoftware.com

HTML Reference Library

Download the Windows HTML Reference Library at http://wubnet.virtual-pc.com/~le387818, or discuss the HTML Reference Library at this Web site.

http://hjs.geol.uib.no/html/htmlibrd/htmlibrd.htm

Insert Page Title Here

This is a perfect example of how not to create a Web site. According to Insert Page Title Here, HTML stands for Hard Text Making Language. Near the breaking point from trying to troubleshoot your HTML? Check out this site for a good laugh.

http://wwwvoice.com/bud/tips.html

IView Pro: Offline Web Browser

Not everyone is rushing toward the millennium at the same speed. Do you have the unenviable task of demonstrating the Web or a Web site to someone without access to the Internet? Try this offline browser; it's small enough to fit on a single diskette yet powerful enough to display most HTML.

http://www.talentcom.com/

A Kinder, Gentler HTML Validator

What's an HTML validator? Does it allow you to park in a yellow zone? Nope, but it will tell you whether your HTML has errors that will prevent it from displaying as it should. Feed the validator the URL you'd like to have checked, and it will identify problem code.

http://ugweb.cs.ualberta.ca/~gerald/validate/

MapEdit

Thomas Boutell is a true Web treasure. He moderates, he writes Web applications, he maintains FAQs. MapEdit is an image map editor for Windows that supports both client and server-side image maps.

http://www.boutell.com

Microsoft's Workshop

Tutorials on intermediate to advanced Web design topics, including Java, ActiveX, color palettes, frames, and much more at http://www.microsoft.com/workshop/. Grab browser add-ons and beta versions of Microsoft software at http://www.microsoft.com msdownload/. And doodads for your Web site from Microsoft can be found at this URL, including wav files, icons, ActiveX controls, clip art, and more.

http://www.microsoft.com/gallery

Mirsky's Worst of the Web

Just like the title says: a sampling of the worst (and funniest) sites on the Web.

http://mirsky.com/wow/

Netscape's Creating Net Sites Reference

A reference for creating Web sites for Netscape.

http://www.netscape.com/assist/net_sites/index.html

PageSpinner for the Mac

PageSpinner is a popular HTML tool that includes a helpful tutorial, and an integrated color picker.

http://www.algonet.se/~optima/pagespinner.html

Project Cool

A very nicely organized HTML tips site, with information on HTML basics and an HTML quick reference page as well.

http://www.projectcool.com/developer

Sausage Software

Sausage makes gee-whiz Web tools for Windows users, including Hot Dog, (a popular HTML editor), FrameGang (a frame HTML editor), and a gaggle of Java applets, including animation effects (Swami, Egor, and ImageWiz), marquees, (Broadway), scrolling text (Flash), and yes, there's more!

http://www.sausage.com

See Lynx for Yourself

Lynx is a text-only Web browser. Curious to see what your site looks like to a Lynx user? Stop in here and see your Web site from a different viewpoint.

http://www.crl.com/~subir/lynx/public_lynx.html

Spyglass HTML Validator

A standalone Windows application that checks your HTML for errors.

http://www.spyglass.com/products/validator/

TableMaker

This little online tool enables you to specify all the attributes of your table, including height, width, number of cells, and so on, then generates the HTML for the table on the fly. You'll also find a frame tool.

http://www.missouri.edu/~wwwtools/tablemaker/
http://www.missouri.edu/~wwwtools/frameshop/

Web Developer's Reference Library

This site has reference material on a vast variety of Web topics, everything from AVI to VRML. It's searchable, up to date, and very helpful.

http://www.stars.com

Appendix A

WebForms

WebForms is a form (also sometimes called guestbook) creation tool for Windows users. You can use this tool to compile the responses to your form into a database as well. You'll also find WebMania and Bookmark Magician at this site.

http://www.q-d.com

Web Mastery Online

An eclectic assortment of links to lots of unusual Web resources, gathered for the sole purpose of saving other people some of the frustration of creating a Web site.

http://fly.hiwaay.net/~nlf/graphics.htm

WebReference

A mega site of information for Web developers. You'll find tips on JavaScript, HTML, Style Sheets, and lots more.

http://www.webreference.com

WebTable

Another Windows Web gizmo. This one takes information from a Web page in table format and allows you to import that information into a spreadsheet. Freeware.

http://www.informatik.com/webtable.html

WebTV

You can find a complete list of specifications for WebTV at this Web site, including what resolution, colors, and HTML tags it supports.

http://www.webtv.net

PUBLICIZE YOUR WEB SITE

Don't get lost on the Web! Make sure that your site gets known by submitting your URL and Web site description to all of these search engines and directories.

A1's Directory of Free Web Page Promotion Sites

This site has a massive, searchable set of links to places you can publicize your Web site for free.

http://www.a1co.com

AddMe

A free URL submission service that sends your information to 30 different places at once.

http://www.addme.com

Broadcaster

A free URL submission service that submits your information to over 200 places.

http://www.broadcaster.co.uk/

Submit-It

A free multiple-submission site that allows you to submit your URL to over 15 places at once.

http://www.submit-it.com

Yahoo's List of Announcement Services

Yahoo has a listing of all of the Web promotional services available at this URL.

http://www.yahoo.com/Computers_and_Internet/Internet/World_Wide_Web/Announcement_Services/

SHAREWARE ARCHIVES

You just can't have too much software. Can you? Check out these sites to find more than you ever dreamed was available!

Filez

This is not an archive, but a search engine for software on the Web. A great way to find difficult-to-locate software.

http://www.filez.com

Galt Shareware Zone

An archive of shareware for Windows users. It's quick loading and has an easy search feature and a brief description of files.

http://www.galttech.com/

Jumbo

I remember when Jumbo was just a few pages of software utilities available for download. Now you'll find utilities; ActiveX controls; Java applications; Internet utilities, fonts, and more. Mac and Windows.

http://www.jumbo.com

Shareware Com

Those tireless folks at CINet have compiled a great archive of software for Mac and PC users. Don't miss the daily featured file.

http://www.shareware.com

Tucows

Mooove over! There are more Web shareware files at this site than you could download in a week! You'll be downloading files until the cows come home! Each file is rated (five cows is an excellent rating, three cows are okay), updated regularly, and contains a link to the author's Web site. If you can't find the Web software you're looking for here, it probably doesn't exist. You'll find browser plug-ins, Web utilities, HTML editors, and much more at Tucows. You can also sign up to receive a weekly e-mail newsletter about the latest files added. Tip: If you can't get through to download a popular file of, for instance, the latest version of a browser, you'll almost always able to get through to a Tucows site. Mac and Windows

http://www.tucows.com

Ziff-Davis HotFiles

Here's the stuff you need, rated, tested, and reviewed, brought to you by the folks who created PC Magazine, MacUser, and every third computer magazine widely available. You'll find some interesting files at this site that may not be listed elsewhere.

http://www.hotfiles.com

NEWSGROUPS

You can search past postings from newsgroups at http://www.dejanews.com or at Deja News. (If you haven't used a newsgroup before, DejaNews also has some helpful information on how not to make an idiot of yourself in front of tens of thousands of Usenet readers.) If your Internet Service Provider doesn't currently carry any of the following newsgroups, it usually will add them if you ask the News Master politely.

news.newusers.questions

This newsgroup is the logical place to start; it is devoted to answering questions from new users.

alt.corel.graphics

A newsgroup for the discussion of Corel Products.

alt.comp.periphs.scanner

Discussion of scanners, scanner drivers, software use with scanned images, and purchasing scanners.

alt.fractal-design.painter

This newsgroup discusses Fractal Design's Painter program.

alt.html

A busy newsgroup that's a little more friendly and less technical than the comp.infosystems.www.authoring newsgroup.

alt.multimedia.director

Discussions of techniques for Macromedia's Director tool.

alt.soft-sys.corel.draw

Another Corel newsgroup.

comp.graphics.animation

This newsgroup discusses animation.

comp.graphics.apps

A discussion of miscellaneous graphics software.

comp.fonts

A busy group, comp.fonts discusses font design, history, and a lot more.

comp.graphics.apps.freehand

This newsgroup covers Macromedia's Freehand program.

comp.graphics.apps.photoshop

This Photoshop newsgroup gets more than a hundred postings a day about Photoshop. Lots of chat and information.

comp.graphics.misc

Like its title says, this newsgroup covers miscellaneous graphics topics.

comp.infosystems.www.announce

You can announce your noncommercial Web site in this newsgroup.

comp.infosystems.www.authoring.html

This newsgroup generates a lot of traffic for its HTML conversations.

comp.infosystems.www.authoring.images

A discussion of graphics and the Web.

comp.infosystems.www.authoring.misc

More on Web authoring issues.

comp.lang.vrml

A newsgroup for the discussion of VRML.

comp.lang.java

A very active Java discussion group.

comp.language.javascript

For the discussion of JavaScript.

comp.multimedia

Covers Shockwave and other multimedia tools.

comp.sys.mac.graphics

A newsgroup featuring graphics software packages, graphics creation, and Mac graphics hardware issues.

misc.writing

This one is for writers, published and hoping to be, of fiction and nonfiction. A busy newsgroup.

Mailing Lists

Mailing lists can be a great way to communicate with other people on the Web, but they are most productive when they focus on a specific topic. And note: Any e-mail sent to the mailing list is delivered to everyone on the list.

If you participate regularly, you'll get to know the regulars. The good news: A mailing list generally has less spam (unwanted advertisements) than a newsgroup.

One of the drawbacks of a mailing list is that a popular topic can generate hundreds of responses in a day, and each will appear as an e-mail to you. This can quickly stuff your mailbox, and prevent other e-mail from reaching you. For this reason, it is a good idea to have mailing lists sent to a secondary e-mail address. (AOL members can have up to five screen names per account). Some mailing lists offer a digest version, which is a daily compilation of the postings that will arrive as a single e-mail.

When you subscribe to a mailing list, you'll get an e-mail about the procedures for unsubscribing. Keep this for future reference.

Corel PhotoPaint

Send e-mail to: discuss-photopaint-sub@discuss.corelnet.com
Subject: none required
In the body of the e-mail: none required

CorelDraw

Send e-mail to: discuss-draw-sub@discuss.corelnet.com
Subject: none required
In the body of the e-mail: none required

Cow-L

Send e-mail to: listserv@thecity.sfsu.edu
Subject: none required
In the body of the e-mail: subscribe cow-l (*your name*)

This mailing list discusses the web message board software known as COW, or Conferencing on the Web. The web site for this mailing list is http://thecity.sfsu.edu/cow2

Direct-L

Send e-mail to: listserv@uafsysb.uark.edu
Subject: none required
In the body of the e-mail: sub DIRECT-L {*your name*}
A mailing list for Director and Shockwave.

FutureSplash Mailing List

Send e-mail to: list-manager@splasher.com
Subject: none required
In the body of the e-mail: subscribe futuresplash

For discussion of the FutureSplash graphics animation tool and browser plug-in.

IE-HTML Mailing List

Send e-mail to: listadmin@lists.msn.com
Subject: none required
In the body of the e-mail: SUBSCRIBE IE-HTML

Join IE-HTML if you're interested in Web content authoring, writing HTML, taking advantage of Internet Explorer, and new/advanced HTML abilities such as Cascading Style Sheets (CCS1), the OBJECT tag, and using ActiveX controls.

JavaScript Mailing List

Send e-mail to: Javascript-request@inquiry.com
Subject: none required
In the body of the e-mail: subscribe

Kai's Power Tools Mailing List

Send e-mail to: majordomo@lists.metatools.com
Subject: none required
Body of the e-mail: SUBSCRIBE KPT, for the usual format; or SUBSCRIBE KPT-DIGEST, which delivers the mailing list as one or two e-mails a day.

This is a very active mailing list for the discussion of MetaTools and KPT (Kai's Power Tools).

Appendix

A

Photoshop Filter Factory Mailing List

Send e-mail to: majordomo@cnu.edu
Subject: none required
In the body of the e-mail: SUBSCRIBE FFACTORY

All about making and using filters for Photoshop with Filter Factory.

Photoshop Mailing List

Send e-mail to: listserv@vm.sc.edu
Subject: none required
In the body of the e-mail: subscribe photoshp *firstname lastname*

Notice the o missing in photoshp.

RayDream Mailing List

Send e-mail to: listserv@cornell.edu
Subject: none required
In the body of the e-mail: subscribe raydream-l *firstname lastname*.

RayDream Designer is a 3D rendering and animation program, also called CorelDream when bundled with CorelDraw 6 and 7. This mailing list is devoted to the discussion of 3D modeling and rendering and related topics, focusing on products developed by RayDream, Inc.

Scout Report

Send e-mail to: listserv@lists.internic.net
Subject: none required
In the body of the e-mail: subscribe SCOUT LIST

Scout Report reports on Internet Resources, especially those of interest to educators and researchers.

WebWomen-HTML

Send e-mail to: Webwomen-html-request@niestu.com
Subject: none required
In the body of the e-mail: subscribe

The WebWomen-HTML list provides a space for women content providers on the Web. Topics include advanced HTML, standards, design issues, graphics assistance, and Java/Javascript. Beginners are welcome but newbie questions will be answered with pointers to FAQs.

Searching for just the right mailing list?

Try Liszt, for a comprehensive menu of active mailing lists. You will also find some helpful tips for participating in a mailing list, too.

http://www.liszt.com

APPENDIX B:
HTML QUICK REFERENCE

<HTML> </HTML>	Begins the HTML page
<HEAD> </HEAD>	Defines the head portion of the HTML document
<TITLE> </TITLE>	Defines the title, which appears in the title bar of the page
<BODY> </BODY>	Defines the body of the HTML page

Attributes:

BACKGROUND

BGCOLOR

ALINK

VLINK

LINK

TEXT

Example:

```
<BODY BACKGROUND="tile.gif" BGCOLOR="#FFFFFF"
TEXT="#000000" LINK="#FF0000" VLINK="#CC00CC"
ALINK="#FFFF00">
```

<P>	Inserts a line space between paragraphs.
<B> </B>	Makes text bold.
<I> </I>	Makes text italic.
<U> </U>	Underlines text.
<A HREF> </A>	Anchor HyperText Reference. Defines a link.

Example:

```
<A HREF="http://www.altavista.digital.com"> Visit my
favorite search engine </A>
```

Example of a mailto: tag

```
<A HREF="mailto:illustratr@aol.com"> Send some email! </A>
```

<FONT></FONT>   Defines size, color, or typeface for text on the Web page.

Attributes:

FACE

COLOR

SIZE

Example:

```
<FONT FACE="Comic Sans Ms, Arial" COLOR="#FF00CC" SIZE=+1> Here is an exam-
ple of the font tag </FONT>
```

<H1> </H1>   Creates a heading.

Attributes:

ALIGN

Example

```
<H2 ALIGN=RIGHT> Here's a Heading </H2>
```

<IMG SRC>   Places an image on a page.

Attributes:

ALIGN

ALT

BORDER

HEIGHT

WIDTH

VSPACE

HSPACE

Example:

```
<IMG SRC="photo.jpg" ALIGN=TOP HEIGHT="200" WIDTH="100"
ALT="a portrait of our founder" HSPACE=10 VSPACE=10
BORDER=0>
```

GLOSSARY

Bit Depth   Refers to the number of colors in an image. An 8-bit image contains 256 colors, a 7-bit image contains 128 colors, a 6-bit image contains 64 colors, a 5-bit image contains 32 colors, a 4-bit image contains 16 colors, and a 3-bit image contains 8 colors.

Browser   The software (such as Mosaic, Netscape, Internet Explorer) that allows you to view pages on the World Wide Web.

CGI   Common Gateway Interface, or scripting that runs on a Web server. Counter scripts, guestbooks, and imagemaps can be created with CGI.

Dingbat   A small ornamental type character, for example, a heart or a diamond shape. Common dingbat typefaces include Zapf Dingbats and Wingdings.

Dithering   In Web graphics, images are indexed to a small number of colors. In order to display complex images with fewer colors, images are dithered, where two or more colors are used to approximate another color, much like the Impressionists used daubs of color.

Domain Name   A unique Web address registered with InterNIC (http://www.internic.net).

EPS   Encapsulated Post Script format. A vector-based file format that includes a low-resolution graphic used for placement and a Post Script file that allows you to print at high resolution.

File extension   Files for Web use must be named with the correct file extension, a three- or four-letter code, at the end of the file name. For example, GIF images should always end in .GIF; for example, flower.gif. HTML files need to end in .htm or .HTML; for example, index.html. Files without the correct extension may not be recognized by the Web browser.

FTP   File Transfer Protocol, the standard for transferring files over the Internet. Generally, FTP is used when uploading (transferring files from your computer to, for example, a remote site) or downloading (transferring files from a remote site to your computer).

GIF   Graphics Interchange Format. A compressed image file format. A GIF image is always composed of 256 colors or fewer.

Header   An image at the top of a Web page. Usually, the main graphic for a Web site.

Hexadecimal   Colors can be specified in HTML using a hexadecimal value, also called a hexcode. The value for black, for example, is #000000.

HTML   HyperText Markup Language, used to create Web pages.

Icon   A small graphic image, sometimes called a button, used to navigate software or a Web site.

Indexed color image An image whose colors are constrained to a specific number of colors. In the case of GIF files, the number of colors is constrained (or indexed) to 256 or fewer.

Interlacing An interlaced graphic will load in a number of stages to a Web browser. Each stage displays a higher resolution version of the image.

ISP Internet Service Provider. A company that provides access to the Web. You'll find a list of ISPs at http://www.thelist.com.

JPEG A 24-bit, lossy compression file format for Web graphics. JPEG allows you to choose the quality of graphic. The lower the quality, the smaller the JPEG file will be.

Lossless A compression method where no information is lost. Using WinZip or PKZip to compress a file or group of files, for example, is a lossless way to compress a file. Once unzipped, all of the original information in the file is still available. Unfortunately, zipped graphics won't display on a Web page.

Lossy A compression method where information from the original graphic is lost during compression. JPEG is a lossy format, which is a good reason to always keep a copy of the original file

Palette Images with 256 colors or fewer store their color information in a palette. Palettes are also sometimes called CLUTs, or Color Look-Up Tables.

Pixel The smallest unit of a bitmapped computer graphic image. Web graphics are measured in pixels.

RGB The color model used by computer monitors. RGB stands for red, green, blue.

Screenshot or screen capture A picture of a computer screen, usually used to demonstrate the features of software. To create a simple screenshot in Windows, use the **Print Screen** key on the keyboard, and then open a paint program and use the Paste command to paste the screenshot from the Windows clipboard into an image.

Thumbnail A smaller version of a larger file. In traditional graphic arts, ideas are usually sketched out first in a small (thumbnail) format. On the Web, thumbnails are used to conserve space. Thumbnails are usually linked to the larger versions of a file, which are downloaded only when a reader doesn't mind the wait.

Transparency A single color of a GIF image may be assigned transparency, so that the background color or pattern of the Web page will show through.

URL Uniform Resource Locator, the format for Web addresses. For example, the URL for the Internet Glossary is http://www.matisse.net/files/glossary.html.

Vector An object-oriented image. Lines and shapes are defined by mathematical formulas.

VRML Virtual Reality Modeling Language.

INDEX

W

Z

PHOTOSHOP TOOLS

Airbrush (A)		Line (N)		Pen (P)	
Eyedropper (I)		Magic Wand (W)		Pencil (Y)	
Ellipse Marquee		Marquee (M)		Rubber Stamp (S)	
Eraser (E)		Move (V)		Smudge (U)	
Gradient (G)		Paint Bucket (K)		Type (T)	
Lasso (L)		Paintbrush (B)		Type Mask	

This is not a complete list of the Photoshop tools, but the tools that are used in the book.

The letters following the tool title are the keyboard shortcut used to access the tool. For instance, to select the Type tool, type the letter T.

Here's a complete layout of the Photoshop toolbar.

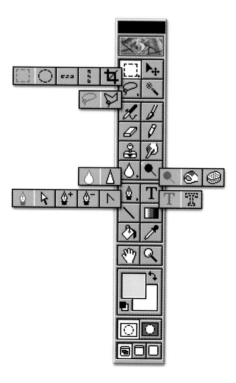

PHOTOPAINT TOOLS

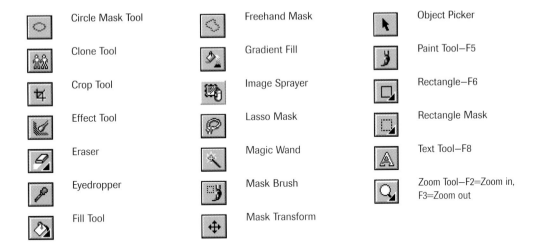

	Circle Mask Tool		Freehand Mask		Object Picker
	Clone Tool		Gradient Fill		Paint Tool—F5
	Crop Tool		Image Sprayer		Rectangle—F6
	Effect Tool		Lasso Mask		Rectangle Mask
	Eraser		Magic Wand		Text Tool—F8
	Eyedropper		Mask Brush		Zoom Tool—F2=Zoom in, F3=Zoom out
	Fill Tool		Mask Transform		

This is not a complete list of the PhotoPaint tools, but those that are used in this book. The following is a complete layout of the PhotoPaint toolbar.

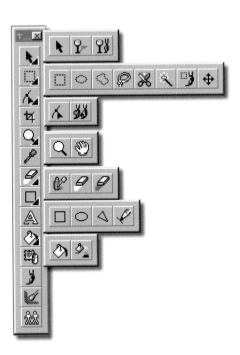

Visit the Web Diner on America Online

When stopping by the Web Diner on America Online, you can take a free HTML class, pick up some graphics tips, and download a new daily graphic, too! This forum (which I developed with three online colleagues) is devoted to helping small businesses put their websites up on AOL.

The Web Diner offers HTML classes twice a week. In thirty minutes, AOL members write their first HTML page and put it up on the AOL server. At the end of class, everyone can see their first web page live on the web!

The two daily changing specials at the Web Diner are:

The Web Diner
keyword: Diner

- the Blue Plate Special, a recommended website.
- the Byte of the Day, a heaping helping of HTML, graphics, or other helpful web tips.

Interested in what other AOL members are doing on the web? Check out Family Recipes, where the Web Diner is offering free links to AOL member websites.

On America Online, use keyword: Diner

The FREE ART Website

If you have enjoyed the graphics and tips in this book, you should visit my FREE ART Website at http://www.mccannas.com, and discover even more Photoshop and PhotoPaint tips and techniques. Learn how to set your type on fire and emboss a graphic. You can download icons, seamless background tiles and examples created in this book.

http://www.mccannas.com